HO

KENNEDY

MME. NHU

KISSINGER

THO

LODGE

MME. KHIEM

CONEIN

VIEN

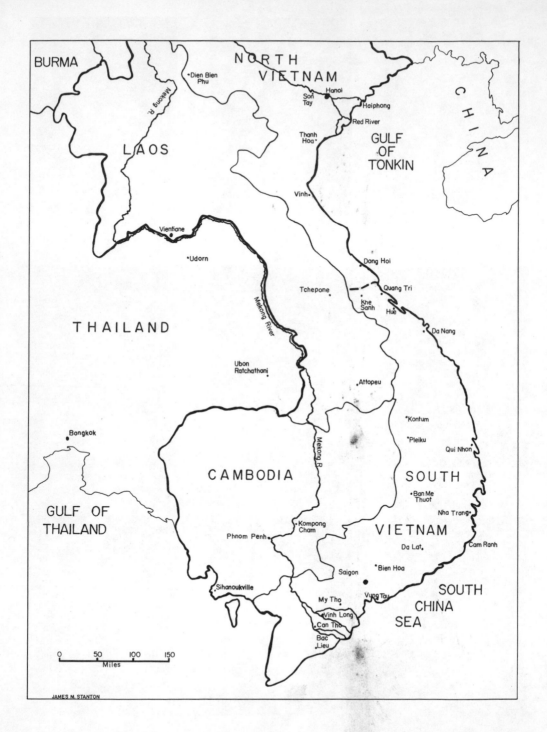

BURMA

NORTH VIETNAM

•Dien Bien Phu

LAOS

Son Tay• •Hanoi
Haiphong•
Red River•

Thanh Hoa•

Mekong R.

GULF OF TONKIN

CHINA

Vientiane•

•Udorn

THAILAND

Mekong River

Tchepone•

•Vinh

Dong Hoi•

Quang Tri•
Khe Sanh• •Hué

•Da Nang

Ubon Ratchathani•

•Attopeu

•Kontum

•Pleiku

Qui Nhon•

•Bangkok

CAMBODIA

Mekong R.

SOUTH

•Ban Me Thuot

Nha Trang•

VIETNAM

Da Lat•

Cam Ranh•

GULF OF THAILAND

Phnom Penh•

•Kompong Cham

Saigon• •Bien Hoa

Sihanoukville•

My Tho•

Vung Tau•

SOUTH CHINA SEA

•Vinh Long
Can Tho•

Bac Lieu•

0   50   100   150
Miles

JAMES M. STANTON

Our Endless War

Our

Endless

War

INSIDE VIETNAM

TRAN VAN DON

PRESIDIO PRESS
San Rafael, California
London, England

Copyright © 1978 by Presidio Press

Library of Congress Cataloging in Publication Data

Trân Văn-Dôn, 1917–
  Our endless war.

  Includes index.
    1. Vietnam—History—1945–   2. Trân Văn-Dôn,
1917–   3. Generals—Vietnam—Biography.
I. Title.
DS556.9.094   959.7'04   78-7914
ISBN 0-89141-019-8

Published by Presidio Press of San Rafael,
California, and London, England, with
editorial offices at 1114 Irwin Street,
San Rafael, California 94901

**Endpaper portraits courtesy of U.S. Army.
All other photographs from author's files.**

Book design by Bruce Kortebein

Printed in the United States of America

With gratitude to those who are still fighting for human rights throughout the world.

Contents

Foreword

Tran Van Don makes a valuable contribution to American history in recounting our Vietnam involvement as it appeared to the Vietnamese. We have many accounts of that difficult experience as seen through American eyes. Officials from presidents on down, journalists and academics in the field and at home, soldiers and rural workers engaged in combat and development, all have recounted their American view of Vietnam. To these we add the fictional and theatrical accounts now becoming popular which focus, as most war fiction does, on the agony and tragedy of military violence and the corruption it brings in its wake.

Vietnam was, indeed, an American experience and a portion of American history, but it was not that alone. For the Vietnamese, it was another in a long list of struggles beginning before the dawn of the Christian era between Vietnamese factions and their foreign overlords and supporters: Chinese, French, then American and Russian. Tran Van Don speaks for those Vietnamese in this century who struggled for non-Communist nationalism, simultaneously contesting the Communist-inclined nationalists and fending off the heavy hands of French and American supporters. In this way, Americans can see themselves as others saw us in Vietnam, where Don played such a prominent role.

Although Don's view of the long and, as he puts it in the book's title, "endless" war is valuable, it is not infallible, reflecting as it does his own background. In particular, I must disagree with his assessments of the efforts of Presidents Ngo Dinh Diem and Nguyen Van Thieu to involve the rural peasantry actively in non-Communist nationalism. During my own active service in Vietnam I knew well and worked closely with both presidents. I therefore had a unique opportunity to observe their several pacification, land reform, and resettlement programs at first hand. Certainly there were problems and some inevitable corruption was present, but both

Diem and Thieu were on the correct path toward winning the peasants' support away from the Communists.

Don very clearly reflects the "state within a state" of the Vietnamese military—a self-contained social entity with its own internal dynamics and a sense of loyalty to that entity vis-a-vis the outside world, be it the enemy, political opponents or government leaders. Don describes the pressures which led his group to move against the Diem government, with encouragement and promises of future support from Washington. He describes the chaotic state which followed Diem's fall, the regimes of Duong Van Minh and Nguyen Khanh, the revolving door series of civilian leaders which finally evolved into the military leadership of Thieu and Ky, the negotiations to "end" the war, and the final collapse of Vietnamese will and American support. In the account, Don makes several critical contributions to history, setting out Duong Van Minh's sole responsibility for the murder of President Diem and his broubther Nhu, and the American pressures and assurances which brought Thieu to accept "peace" in 1973.

Don's book is an important building block in the construction of a complete history of the Vietnam experience. He was a prominent participant in an influential group of military officers. In the swirl of the Vietnam contest, however, this group played but one role, and its voice was only one amid the cacophony of sound from other participants—military and civilian within the American government, non-Communist Vietnamese of all social classes and factions, and, of course, the eventually victorious Vietnamese Communists, themselves divided between Southerners and Northerners. Each of these participants had a role and an influence, and each now has a contribution to make to a final understanding of the Vietnam experience.

One could find whatever one wished to look for in Vietnam—courage or cowardice, corruption or integrity, wisdom or stupidity—and no single soldier, statesman or civilian had a monopoly on either the good or the bad qualities. As we try to assess the experience and learn what lessons we can on a national and individual level, we Americans must remember that the conflict took place in Vietnam and that Vietnamese such as Don have a vital contribution to make to our understanding of what really happened there.

William Colby

Fishing boats in small coastal port, South Vietnam.

CHAPTER ONE

A Retrospective Look

On the eve of the First World War, my father, a doctor of medicine, left Vietnam with my mother and two older brothers for France to complete his training in medicine. He finally settled in the vicinity of Bordeaux where I was born. Therefore, by birth I became a French citizen and later an officer in the Army of France. I never, however, forgot my Vietnamese heritage and remained a Vietnamese in heart, by blood and by law. The fate of the Republic of Vietnam has been my greatest concern and the cause of my deepest sorrow.

I can still remember clearly an event of my youth that illustrates my early dedication to my country and expresses what turned out to be a forlorn hope for its future—at least, so far.

In 1944, my dear friend and classmate, Tran Van Xuong, and I were studying at Tong, a French military academy in Son Tay, which is about twenty miles north of Hanoi. We were preparing for regular commissions in the French army.

One afternoon the bugle sounded, calling us to fall in ranks for a special ceremony. The symbol of the foreign country we were serving, the French tricolor, flapped in the gentle evening breeze. The flagstaff flew no other; nothing of our own to honor as we stood at rigid attention.

The ceremony came to an end and we were dismissed. Xuong and I faced each other, evidently moved by the same thoughts. There were tears in our eyes. At that moment, in the splendid effusiveness of youth, we swore that we would from now on dedicate our whole lives to serve only one country, Vietnam, and to defend only our own national colors in independence and freedom.

When we completed the course of instruction, Xuong and I parted company; he remained in the North, I returned to the South. We never saw each other again, but we both kept our oaths made on that French drill field.

I went on to a thirty-year career of service to Vietnam as soldier, politician, and cabinet minister, during which I helped shape the Vietnamese National Army from its birth to its final tragic end. Xuong, on the other hand, heard a different drummer and rallied to the Communist ranks of Ho Chi Minh. He gained repute as an effective guerrilla fighter and later commanded one of the Viet Minh's most troublesome provinces, Hung Yen. I lost track of him in 1954, but am confident that he has never forgotten the vows taken freely so long before.

If 1944 can be said to have been the beginning of my resolve, 1975 was its defeat.

I met with Nguyen Van Thieu on April 25, 1975. Thieu had already resigned his office as president of the Republic of Vietnam after American Ambassador Graham Martin had requested that General Duong Van Minh be appointed premier with full power to negotiate with Hanoi. He spoke about three occasions in 1973 and 1974 when I had presented him with concrete and feasible plans for making peace with his Communist enemies and non-Communist opponents. He referred to these missed opportunities and with a long sigh, said:

"General Don, I should have done at that time as you asked. But, I could not bring myself to do it because of my implacable opposition to Communism."

Then, impassively, Thieu left me, proceeding into exile with his inseparable friend, Tran Thien Khiem. They went to join their families in Taipei. Sixteen well-equipped North Vietnamese divisions closed in on our besieged capital. The previous week neighboring Cambodia had fallen amid a sea of blood.

I, too, am now in exile but I cannot help thinking back on my life, and on the history of my country, and trying to untangle the happenings of the past decades.

After World War I, in 1920, our family returned to Vietnam. I was sent back to Paris in 1937 at age 20 to attend the university there with no ambition whatsoever to be a soldier. A banker's life is what appealed to me, but the Second World War interfered. I was drafted into the French army in 1939 at the start of the war and was sent to a reserve officers' training school

2

at Saint Maixent. This schooling was interrupted by needs at the front, so as a cadet I joined a unit fighting Germans. After several campaigns, during one of which, at the Loire, I was awarded the Croix de Guerre, France fell and I became a prisoner of war.

After the partition of France in 1940, the Germans released us and I was sent back to Vietnam. In 1942, I was promoted to second lieutenant in the French Army Reserve, and an unlooked-for military career began.

Before embarking on the narrative of those years, I would like to describe my country and my family.

Both my father and mother came from the Saigon area of South Vietnam which was called Cochinchina* by our French masters. In addition to being a physician, my father was a landlord, owning and operating some 2,700 acres of rich rice-paddy land in Long Xuyen in the lush Mekong Delta. The rice and the other vegetables and fruits growing in this fertile land were a beautiful sight. The immense delta was truly a breadbasket, similar to its counterpart in the Red River Delta in the north.

Although my father was a professional man and a landowner and therefore relatively prosperous, we as a family were of humble origin. My grandfather was actually a boatman who had a small sampan, delivering goods from one place along our inland waterways to another. Since he was extremely poor, my father and other family members helped him by working on the boat.

One day at the market of Ba Chieu near Saigon, my father who was then only eight years old was sitting in a corner waiting for his father to complete some business. To pass the time, he was trying to read a book of French grammar. A Frenchman happened to see my father struggling with the French language and became interested in the young lad. He asked my grandfather if his son liked to study. Grandfather replied that he did, but because of his poverty he could not go to school. What education he did have was provided directly in the family as time permitted.

*Cochinchina was one of five separate sections of French Indochina and was considered to be a true colony. The other two parts of Vietnam, Tonkin and Annam, were protectorates and had a slightly more autonomous status. Laos and Cambodia were the other two parts of Indochina, but were administered separately by the French.

3

The Frenchman, who was a doctor of medicine, apparently was touched at their plight and felt that my father had potential for higher learning. He said that he would like to offer the boy a scholarship to primary school, which was, of course, eagerly accepted. My father did so well in this school that the kindly French doctor continued his support through a good French high school in Saigon and finally to the medical school of the University of Hanoi, where my father graduated after a five-year course with his coveted initial degree in medicine. Then the same French mentor helped my father go to France to obtain his final medical degree.

This was at about the time of the start of the First World War. Our French friend invited my mother and two elder brothers to live near his family in Bordeaux, where my sister and I were born.

After that war, we all returned to Vietnam and, since my father was the first Vietnamese graduate of a French medical school, he immediately established an extensive practice and began to prosper financially. He became active in many social activities and, remembering his own good fortune, emulated his French sponsor by providing scholarships for many poor and capable youths. He told me that he bought his rice fields so that he would never forget that he originally came from the land.

As a French citizen he dismayed many of the officials of the colonial government by openly advocating the cause of Vietnamese nationalism. In 1931, as one of the Representative Council of Cochinchina, he gave a speech about the future Vietnamese army which would be officered by Vietnamese. This shocked the French who denounced it, but he was immune from arrest because of his French citizenship.

My father was an inspiration to me in my own life. He treated the illnesses of many poor people for nothing and frequently provided out of his own pocket for their medicine. When World War II began, he again volunteered for service in France as a doctor, so we found ourselves together in a repatriation camp in southeast France in 1940. In later years he became the first Vietnamese mayor of Saigon (1949), and our ambassador to London (1951) and Rome (1953-1957).

I have four brothers and one sister. Two of my brothers followed my father and became doctors, while two became diplomats in our foreign service. And, my dear sister married my best friend, Le Van Kim, about whom I will have much to say as my narrative unfolds. My revered mother died when I was twelve, so she was not able to know my wife whom I married in 1942. We have two boys, a doctor educated in France and a banker who gained his degree from Cornell University in the United States, and a girl who is currently attending college in Paris.

As a glance at a map will show, our country is long and narrow, widening at the ends and pinched in the middle. It is said to resemble a bamboo pole with a rice basket at each end, an accurate analogy, both geographically and economically.

I grew up in the relatively easy life of Saigon and the southern provinces. My eyes were not really opened to the rest of my country until 1935 when my father took me on a memorable train trip to Hue in Central Vietnam (Annam) and then to Hanoi in the North (Tonkin). We went for the ceremonies commemorating the completing of the first railway line between Saigon and Hanoi. On this trip, for the first time I became acutely aware of the differences in my country. I was so used to the flat rice-producing areas by the Mekong that the terrain in the central section, near Hue, came as a shock: rugged, tall mountains with dense forests coming almost to the sea. It was, as time later proved, land most suitable for guerrilla fighting. Our guerrilla enemies were indeed able to live undetected in the remote mountains from which they could raid our settlements with impunity. The Imperial City of Hue, with its Perfume River, I also saw for the first time. I couldn't know then, of course, that later I would be a general commanding an army corps here.

The people who lived in the rugged area of Central Vietnam could certainly not grow sufficient rice for their own needs and had to depend on the southern and northern rice baskets for their basic food. The unequal distribution of natural resources is characteristic of our country. The central sector is rich in forests and marine life while the high plateau region is well suited to raising rubber, tea, coffee, and jute. Interregional economic cooperation, therefore, is essential for effective development of the country.

From Hue, our train proceeded to Hanoi. Here the Vietnamese people lived still another way of life. The vast rice-producing areas of the Red River Delta were familiar but other conditions seemed downright foreign.

The most obvious difference was the much higher population density; some 2,000 people per square mile, perhaps four times what I knew in the

5

South. Life seemed much harder. Longer work hours were necessary to produce enough to sustain the population. In addition, the climate is different. Instead of the gentle monsoon, which gives a warm, "tropical paradise" feeling to life for southern rich and poor alike, the northern wind produces cold and highly disagreeable weather. I have seen peasant girls standing up to their bare knees in rice paddies in January planting rice, bravely suffering the effects of both low temperatures and chilling winds. Their more frugal existence and more difficult life make the northern people "harder." Used to the perversity of nature and the frequent privation of insufficient food, the North Vietnamese have a quite different attitude toward life than we do in the South. They work harder, endure more, and know less of creature comfort. It is no wonder that they were able to fight so courageously and continuously over so many years while living an austere and cheerless existence.

Until this trip I had believed that all Vietnamese at least shared a common language. We do, of course, but even here I found a difference. We don't have different dialects, but we do tend to pronounce certain words differently, so it was difficult for a southerner like myself to understand my language as it was spoken in both Central and North Vietnam. Gradually, I got used to the changes as I moved from one sector to another, but people I conversed with knew immediately that I was a foreigner, at least in speech. (When Ngo Dinh Diem imported officials as district, province, and village chiefs from North and Central Vietnam to govern in the South, their speech patterns gave them away immediately and they were instantly mistrusted by the people.)

Physical appearance also differs. The various migrations from Indonesia in the south and from China in the north have left their marks. My southern neighbors tend to be darker and to resemble somewhat the Cambodians and Thais, while the northern Vietnamese look more like Chinese. Neither, however, look like the indigenous people who retreated to the highlands from the migrations, called "Montagnards" by the French. These people are truly ethnic minorities, having their own customs and individual languages.

The impressions of my historic train trip remained with me and were reinforced by numerous later journeys throughout the country. Despite these surface differences, however, many similarities bind us together, such as our written language. Vietnamese is unique as a *written* language. It was perfected by Catholic missionaries in the seventeenth century; it uses common Western style letters, with diacritical marks to denote its tonal aspects. This development has led to a relatively high rate of literacy and has enabled the rapid spread of our culture. Numerous works of literature, philosophy, and science have been published by Vietnamese authors.

Traditions and customs do not differ from one region to another, except for a few insignificant local features. Vietnamese family structure is patriarchal, with the authority of the father and the eldest son remaining unchallenged in spite of many revolutions and political upheavals. Dwellings, clothing, tools, food, and cooking are almost the same everywhere. The arts (painting, sculpture, music, theater, and singing) are practiced with the same gusto in both towns and countryside. During the seasonal lulls in fieldwork, in spring and fall, all our people enjoy religious processions, regattas, boxing matches, lively chess games in the public squares, and singing competitions between young boys and girls. I hope that such activities are still part of Vietnamese lives in Ho Chi Minh City, the new Communist name for beautiful Saigon.

Because 80 percent of our people live on farms we tend to be not very mobile, especially in the South where so many of a person's wants are supplied locally. The villages I visited in the north and central sectors were much like those I knew at home, islands of green vegetation enclosed by a bamboo hedge. Village authorities have for centuries been chosen by the local people, and have always jealously guarded their individual authority even against their overall rulers. As a child, my father taught me a popular adage, "Royal edicts defer to communal practices," a bit of wisdom that appeared lost on most of our political leaders such as Ngo Dinh Diem.

In Saigon, I was used to religious tolerance as a way of life, a situation I found duplicated in the rest of our country. Not only did my Buddhist family live in complete harmony with our Catholic, Taoist, and Confucian neighbors, but the various religious groups cooperated in the conduct of religious services. It was not uncommon at all to have parts of a Buddhist pagoda used by different Vietnamese elements to venerate their ancestors. I was taught by my family, for example, to pray to my ancestors whenever embarking on some new venture such as occupying a house for the first time. Many Catholics did the same thing.

7

As a schoolboy, I learned that my ancient country had a rich tradition and desire to be independent, but had been beset over the years by factional disputes internally and by invasions from China externally. Periods of warfare between competing royal factions had been interspersed with periods of Chinese domination, when the nation had united to throw out the northern invaders. In general, there had been two opposing regimes, but these were crushed eventually under Emperor Gia Long when Vietnam became a united nation. But, this independence had been short lived. France, in the second half of the nineteenth century, invaded Vietnam, transforming it into a colony. Her dominance over us lasted until World War II, when Vietnam entered a new era. France alternated peaceful gestures for Vietnamese independence with a French-sponsored war of southern Vietnamese against northern.

French influence had both positive and negative aspects, as my own life so clearly shows. The Vietnamese benefited greatly from French advances in science and technology, health services, modern farming methods, disease prevention, and the encouragement of industrial and business development. Our youth, including myself, learned of free enterprise and social justice, and respect for Western democratic principles. We also attended French schools, learned the French language, and came to realize that we could compete favorably with Westerners in a variety of disciplines. As a by-product of all this education and example, many of us became political militants, prepared for the coming struggle against oppression. We learned from France herself, not the French colonists, that we should fight to better the lot of the underprivileged and to recover independence and national unity.

Although we found much to admire in France as a nation and in French culture, we could never be content with the negative aspects of a colonial administration in Vietnam. The most remarkable attribute of this French political regime was that racial discrimination was practiced universally. The native Vietnamese were represented either poorly or not at all, and thus could not articulate their legitimate aspirations. Many Vietnamese functionaries were better qualified to fill positions in the government than the Frenchmen who held them, but these locals were excluded. We were deprived of essential liberties by a prying, arbitrary police network which was aided by courts that systematically denied accused persons elementary

8

rights of defense. This was especially strange to my family and myself who had found in France the opposite type of treatment. While residing in that country, we had been led to expect some implementation of the noble principles of liberty, equality, and fraternity, but this was completely denied us at home.

Agriculture and mining were financed almost entirely with French capital and directed by French technicians, with the greatest benefits going to the French, while local manpower was exploited and mistreated. A Vietnamese youth could go to France, spend five years there and graduate from a university with a first-class diploma, only to find when he returned to Vietnam that he would be given a menial job, subordinate to a semiliterate Frenchman who had never completed high school.

Economic development always involved what benefited France and her French colonists, not the Vietnamese. Vietnam was kept as dependent on the mother country as possible, both as a source of raw materials and as a captive market for French manufactured goods. Customs regulations were designed to promote French products and discourage competition from foreign goods, thus restricting the consumer in what he could buy.

A less shortsighted administration could have predicted the eventual outcome of these restrictive policies, but it took raw armed force to shock the French and the rest of the world into the realities of the situation. In a few words, the people were getting fed up. An early example of this can be demonstrated by summarizing briefly the life of an early Vietnamese nationalist, Phan Chau Trinh.

Trinh was born of a middle-class family in 1872. His life was dedicated to the eventual independence of Vietnam, promoting social and economic modernization, fighting against corruption, and revolutionizing education. He worked for a time with the French, helping found the University of Hanoi in 1906, but eventually proved to be too much of a thorn under the French saddle, so they deported him to Poulo Condore Island in 1908. He was released in 1911 and exiled to France, returning to Vietnam in 1925. He died finally on March 24, 1926.

I attended his funeral procession with about 140,000 other Vietnamese, which, considering the population of Saigon at that time and French repressive measures, was a fantastic manifestation of nationalist support and sympathy. Even as a nine-year-old boy, I could sense the deep feelings

9

of our people, and knew that we had lost a real man. Signs like this obvious nationalist sentiment and sub-rosa resistance were everywhere to be seen but failed to have any effect on the unseeing French.

Resistance to French rule was frequently not assessed for what it was, simple nationalist sentiment trying to achieve independence for our country. Shortly after the First World War, the French came to see political opposition to the colonial regime as a manifestation of Communism. Some of our nationalist leaders, myself included, tried to work with the West toward Vietnamese independence. We were in a difficult position. To the French, and later the Americans, if we failed to agree with them we were either Communists or neutralists, while to the other side, by cooperating, we became puppets.

We therefore had a grave internal problem to solve when the great struggle began in 1945. I chose to follow the Western side while other equally patriotic Vietnamese took the Marxist path under the direction of Soviet Russia.

Emperor Bao Dai as a young man.

Empress Nam Phuong, Bao Dai's wife.

CHAPTER TWO

The Misty Period:

Pre-Independence

The explosion of the Second World War in Europe profoundly altered conditions in both France and Vietnam.

After the Germans' blitzkrieg victory on June 17, 1940, Marshal Petain asked for an armistice, which was agreed to on the 25th. A new government was installed at Vichy, directed by the aging hero of Verdun. At first limited to Europe, the conflagration spread to the Far East and Southeast Asia following the September 27, 1940, three-power agreement allying Germany, Italy, and Japan.

In spite of France's capitulation, she retained almost all her colonial possessions, including the Indochinese peninsula. Japan, however, was becoming increasingly aggressive and was already at war with China and Chiang Kai-shek. French civilian and military authorities in Indochina found themselves facing greater and greater difficulty dealing with this pressure, since their parent government was so far away and so shackled by the Nazi regime.

Militarist Japan had long nurtured grand expansionist aims which were manifested in the invasion of China in 1937 and the occupation of Nanking, Canton, and the island of Hainan. In 1939, Japan tried to cut the Chinese lines of supply that ran through Tonkin, particularly the crucial railroad linking the port at Haiphong to Kunming in Yunnan province.

General Catroux, then Governor General of French Indochina, received an ultimatum on June 19, 1940, demanding that the Sino-Tonkinese border be closed and placed under the control of Japanese officials. Catroux, after much arduous bargaining, agreed to the closure, but refused to grant control to the Japanese. He believed he would be able to resist Japanese pressure with the expected arrival of reinforcements from France, plus American materiel that had been ordered earlier. He was soon disabused of that notion because nothing came. Instead, he was dismissed and replaced by Admiral Decoux, who was confronted with new Japanese demands, this time for the right of transit in Tonkin for their army and the use of Indochinese airports.

Because of the disproportionate number of French and Japanese troops in Indochina, the Vichy government negotiated a pact with Tokyo, signed September 22, 1940. According to its terms, the Japanese army at Canton could march through Tonkin and could use the airfields at Gia Lam, Lao Kay, and Bac Giang.

On the same day, at Lang Son in northeast Tonkin, several units of Japanese soldiers stationed in Chinese territory decided on their own to forcefully cross the frontier. The French garrison attempted to block their passage but suffered heavy casualties and had to surrender to the invaders. The soldiers taken prisoner were not released until the 27th, five days after the agreement reached between General Nishihara and the French went into effect.

The decline of French hegemony in Indochina was to follow the pattern set by this unfortunate event. The Japanese filtered beyond Tonkin into Annam and Cochinchina, preserving as they went the communication and supply route for their army. In the beginning, they preferred to deal with French authorities for the rapid satisfaction of their requirements, but gradually, in some localities, they started to go directly to local authorities for workers to repair roads, bridges, and railbeds. The people were required to grow certain textile crops (cotton, flax, jute), as well as rice for the Japanese.

We Vietnamese watched developments in the war very closely. We were apprehensive about the Japanese presence in our country and wondered to ourselves how long they would permit the white French government to stay in power. They seemed to have a policy of expelling white governments wherever they conquered. Their attack on Pearl Harbor and subsequent occupation between 1941 and 1942 of Thailand, Guam, Hong Kong, the Malay peninsula, Singapore, Burma, the Philippines, Wake, and the Indonesian islands of Java and Sumatra made them seem to us a

14

practically irresistible force, bolstered by their considerable prestige and the natural power of the sword.

The political situation in Vietnam, which had already been strained in the years preceding the outbreak of World War II, did not improve. The Japanese action was favored by the nation's patriotic groups who were ready to rebel against the tottering and unpopular regime of France, and hoped to regain independence. In 1941, the Japanese diplomatic mission and intelligence arm began to multiply its contacts with these groups, with the intention of fostering the creation of a front strong enough to overthrow the French and set up a pro-Japanese national government.

While the rest of the world was engaged in a life-and-death struggle, we people in Vietnam, Vietnamese and French colonists alike, lived a rather unreal life. When I returned from Europe in 1941 after the fall of France, I found the countryside in Cochinchina almost the same as when I had left to go to school in France in 1937. Except for sporadic incidents, life was calm and peaceful, the people relatively happy. The abundant harvests of rice and other crops were uninterrupted by wartime conditions, and nobody was ever hungry. About the only complaints came from Frenchmen who were running out of their favorite wines and luxury foods from France, but for the rest of us, all seemed idyllic if not ideal.

I joined a French unit engaged in the usual garrison type training that has bored military units since Julius Caesar's time. Suddenly, however, we were alerted for movement to Cambodia to defend that part of French Indochina from invasion by Thailand. A brief war ensued which resulted in the sinking of the Thai navy in a one-day engagement. The Thais nevertheless succeeded in occupying a portion of Cambodia which they alleged belonged originally to them. Not much was involved, but they did take control of Angkor and the famous ruins of the ancient Khmer civilization there. They retained this until the end of the Second World War when Angkor reverted peacefully to French and Cambodian control.

After this uneventful episode in Cambodia, in which my platoon suffered no casualties, I was sent to Hanoi to teach basic military training to recruits. This was agreeable duty and it gave me a chance to renew my acquaintance with this part of Vietnam which I had not visited since my train trip in 1935.

In 1942, I was placed on detached service as deputy chief of the French outpost at Pholu on the border between China and northern Vietnam. This was also fairly boring duty with nothing particularly exciting happening, but at least we were in the field and were our own bosses; it was much better than city garrison duty, with its ceremonies and shined shoes.

Our routine was interrupted one day in August. We sighted three planes heading in our direction from the north out of China. We alerted our antiaircraft battery. Then we noticed that the aircraft bore United States markings, so we felt secure. Suddenly, to our amazement, the planes peeled off and made a bombing run on our little camp, dropping nine bombs on us. Fortunately for us they were quite inaccurate, only making some large holes near our position. We were not damaged and sustained no casualties. I never could understand why they attacked us with our French flag bravely flying, but perhaps they had mistaken us for Japanese. I hope their accuracy improved when faced with a real enemy.

The troop trainers in the army apparently missed me, so in 1943 I was transferred to Tay Ninh (50 miles northwest of Saigon) where the French had set up recruit instruction in the Cao Dai* temple there. Later during the war against the Viet Minh, the French were happy to make friends with and support the Cao Dai and other sects, but in 1943 they were doing everything to suppress them. Japanese agents were trying to incite the Cao Dai against the French, so the colonial government had reacted vigorously, seized the temple, and put it to military use.

In 1944 I returned again to Son Tay near Hanoi, but this time, as I mentioned before, as a student working for a regular commission. Our training was interrupted by the Japanese surprise attack on March 9, 1945. The French army was in no position to offer any real resistance, so our school units were marched north to sanctuary in China where we were

*The Cao Dai is a complex religious group based in the area of Tay Ninh. It was founded by Ngo Van Chieu in 1921 and gained a large following, of perhaps 3 million. They believe that there is a universal god for Christians, Jews, Buddhists, Hindus, and Muslims. The church is organized along Western lines, having a head similar to the Pope and canonized saints such as Victor Hugo and Woodrow Wilson. They also had an organized military force and from time to time were able to control several provinces.

16

aided by the Nationalist troops of Chiang Kai-shek. The Allies wanted to establish a special intelligence network in northern Vietnam, so several of us volunteered for this duty. We infiltrated back into the country and set up several posts which began to send information on the Japanese forces back into China. Part of our job was to contact Ho Chi Minh's Communist underground, which was possessed of the latest and most reliable information.

I had been at my post in a small village for only two months when my intelligence career came to an abrupt halt. A villager turned me over to a Japanese patrol when I refused to marry his daughter as he desired. I did not want to enter into such a contract, and told the man that I was already married. Apparently I was not very persuasive, because the next thing I knew I was back in Son Tay, this time as a prisoner of war. Fortunately, I was able to escape from the Japanese and started a long trek back to Saigon.

In looking back on that confused situation in 1945, it seems a little absurd for the Japanese to have made their attack when it must have appeared obvious that the war was about over for them. I suppose they feared an Allied operation into Indochina which could have cut off their forces scattered throughout Southeast Asia, so they took immediate steps to avoid the worst.

The Japanese attack and occupation thoroughly convulsed both the military and political scene. In a short twenty-four hours, spectacular changes were produced which pointed up the fragility of the French colonial administration in spite of its having been in control for almost a century. Based solely on weapons and a police apparatus, the administration fell apart when these props were removed. To the French, it was a disaster. To the Vietnamese it was an opportunity to seize what power we could for our own advantage. We desired neither the return of the old French regime nor a continuation of the newly imposed Japanese dominance.

The Japanese had not invaded Vietnam to make it a solid milestone on their path to military or political supremacy, but rather to ensure the safety of their troops and their supply line. In their *coup de force,* the Japanese arrested and imprisoned all French officers and other political officials not absolutely essential to the overall functioning of the country. Except for a few army units like my own which had managed to escape to China, all

17

French military were made prisoners of war. Political and governmental posts, such as chief of province, vacated by the coup were filled with the best qualified Vietnamese available, some of whom had previously been deputies under the French. The only French retained in key positions were technicians or engineers, who were needed to direct such activities as power stations and waterworks.

To establish a central government for the three sections of Vietnam, the Japanese turned to Bao Dai, the reigning monarch of Annam, the central sector. The three sections of Vietnam, Tonkin, Annam, and Cochinchina, had been administered separately by the French under an overall governor general for Indochina, but now the Japanese catered to our desire for independence and unity by creating a single central government.

We were somewhat surprised at this turn of events, since the Japanese had previously supported other pro-Nippon revolutionary elements such as the Alliance for the Restoration of Vietnam of Prince Cuong De, an anti-French uncle of Bao Dai, and politico-religious groups such as the Cao Dai.

So, on March 11, 1945, Emperor Bao Dai proclaimed that, ". . . from this day, the protectorate treaty with France is abolished and the nation will recover its independence. The Government of Vietnam has faith in the loyalty of Japan and is determined to collaborate with that country, lending its resources to aid the common prosperity of Greater East Asia. . . ." I suspect that the emperor swallowed hard.

I am sure that Bao Dai did not mean those last words since he and all his advisors knew full well that Japan was on her last legs and that the war was lost for her. Our people wanted to obtain as much power as possible and get our political apparatus established throughout the country, so as to face the Allies with a functioning, unified Vietnamese government if the French tried to return.

The nomination of a premier for Bao Dai's new government proved to be a little difficult since his first choice, the future president of the First Republic, Ngo Dinh Diem, refused the honor twice. He did finally get an excellent man in Professor Tran Trong Kim, a non-Communist nationalist who was an eminent writer and historian with an excellent reputation in academic and political circles. Kim had been living in exile abroad, having escaped to Singapore from the claws of the Sûreté, Admiral Decoux's federal police.

Other splendid men were chosen, men of Kim's nationalist non-Communist persuasion who were respected throughout the country for their competence and integrity. They included Professor Hoang Xuan Han, graduate of the Ecole Polytechnique and l'Ecole Normale Supérieure de Paris, four lawyers (Tran Van Chuong, Trinh Dinh Thao, Vu Van Hien, and Phan Anh), four doctors of medicine (Tran Dinh Nam, Ho Ta Khanh, Nguyen Huu Thi, and Vu Ngoc Anh) and a government civil engineer, Luu Van Lang.*

This team of technicians, mostly young and enthusiastic, were willing and able to form a solid foundation for newly regained independence, prepare a new constitution consistent with the wishes of the people, and implement wide-ranging and profound social and administrative reforms.

The strongest man in the government was Tran Van Chuong, an old friend of my family whom I had known since I was a small child. He had practiced law in the Mekong Delta area southwest of Saigon, but had moved to Hanoi in 1942. He later became our ambassador to Washington (1954-1963) while his politically astute wife, a cousin of Bao Dai, was our official observer to the United Nations. This remarkable couple had one other claim to fame: they were the parents of the beautiful wife of Ngo Dinh Nhu, the "first lady" of Vietnam during the regime of Ngo Dinh Diem. In this new government he was deputy premier and foreign minister.

While these important events were taking place, I was simply trying to survive as an escaped prisoner of war. It had been quite easy for me to escape from my Japanese captors since security measures were very lax and I had made friends with some Japanese officers. One day when they were not watching, I simply walked away and headed south. I soon found that it was much easier to evade the Japanese than our supposed Allies. Again, I had to dodge American aircraft which attacked any movement they saw on the roads during daylight hours. By moving at night, I was able to make fairly good time, however, and thus was able to accept some much

*A few months later, Phan Anh went over to the Communist side, and was appointed a government minister by Ho Chi Minh. Trinh Dinh Thao, a respected neutralist, waited until 1968—when the Communist troops launched their nation-wide Tet offensive—to join the pro-Hanoi National Liberation Front. Dr. Tran Dinh Nam afterwards became a prominent opposition leader in South Vietnam.

appreciated hospitality from Mr. and Mrs. Chuong at their home in Hue in June 1945. It was good to see some old friends in comfortable surroundings after several months of prison and fugitive life.

We had a splendid lunch and an excellent conversation, during which they brought me up to date on the latest military and political news as well as their aspirations for the future. Chuong especially wanted me to tell my father and other friends in Saigon that Bao Dai, Kim, and all his associates were fully aware that theirs was only a puppet government now, but that the days of the Japanese were definitely numbered. He said that they were trying to seize as much power in as short a time as possible to pave our way for unity and independence after the departure of the Japanese.

Unfortunately for my friend Chuong and his associates, their good intentions ran afoul of more pressing and imperious Japanese military and economic demands. Requisitions of manpower and especially of rice to feed their troops and secret police stirred up a general undercurrent of dissatisfaction. The disastrous effects of floods in the Red River Delta, with resulting crop loss and famine, combined with the Allied economic embargo and bombings, made the situation critical. A great popular insurrection could have been instigated at any moment by militants of any political tendency. But the new government was powerless to act because most of the problems were caused by matters quite out of their control.

By this time I had arrived in my home area, managing to elude both the Japanese police and American aircraft. Here I found conditions not as bad as in Tonkin and Annam, probably because of the overall capability of my region to produce immense quantities of rice. It was much as it was when I left to go to Son Tay except that the French were conspicuous by their absence.

Here I was reunited with the person who was to play such an important role in my future life, Le Van Kim who had married my sister, Gaby, in 1942. Kim was a young French officer. My family and I had met him in a repatriation camp for "colored" French citizens who were returning to their homelands, and we have maintained a life-long friendship since then. He had been in an artillery unit south of Saigon at Vung Tau when the Japanese coup occurred. When I got back home, I found him sheltered in the home of a doctor and politician, Tran Nhu Lan.

20

Later he told me of an amusing event that happened at Lan's house. Some Japanese officers arrived with a Vietnamese disguised in uniform as one of them. He was Ngo Dinh Diem, later destined for fame as our president. Diem had been struggling against the French for years, and he wanted to remain incognito. Much later I asked Diem why he was masquerading as a Japanese. Did he approve of their policies? He responded heatedly that he much preferred the French to the Japanese, but he could see that by then Japan was finished and that there was a chance of using them for the good of Vietnam.

My father and his friends were very interested in the news I brought from Mr. and Mrs. Chuong, but of equal interest to them was information about the Viet Minh and its leader, Ho Chi Minh. I repeated to them the prevailing sentiment of the Vietnamese prisoners of war at Son Tay who were laudatory of Ho and his valiant resistance efforts against the Japanese. They saw him as a truly patriotic and effective leader. Some of my old friends wondered if I had become some kind of propaganda agent for Ho, since they were aware that he was definitely anti-French. Others saw Ho as a true nationalist because he fought against both French and Japanese. He was indeed, and continues to be, a real enigma to the Vietnamese people.

As it turned out, we had two kinds of Vietnamese nationalists. The first, like Premier Kim and Vice Premier Chuong, were what I will call non-Communist nationalists. They did not agree with Marxist principles, believing that the free enterprise system practiced in France, England, and the United States was the best course for our people to follow. The second group followed the teachings of Marx, Lenin, and Stalin, seeing a class struggle that did not really exist in Vietnam. We had rich and poor, of course, but nobody, in my view, was being exploited except by the French colonial government. Ho Chi Minh was the leader of the Viet Minh, a so-called Nationalist Front secretly but effectively dominated by hard-line Communists like Vo Nguyen Giap and Pham Van Dong.

By 1941 they had managed to build a firm base in the provinces of northeast Tonkin (Bac Kan, Cao Bang, and Thai Nguyen) for their future push into the northern delta posing as a non-Communist Front. They had already obtained arms and munitions from the Nationalist Chinese, with the understanding that they would help resist Japanese troops in Vietnam. The

21

Americans, too, had been providing weapons via the Office of Strategic Services (OSS), and even the French military mission at Kunming did similar work for them in 1945 after the Japanese takeover.

Jean Sainteny, the French diplomat, later told me that an American OSS team was parachuted to Ho's Viet Minh headquarters at a remote village in August 1945. They found Ho very sick and the medical member of the team, Paul Hoagland, saved his life. Major Allison Dawes was the team leader who accompanied Ho on his triumphal march to Hanoi later in August.

The Viet Minh was without doubt the strongest, most disciplined, and best organized of the several groups of nationalist militants, who could not manage to agree on programs of action or leadership. In truth, the Allies had no real choice of whom to back initially since the Viet Minh had an operating network already established, while the non-Communists were notable only by their disorganization. Their lack of cohesion and mutual trust was due partly to the "divide-and-rule" tactics of the French colonial administration.

In mid-August 1945, the Dai Viet (Greater Vietnam) Party, a revolutionary right-wing organization made up of intellectuals, students, and city dwellers, was ready to take control of Hanoi with its well-trained and well-equipped commandos before Ho Chi Minh's cadres moved into the city. The plan drawn up by Truong Tu Anh,* the party's young, but charismatic and uncontested leader, failed because of hesitation and lack of coordination with the other prominent nationalist party, Viet Nam Quoc Dan Dang (VNQDD).

Like the Dai Viet, the VNQDD was a right-wing party. It was organized in the late twenties by Nguyen Thai Hoc, who was executed, along with other members of the party's central committee, for his leadership of an abortive but spectacular revolt against the French colonists in Tonkin. The party had been almost decimated by the French, but some of its leaders escaped to China. The VNQDD was able to make a political comeback in 1945 when its strong ally, Chiang Kai-shek's Nationalist China, assumed military control of Tonkin in the wake of Japan's surrender.

*Anh was killed in early 1946 by the Viet Minh.

Both the Dai Viet and VNQDD parties were opposed to the Communist-led Viet Minh, but differed in their approaches to Communism. The Dai Viet maintained that no cooperation was possible with the Communists, while some more flexible VNQDD leaders responded favorably to Ho Chi Minh's appeal for a coalition government. Among them were Vu Hong Khanh and Nguyen Tuong Tam.

Tam, Vietnam's most prominent novelist in the thirties and forties, soon became disillusioned with Ho. Later he was wrongly accused by President Diem of participating in an abortive antigovernment coup d'etat. As a sign of protest, Tam took his own life, to the sorrow of thousands of Vietnamese who admired his literary genius and political integrity.

Toward the end of 1945, threatened with persecution and liquidation, the leaders of Dai Viet and VNQDD succeeded in forming a unified anti-Viet Minh front and a unified leadership. Unfortunately, this was too late.

Ho was known as Nguyen Ai Quoc prior to 1943. He changed his name before negotiating with General Chiang Fa-kwei, the Nationalist Chinese commander of Kwang Si province, feeling that his new name would not immediately expose him as a Communist to the Allies.

In addition to changing his name, he sought to disguise even his political party, calling it from about 1940 "The League for Vietnamese Independence" (Vietnam Doc Lap Dong Minh, abbreviated to Viet Minh). Later he organized what he called his "Labor Party" (Lao Dong), and after 1945 the Communist regime of North Vietnam was called "The Democratic Republic of Vietnam" (Vietnam Dan Chu Xa Hoi). Not until 1975, when its victory was complete, did the party openly put the name "Communist" to its political apparatus.

The events of this same general period, which seemed so important to us in Vietnam at the time, were relatively insignificant in an historical sense. World War II was winding down; it had already ended in Europe and was rapidly coming to a close in the Far East. President Roosevelt of the United States died in the spring of 1945 and was replaced by Harry Truman. Finally, Hiroshima was bombed on August 6 and the Japanese surrendered on August 14.

Seeing his chance for a successful coup of his own, Ho Chi Minh called for a general uprising, with August 19 as the actual revolution day. A huge

23

demonstration was organized in Hanoi that day, supposedly by a nationalist committee loyal to Bao Dai's government to celebrate the surrender of the Japanese. The committee was seated in chairs facing the large crowd when suddenly six armed Viet Minh soldiers appeared to intimidate the members of the committee. One of this squad climbed the flagpole and tore down Bao Dai's yellow imperial standard, substituting the red Communist flag for it. More Viet Minh flags magically appeared in the crowd and the demonstration turned into a noisy victory for Ho Chi Minh.

Bao Dai abdicated on August 25, after learning of the revolt against his rule that had taken place in Hanoi on August 19, but word of this action did not reach the masses in Saigon. It became abundantly clear to us, however, in demonstrations on August 25 and September 2, when we observed the coup that suddenly took place in Saigon. One minute the people were waving their arms in the air with palms open in a friendly way; the next, they changed the gesture into the ominous closed-fist salute of the Communists. The results were much the same, with the Viet Minh taking over all important governmental posts. The efforts of Professor Kim and my friend Chuong thus came to naught.

Ho Chi Minh also chose September 2 to formally proclaim independence in the Ba Dinh public square in Hanoi. The fact that we already had established a legitimate, independent, and unified government headed by Bao Dai made no difference to the Communists. They, of course, had the weapons and ammunition, so there was not much the Bao Dai government could do to avert destruction.

In the organization of this provisional government, Ho, himself, became president and foreign minister and logically appointed his close Communist collaborators to various essential posts: Vo Nguyen Giap at Interior, Pham Van Dong at Finance, Chu Van Tan as Minister of Defense, and Tran Huy Lieu as Minister of Information. Bao Dai, now considered to be a simple citizen, was named Supreme Government Counselor. In a short time he voluntarily exiled himself abroad to live in Hong Kong.

Thousands of words have already been written about Ho Chi Minh, Vo Nguyen Giap, and Pham Van Dong detailing their lives and philosophy. I shall confine my commentary to reporting the opinion prevailing among many Vietnamese, including those in zones long controlled by the Communists. They recognized fully the dynamism, steadfastness, and shrewdness

24

these Communist leaders exhibited in their victorious struggle to eliminate successively the Japanese occupation, the French colonial regime, and what they labeled "American imperialism." They also accomplished the remarkable feat of unifying by force North and South Vietnam and installing a single Communist government.

But, this was done at a fearful price in terms of human dignity and Vietnamese customs and tradition. They sought to generate a struggle between classes in a backward country where class differences were never known. Our single most important characteristic was a heartfelt desire to be unified and independent. We had suffered under foreign domination for centuries. We had had enough of foreign exploitation by Chinese, French, and Japanese. What we really wanted was to be left alone to chart our own course in the ocean of the world.

From my conversations with many Western friends, it is apparent that Vietnam and the Vietnamese are lumped together with our immense neighbor, China, or with other Asian countries like Japan. Nothing could be farther from the truth. The Chinese existed for centuries under a warlord type of feudalism, while the Japanese had a strong monarchy with a noble class who governed the country. We had neither of these traditions, no peasants exploited by rich landowners, and no hereditary nobility to create artificial class distinctions. There were no industrialists forcing degrading work on dissatisfied laborers in the cities.

We were an agrarian society and, except for a few French planters who had large land holdings, the bulk of the land was held by individual Vietnamese who owned only small parcels on a highly democratic basis. Vietnamese families tended to be large, so the land was divided among succeeding generations, ensuring a fidelity to it because of the veneration we owed our ancestors. Additionally, in each village there existed communal land which was divided into small portions for allocation to all inhabitants over eighteen years of age. This was done by lottery every three years, so a young man could always hope to better his lot by being lucky in the selection.

Therefore, we could all be practically sure of owning a good piece of land, having our own home, and being able to cultivate food for our personal use. We could make the small amount of extra cash we needed by selling the excess production in the cities or even for export.

25

Government posts were also filled on a democratic basis, using competitive examinations, without consideration of the native origins or initial work stations of the applicants. Industries and trade were in the primary stage of development, so there were very few wealthy businessmen who might seek to exploit our people as workers.

By contrast, a "new class" of privileged people, the Communist hierarchy, has now imposed a stern and joyless political system on the people, and has resorted to force and intimidation to maintain itself in power. We Vietnamese do not need centralized planning of the economy; our tradition has taught us that governmental control should cease at the hedge surrounding the village. We Vietnamese do not need to have our farms collectivized; they belong to our honored ancestors and are thus sacred to us. We want the freedom to pick our own employer if we choose to work in a trade. We want the freedom to join labor unions and to go on strike if we choose to try to better ourselves. And, we want to be able to demonstrate against inept or corrupt politicians when they do not govern us properly.

I have spoken of several patriotic nationalists so far in this book and will mention others later. These good men were truly after what the people wanted. They could see no advantage in the Communist system for our country. But, they were vilified as "traitors" and "imperialist lackeys" because they tried to work with the Western powers to achieve our independence.

And so we watched as the Viet Minh took over in the north, exploiting daily their successes of August and September, 1945. A first order of business was the legitimization of their provisional government by the use of elections held throughout Tonkin and Annam on January 6, 1946. A government headed, of course, by Ho Chi Minh, was elected as well as a National Assembly. Some interesting innovations were used in this orchestrated election.

The citizens were obligated to vote or they could not obtain an identity card. Without this card, they could not transact even the most simple business, so naturally everybody voted. They were faced with a single slate of candidates, and at all polling places were armed Communist functionaries who, through their intimidating presence, insured a "Yes" vote from all. As a result, the overall election tally showed a landslide of 99 percent for the

26

party's candidates, not a surprising result considering the circumstances.

On this unopposed slate, the party had included a few non-Communist nationalists to give the appearance of a coalition government and opposition members in the Assembly. Their numbers were so few, however, and their positions so obscure, that there was, in fact, total domination by the Viet Minh element.

The Communists even went so far as to give fictitious political designations to various parts of the room where the Assembly was convened in Hanoi. The body was divided into right, center, and left sections as in France—again to give the appearance of democracy in action. In fact, the bulk of the delegates sitting in those various chairs were Communists and Ho's picked men.

Even this ineffective coalition proved ephemeral as the Viet Minh began to feel more secure. In March 1946, Ho and his Communist-dominated Front began the liquidation of other non-Communist parties, with some 5,000 nationalists being executed. Ho's Minister of Defense, Vo Nguyen Giap actually directed this purge against the nationalists. Khai Hung, Vietnam's well-known novelist, was stuffed in a bag and drowned in a river. About 25,000 other nationalists found themselves in labor camps, and another 6,000 managed to escape by fleeing into China.

But I must go back in time, because the overall situation was so confused at the time of the Japanese surrender and differed greatly from region to region. In the south, in Cochinchina, where I was keeping myself as inconspicuous as possible, control over the government passed quickly from the Viet Minh officials who were representing Ho's Democratic Republic of Vietnam to the returning French. This occurred as a result of the greatest duplicity possible on the part of the British.

At previous conferences of the victorious Allies, it had been decided that British influence would prevail in Southeast Asia, and that disarmament and repatriation of the Japanese and restoration of civil law and order in Vietnam would be accomplished by the British south of the 16th parallel, and by the Chinese north of that arbitrary boundary (near Da Nang in Annam). Accordingly, British officials entered Saigon toward the end of August, 1945, to find a de facto Viet Minh government in place with the Japanese waiting to begin their repatriation homeward.

Major General Gracey, the overall British commander, arrived in

27

Saigon on September 6, but was preceded by a Colonel Jean Cédile, France's delegate to Indochina. Cédile, from France's High Commission and Administration of Colonies, had dropped by parachute, with Japanese assistance, at Tay Ninh on August 22. Cédile proceeded to Saigon where he contacted the British, persuading them to help him restore the tricolor to its former position of preeminence over Saigon.

The British cooperated beautifully, not only rearming the French who had remained in the area, but using armed Japanese in conjunction with their own troops to suppress the Viet Minh soldiers who were attempting to maintain their authority there. Although the British found a functioning Vietnamese government operating in Saigon, they refused to enter into any kind of negotiations, declared martial rule, and by force of arms gradually overwhelmed the Viet Minh. Finally on September 23, 1945, Cédile managed to seize power over the civil administration of Saigon.

During this time, Cédile tried to get himself well informed on the new situation in Vietnam and organized an information committee. At one of his meetings with this group he asked, "What must I do? What should I say during my first contact with the Vietnamese people?"

A French friend of mine, Jean Orsini, suggested: "There are two magic words, *Doc Lap* (Independence), which will make all Vietnamese enthusiastic. Say something about independence and pronounce the words. We all know that you cannot give independence by yourself, but at least say the words."

Cédile answered, "I am authorized by de Gaulle to do and say anything except *Doc Lap*." His noncommittal position made it obvious to us that the French position had not changed.

French reinforcements arrived in Saigon in October and in combined operations with British and Japanese troops, they extended their control of the area around the capital city of Cochinchina. The British finally withdrew at the end of the year, but by that time, control of our lines in the south had passed back to the French. This was, of course, considerably different from the situation in the North where the Viet Minh were still firmly in control.

The Nationalist Chinese of Chiang Kai-shek were given the task of disarming the Japanese north of the 16th parallel. They viewed their mission in an entirely different manner than did the British, not caring if the French ever regained control over their former colony. Instead of cooperating with the French, they proceeded to disarm the Japanese without incident and worked directly with Ho's government to maintain order in the area.

Big power politics became a definite factor in early 1946, however, with negotiations beginning in Chungking, China, between the Chinese and the French. Both were after concessions. France had certain territorial rights in China which she renounced in exchange for Chinese recognition of French sovereignty over Indochina. Treaties were signed on February 28 and March 6, 1946, jointly by Jean Sainteny for France, and Ho Chi Minh and Vu Hong Khanh, a non-Communist nationalist, for Vietnam. Among other provisions, the March 6 treaty contained a clause pledging France to consult the Vietnamese people by referendum in regard to unification of the three sections, Tonkin, Annam, and Cochinchina.

General Phillippe Le Clerc, the French hero of the final fight against the Germans in the Second World War, was sent at this time to Vietnam by de Gaulle to supervise the French in reinstating their colonial administration. To do this and to ensure the safety of some 30,000 French living in the North, Le Clerc had also to negotiate with Ho Chi Minh's government.

With Chiang Kai-shek's approval, France began to relieve Chinese troops on March 15, a mission to be completed by March 31 when the French army would assume the responsibility of completing the disarmament of the Japanese and maintaining order north of the 16th parallel. At this time an extremely bizarre thing happened.

As I mentioned earlier, Ho's government was a kind of coalition affair with various nationalist elements present. In addition, some nationalist militia formed part of its troop strength under Vo Nguyen Giap, the Minister of Defense. Ho Chi Minh thought it greatly to his advantage to eliminate as much nationalist influence as he could, so he persuaded the newly returned French to help him disarm this dissident political fighting force. These strange bedfellows cooperated to remove the nationalist force from the scene, immensely strengthening Ho's hold on the people. Such cooperation with his supposedly avowed enemy did not seem to bother him at all. What counted was the advantage to be gained at the time. Ho also cooperated fully with the French in getting the Chinese out of Vietnam as quickly as possible, seeing them as natural allies of the right-wing nationalist politicians who would eventually be in concerted opposition to him.

Sainteny and Le Clerc were willing to recognize Ho's government as a

29

free state in the Indochinese Federation and in the French Union. They saw clearly that it would be better to grant the Vietnamese a degree of autonomy within the French sphere of influence than to have to oppose them on the field of battle. Le Clerc, especially, could profit from his personal experience as an old resistance fighter against the Germans in occupied France and predict what a determined guerrilla force like the Viet Minh could do against his conventionally organized forces. These two practical Frenchmen had not reckoned, however, with the balky reaction of the French colonists, investors, and administrators, and especially of Admiral Georges Thierry d'Argenlieu, High Commissioner of Indochina and Commander-in-Chief of all French forces in the Far East.

Cédile, speaking for d'Argenlieu and the French government, declared that the March 6 pact, which recognized Vietnamese independence within the French Union, was only a local agreement for Tonkin and did not apply to Cochinchina, which was soon to have its own government, parliament, army, and financial situation. This was confirmed by French Overseas Minister Marius Moutet on March 14 when he stated that Cochinchina, too, would become a free state equal to the others in the French Federation (Laos, Cambodia, and Tonkin). These assertions were not at all what Sainteny had agreed to during his negotiations with Ho Chi Minh and the other Vietnamese nationalists. Under the old colonial administration, the small states of Laos and Cambodia were always considered separately since they were composed of different ethnic groups from the Vietnamese and had different languages, so it was logical to see them continue this way. There was no logic, however, in considering Tonkin as separate from Cochinchina with no reference to Annam. Previously the three sections of Vietnam— Tonkin, Annam, and Cochinchina—had been administered separately by the French, but now all Vietnamese nationalists passionately wanted unity along with independence. Sainteny and Le Clerc were perceptive enough to see this and tried to solve the Vietnamese problem from this viewpoint, but were foiled in their efforts by the short-sighted Frenchmen in Saigon and Paris.

On March 24, 1946, Ho Chi Minh and d'Argenlieu met at the Bay of Along in the admiral's flagship and agreed to a preparatory conference in Dalat in early April to be followed by a definitive meeting in Fontainebleau later in the year to try to settle the provisions of the March 6 agreement.

On March 26, a French batallion entered Hue, capital of Annam, and on the same day, the Cochinchina Advisory Council appointed Dr. Nguyen Van Thinh as head of the provisional government of the Republic of Cochinchina. This was an obvious attempt on d'Argenlieu's part to have some kind of Vietnamese government operating in Saigon before the start of the preparatory conference with Uncle Ho.

Thinh was a physician, a French citizen, and one of the most respected personages in South Vietnam. He was honest and wealthy and chairman of the Democratic Party in Cochinchina. Very influential, he had organized rice shipments from large stockpiles in the south to alleviate the suffering caused by the famine in the north in the spring of 1945.

Since he was an old and very dear friend of my family, I saw him frequently during his term as president and even made some trips on his behalf to inform supporters in the Mekong Delta of his policies and programs. During one of our meetings, he told me that the main reason he accepted the presidency from the French was that it seemed to him to be the best way of working for true unity of the country. He saw himself as being the modern-day unifier of Vietnam, as was Gia Long in 1802 whose movement started in the south and eventually encompassed the entire country. Thinh was French-educated and married to a Frenchwoman, so he seemed like an excellent choice to fulfill this mission; he was popular with his fellow Vietnamese and had close ties to the French.

The Viet Minh, of course, saw Thinh's appointment and the establishment of a new republic in Cochinchina as an example of French duplicity and as a contravention of the provisions of the March 6 agreement which called for a referendum of the people as a first step to unification of the country. Ho Chi Minh was totally correct in his view since this was d'Argenlieu's maneuver to circumvent Sainteny's agreement. From the start of their colonizing in the 19th century, the French always tried to keep Vietnam divided, so this was nothing more than a continuation of their "divide and rule" policy.

By this time, my comrade Le Van Kim and I were back in the French army. We were living together in Saigon at the time of the Japanese surrender in August 1945 and witnessed the great demonstrations I have already recounted. We were seized by the spirit of the time and tried to join the newly organized Vietnamese army. Much to our surprise, we were rebuffed by the Viet Minh authorities because of our French citizenship. We were told we were not worthy to join them, so as the only choice open to us as young military men, we joined the newly released French troops under Cédile. We operated with them for a few weeks, but then General Le Clerc decided that we should not be in a position where we might perhaps have to fire against our countrymen. He therefore sent Kim to be Admiral d'Argenlieu's aide and gave me a similar position in his own headquarters.

As a result of these appointments, Kim and I were able, each night after returning from work, to compare the policies of Le Clerc and d'Argenlieu and the qualities of the men themselves. In our view, Le Clerc came out looking much better. He was a capable and forthright soldier who believed in living with and honoring the accords that Sainteny had made for France with the Vietnamese. He also saw the practicality of French-Vietnamese cooperation in governing the country. D'Argenlieu, on the other hand, was a disaster in his role as high commissioner. We could not understand how he could have been appointed since he was not a real admiral at all, having been a monk in a monastery before the war. But, he was a friend of de Gaulle and thus had been appointed to a post for which he was completely ill suited. When replaced as high commissioner in 1947, he returned to the tranquility of the monastery.

The preliminary conference agreed to by d'Argenlieu and Ho convened on April 17 in Dalat. The Vietnamese delegation included Vo Nguyen Giap and several eminent lawyers, engineers, doctors, journalists, and politicians. The French argued for a division in the country, especially for the new Republic of Cochinchina with the five* separate states related politically to the overall French Federation of Indochina. The Vietnamese delegates were just as adamant in their nationalist arguments for a unified Vietnam, within the French Federation if necessary. Thus, this conference ended in an impasse with nothing decided.

Le Van Kim in his role as Admiral d'Argenlieu's aide attended this conference and came back with stories of his admiration for Vo Nguyen Giap. Eight years later at the 1954 Geneva Conference, Kim attended as a

*Tonkin, Annam, Cochinchina, Laos, and Cambodia.

military representative from South Vietnam. In a break from the latter conference, a member of the Viet Cong told Kim in a restroom very confidentially, "Now Vietnam is divided. Try to keep the South free."

The next step in the conference agenda was the planned follow-up meeting in Fontainebleau, which opened on July 6, 1946, with Pham Van Dong and Max André heading the Vietnamese and French delegations respectively. Because France had not committed herself to a precise date and procedure for the reunification referendum, the Vietnamese delegation refused to sign the draft of the *Modus Vivendi* which was prepared on September 10. But on the night of September 14, Ho Chi Minh visited Marius Moutet, French Minister of Overseas Territories, to say that he would sign the provisional *Modus Vivendi* before returning to Vietnam. These are some excerpts:

> The governments of France and Vietnam are firmly agreed to follow, in the spirit of mutual trust, the policy of collaboration and accord first stated at the preliminary conference of March 6, 1946, and elaborated at Dalat and Fontainebleau.
>
> The two governments agree to cease all acts of hostility and violence on both sides in Cochinchina and South Annam.
>
> The two governments postpone the fixing of the date and procedure for the referendum decided on at the March 6 preliminary conference.

After Ho returned to Vietnam, he assigned Vo Nguyen Giap to supervise the execution of the accords he had made with the French. There were numerous violations on both sides which made his supervision extremely difficult. Especially irritating to the Vietnamese was the reopening of a customs office in Haiphong which gave the French virtual control over all trade coming into that port city.

While Kim was in France with d'Argenlieu, I remained in Vietnam, continuing to work for both General Le Clerc and President Thinh. Because of my position on Le Clerc's staff, I moved around the country a lot and thus

33

was able to meet many politicians and army officers. On a trip to Hanoi in June 1946 to gather information for Le Clerc and his staff at first hand, I saw one person I especially wanted to meet, Dr. Tran Van Quy, a medical school classmate of both my father and President Thinh.

Quy was an ardent nationalist who had managed to escape Vo Nguyen Giap's purge because he also happened to be Ho Chi Minh's personal physician. Both Dr. Quy and his two sons questioned me at length about his friend, Dr. Thinh, and his new Cochinchinese government and how many of us were trying to work for unity in the country. He seemed to understand and sympathize with our predicament, but his sons were extremely hostile, so much so that he feared for my safety.

I saw him again in 1948 when he had become mayor of Hanoi and I asked him if he and Ho Chi Minh had discussed Dr. Thinh and his conciliatory policies aimed at reunifying the country. Quy responded that Ho understood Thinh's situation, but had to go along with other leaders in the Communist party.

I also saw our old friend, Tran Van Chuong in Hanoi. He had returned to the practice of law after his short-lived post in Bao Dai's government had been dissolved. Chuong was bitter over the French creation of the Cochinchinese Republic, even though Dr. Thinh was one of his dearest friends, believing that this was one of the typical French methods of dividing and conquering. He was even more upset at the French for their collaboration with the Viet Minh against the nationalist elements during Giap's purge. When open hostilities between the French and Viet Minh broke out later, he removed himself and his family from Hanoi and went to live in the country for three years.

After these trips around the country, I passed on my impressions to Le Clerc and President Thinh. To visit Thinh at that time was very discouraging because of the way the French were treating him. They had completely underestimated him, thinking that he would be a docile puppet. He had to use his own house as both office and official residence because the French gave him insufficient means for getting his work done. They did give him an official car, but the license plate was marked with five zeros in order to make him an object of ridicule.

Furthermore, he was on an obvious collision course with d'Argenlieu's policies and was vilified by the Viet Minh administration in the North as a

34

French puppet. As time went on, more and more French support was withdrawn from him. I visited him at his home on November 9, 1946, to find him in an extremely morose state. I knew he was discouraged, but not to this extent.

He told me, "France is not fair. I have not been enough of a puppet for them, so they are trying to replace me."

The next day he hanged himself as a protest to French misrule.

The French put on a real show for his funeral, a true comedy. A state funeral was organized, with Admiral d'Argenlieu and most of the high French officials present to pay their respects. It made his Vietnamese friends both sad and angry, and played again into the hands of the Viet Minh. He was replaced by the more complacent Le Van Hoach.

As a by-product of the French reopening of their customs office, which to the Vietnamese in Hanoi contravened both the March 6 agreement and the French-Vietnamese *Modus Vivendi* of September 14, an incident occurred in the port of Haiphong in the North on November 20. A Chinese trading boat was seized by the French because they believed that it was smuggling contraband motor fuel. Vietnamese militia, seeing the action aboard the boat, opened fire on the French. Both sides were reinforced and in the resulting fracas, both sides sustained casualties.

This precipitated a strong reaction; the French hierarchy issued an ultimatum requiring the withdrawal of all Vietnamese military from Haiphong and ordered that a broad zone around the city be occupied by French troops. These measures caused great resentment among the Vietnamese in both Haiphong and Hanoi and steeled Ho Chi Minh to resist the French demands. After many demands by the French and refusals by the Vietnamese, on November 23, a severe attack was launched by combined French artillery and naval gunfire against the city of Haiphong. As a result of this brutal and excessive action, some 6,000 people were killed, including many innocent civilians.

Things went from bad to worse in the North and even a visit from Jean Sainteny to his friend Ho Chi Minh on December 2 did little to ameliorate the situation. Finally, on December 19, 1946, General Giap ordered an attack on Hanoi, seizing the central power station. At the same time, Giap called for general fighting on all fronts against the French. This, then, was the effective start of the French-Vietnamese war which ended only after seven years of bitter fighting with the disaster of Dien Bien Phu.

The French naturally responded to the Viet Minh armed attacks in kind, initially with some success. They did, however, recognize that a political solution was an indispensable part of any overall victory over the dissident Communists. They therefore tried to advance various Vietnamese to positions of political authority in the governments they established. One of these was Nguyen Van Xuan, deputy premier in the previous Thinh government.

Xuan was a French citizen and a colonel in the French army. Mistrusted by the French, however, because of his known nationalist views, he was not allowed to participate in the government that succeeded Thinh's. Disappointed, he returned to France where he was promoted to brigadier general in early 1947. I was sent to Paris to brief him on the latest developments in southern Vietnam and to urge him to return to Saigon because the government of Le Van Hoach was having difficulties. My persuasions proved successful and Xuan returned to Cochinchina on September 15 as premier.

He immediately tried to change the overall political situation, finding that matters were even worse than I had depicted. A new election was held, and on October 1 Xuan was elected president by the Council. He immediately appointed me his aide-de-camp. One of Xuan's first actions was to change the name of Cochinchina to South Vietnam, an important move politically because it denied the French notion of keeping that section of Vietnam as a separate colony of France, like Laos and Cambodia. This, coupled with Xuan's further work toward unifying the country, did not set well with the French colonists, but his views tended to prevail in negotiations at high levels.

The idea of an independent, self-governing Vietnam within the French Union was rather a popular notion with de Gaulle and his personal advisors in Paris. Constant opposition came from the French in our country, however, so government by someone like Thinh or Xuan proved difficult. To demonstrate this point, I will describe one little-known plan of de Gaulle's.

At an early date, General de Gaulle had thought of establishing a central government for the entire country as a counter to the Communists.

The first attempt at this occurred in late 1945 and involved Duy Tan, a former king of Annam and a cousin of Bao Dai. He had been exiled to Reunion Island in 1917 at the age of 17 for a revolt he had instigated against the French colonists.

De Gaulle himself authorized Jean Sainteny to bring Emperor Duy Tan back to Vietnam. He sent a French lieutenant named Bousquet to Saigon as his personal representative to implement the plan. Bousquet, a Communist fellow-traveler, was close to a French government minister, Bonnard, another Communist.

Lieutenant Colonel Trocard, my superior, introduced Le Van Kim and myself to Bousquet. His plan called for a lightning raid against Hue, the imperial city in Central Vietnam. A 100-man commando force was to be dropped into the city, with orders to seize it. At the same time, a council of notables representing the population, who still remembered Duy Tan as a great patriot, was to be formed, petitioning for the king's return.

On December 20, 1945, about three weeks before the planned raid, Duy Tan met with a close Vietnamese friend in Paris. The soon-to-be emperor told him that he had a hunch that his long cherished dream of returning to his homeland and leading it toward independence would never come true.

In the meantime, in Saigon we had begun to train for the raid with commando forces and became extremely enthusiastic about it. It seemed a good compromise solution for obtaining independence within the framework of the French Union.

Duy Tan embarked on a flight to Reunion Island off the coast of French-controlled Africa to see his wife and children prior to his return to Vietnam. He had spent several years in exile on this island, before volunteering to serve in the French Foreign Legion during World War II. A courageous officer, he was promoted to lieutenant colonel at the end of the hostilities.

The plane carrying Duy Tan crashed near Bangui, now the capital of the Central African Republic, on December 24, 1945. Rumors made the rounds that the accident was the work of British or Soviet Intelligence, but I have no way of knowing it. Certainly, accession to power by Duy Tan in a former French colony might have proved embarrassing to the British who were then trying to preserve their own colonial structure against various nationalist movements. The Soviets might have been interested in thwarting the French plan, since its success would have caused considerable difficulty for Ho Chi Minh.

In 1973, while on a visit to Bangui, I paid my respects to the late Emperor Duy Tan. His tomb is located some 50 miles from the republic's capital. The republic's ruler, Mr. Bokassa, who for the first time learned that the anonymous tomb contained the remains of one of Vietnam's great kings, promised to place flowers on it on December 24 each year.

The next French attempt to find a compromise solution to their problem occurred in December 1947 when they sought to have Bao Dai return to Vietnam to form a centralized government. As a result, I accompanied President Xuan to Hong Kong to confer with his royal highness. In our party were Ngo Dinh Diem and governor Tran Van Ly of Annam. The French government had been in secret contact with Bao Dai, conceding a statement of independence to the people providing he agreed to form the new government and, in effect, become France's spokesman for Vietnam. In our conversations with him, Bao Dai seemed to be having trouble grasping the significance of "independence" as a concept vis à vis the French.

Bao Dai was the son and heir of Emperor Khai Dinh who died in 1924, so at 9 years of age he became emperor. He lived in France and came back to Vietnam in 1932 when he was 19. From then on, various nationalists thought of him as a real hope, but every time there was a good chance for independence he disappointed them. He was very intelligent, but had been raised by the French to be a king without power. He was an ardent sportsman, gambler, and hunter, but was not apt to devote much energy to the actual work of government.

From time to time, as in 1938 with the French Colonial Minister Mandel, he tried to gain more power for Vietnamese self-government, but his heart was not really in it. In conversations with me in December 1949 he spoke of his aspirations for a free Vietnam, so I advised him strongly to get the French to let us organize a separate national army. There had been Vietnamese units within the French army for some time, but not as an independent fighting force. Bao Dai listened to my entreaties, but responded that he did not believe the French would grant him authority to create such an organization outside French immediate control. He was much more excited, however, over the tiger he had shot the night before and spent a long time telling me about it. Bao Dai was a good man who well understood everything going on, but he had no real capacity for leadership, a fact the French, the Viet Minh, and finally the Americans thoroughly understood.

On April 24, 1948, we again visited Bao Dai in Hong Kong at his request, to discuss further the establishment of the central provisional government proposed by the French. He first asked Ngo Dinh Diem to be the premier in his government, but Diem refused. Nguyen Van Xuan accepted, however, and he got directly to work on it. On our return to Vietnam, Xuan organized a congress of forty members representing the three sections of Vietnam and comprised of all types of political thought, but, of course, excluding the Communists. This congress invited Xuan to become premier and form the new government.

Le Van Kim and I were working full time for Xuan at this time and, in addition to helping organize and support the congress, we proposed a new Vietnamese flag (yellow with horizontal red stripes) and a national anthem.* These were adopted unanimously by the Congress and remained our symbols until the final defeat in April 1975. On May 27, the new government went to Hong Kong to be presented to Emperor Bao Dai.

On June 5, 1948, at the agreement of the Bay of Along, Emile Bollaert, the French High Commissioner for Indochina, signed for France while Xuan signed for Vietnam, and the agreement was countersigned by Bao Dai. Although the agreement recognized the unity of Vietnam under the French Union, an immediate confrontation occurred between Xuan and Bollaert over our right to designate ambassadors to foreign countries. The agreement made no mention of Vietnam being able to designate ambassadors to foreign countries, but Xuan and his staff wrote into a separate charter that we could send such emissaries abroad as we desired. Bollaert was shown the charter and got quite upset about it, precipitating a rather strong discussion between them. Bao Dai was not present at the argument

*The yellow field in the flag symbolized the land of Vietnam itself, while the three horizontal red stripes stood for unity of the three sections of the country. The anthem was a revolutionary song written in 1945 to inspire youth to fight for independence from the French. It was sung during anti-French demonstrations then. Its author, a Southerner, Luu Huu Phuoc finally followed the Viet Minh, so the song, which was modeled after France's "La Marseillaise," was used by both sides. This shows that the Viet Minh did not have a monopoly on the fight for independence, despite the fact that we cooperated with the French to the same end.

39

so I went to his cabin to tell him about it. He smiled and said, "Don't worry. Everything will be settled in the end. Be patient."

Bollaert threatened to cancel the naval review for Bao Dai and the new government if the language about ambassadors was left in the charter. Xuan answered him with the single French word made famous at Waterloo, "Merde." Bao Dai then appeared and asked Bollaert if the review was ready, so he had to follow the program as planned.

The French did not try to publicize the importance of the agreement of the Bay of Along, probably because the word "independence" was used officially in it for the first time. As in many other negotiations conducted in behalf of the Vietnamese, our supposed friends did not play fair with us.

Xuan finally had to withdraw the charter provision about ambassadors which was, of course, a real defeat for him and the new government. The French were determined that there would be no separate foreign policy determinations made by us, such as independent representation in foreign capitals. We could not truly call ourselves "independent" if we could not make foreign policy. I think the French erred in this. Had they granted this concession, the Viet Minh position would have been greatly undermined. As it turned out, the French had no intention of letting us operate as an independent country. This event was merely the first real indication.

Xuan remained premier from 1948 through 1949, but Bao Dai was reluctant to return to the country himself. Xuan could not govern effectively, however, because the French would not transfer to him the requisite power and backing until Bao Dai returned. Bao Dai finally, after negotiating a new agreement in Paris on March 8, 1949, agreed to come back. Xuan was called by Bao Dai to meet him in France on March 15. On April 23, a new assembly composed of 1,700 delegates (700 French, 1,000 Vietnamese) was organized which voted that Cochinchina would be attached formally to the other two sections of Vietnam, Tonkin and Annam, producing a united nation for the first time in 87 years. Bao Dai finally returned to Vietnam on April 28, 1949, and made his residence in Dalat.

Bao Dai had missed at least two previous opportunities to take national power away from Ho Chi Minh in early 1946.

After the death of Emperor Duy Tan, France was compelled to throw its weight behind Bao Dai. In late February 1946, while in Hanoi serving as a powerless "supreme advisor" to Chairman Ho, Bao Dai tried to contact the French delegate, Sainteny, because he had been informed secretly by his aides that France was willing to help him against Ho.

Sainteny arranged a secret interview but Bao Dai failed to show up. He missed a second appointment with Sainteny and the French plan was scrapped.

On March 6, 1946, when France signed its reunification agreement with the Vietnamese, the cunning Sainteny made another attempt to prod Bao Dai into unseating Ho. Sainteny told Ho that France would sign the treaty only with the representative of an organized government, not the leader of a political front. As Sainteny expected, Chairman Ho requested Bao Dai to form a new government on two different occasions. The French predicted that Bao Dai would jump at the offer, but he was unable to come to a decision. In the end, the French had to accept a Communist-led coalition government.

Toward the end of 1949, Bao Dai appointed himself prime minister, demoting Xuan to vice premier. This move was viewed by my boss, Xuan, and many Vietnamese politicians as a Bao Dai attempt to obtain more power from the French. They soon were disappointed.

In November 1949, Vice Premier Xuan and I accompanied French High Commissioner Leon Pignon to the highland resort of Dalat to meet with Emperor and Premier Bao Dai. Pignon had a 60-minute private talk with him.

Pignon had been asked by the French government to keep Bao Dai informed of the situation in China, where Mao Tse-tung's Communist troops, after defeating Generalissimo Chiang's Nationalist regime, were approaching the Vietnamese border.

"In close consultation with Washington," the French envoy told him, "Paris has decided, with U.S. support, to transform Indochina into a strong anti-Communist bastion in Southeast Asia."

Bao Dai was urged by Pignon to issue a statement against newly formed Communist China: "Such a declaration from Your Majesty," Pignon added, "would have a divisive impact on the Ho Chi Minh-led armed resistance in the Tonkin. There are many adherents to the Viet Minh who

41

don't like Communism. A Communist-held China, coupled with Your Majesty's declaration against it, would prompt a return of these patriots to our camp."

Bao Dai politely listened to the French envoy's eloquent suggestions. But he said nothing. Later Pignon told Xuan that he was disappointed. "Bao Dai grumbled, grumbled, and grumbled. That's all," Pignon said.

One of Bao Dai's methods was to try to gain advantage from one side or the other. If he could not get what he wanted from one source of power, he would turn to another. Stalemated by the French, but understanding that the United States was backing them, he decided to approach the Americans. The obvious person for this type of negotiation was Ngo Dinh Diem with his myriad connections in America, so Bao Dai sent him to the United States as a special secret emissary to gain support.

I remained Xuan's aide, along with Le Van Kim, while he was both premier and vice premier of Bao Dai's government. From what I could see of the military situation, I was not at all encouraged. It seemed to me that the Viet Minh forces continued to get stronger while the French employment of conventional tactics against them proved almost totally ineffective. The Viet Minh was cunning in its military operations, using the art of ambush and surprise attack against vulnerable opponents. On the other hand, they avoided set-piece battles against regular French units, melting into the jungle when their enemy appeared to have numerical or fire-power advantage. The French had trouble fighting this will-of-the-wisp and did not have enough troops to garrison adequately all strong points in the country.

When Xuan was relieved as vice premier, Kim and I were sent back to France to attend a year's course at the Command and Staff College. We were the first members of the Vietnamese Army to attend this coveted course of instruction. We returned to Vietnam in July 1951 where Kim and I were finally separated. I was made captain and Chief of Military Security, and Kim was sent to be a deputy region commander in the Highlands. I became a major in 1952.

By this time the military situation had deteriorated further, so the French assigned one of their most able soldiers, General de Lattre de Tassigny, as Commander-in-Chief and High Commissioner with full power in all Indochina. Seeing clearly the needs of our country, he decided to create the first national army of Vietnam which would be trained, equipped, and directed by the French. He pushed Bao Dai for support in this new development to mobilize the youth of the country to fight for their own freedom in opposition to the ideology of the Communists. Vietnamese officers were appointed as commanders of units of this new force up to battalion level to gain experience fighting beside their French counterparts. De Lattre was in favor of providing the new national army with heavy weapons and all support required to make it a truly effective fighting force, but he died in January 1952 before his ambitions could be realized. His successor, General Salan was reluctant to give the new formations the support they needed. He trusted neither our capability nor our loyalty.

In April 1952, General Nguyen Van Hinh became the Chief of the General Staff of the new Army of Vietnam. He tried to organize an army composed of light battalion formations officered by Vietnamese. In 1953, as a new colonel, I was assigned as Hinh's chief of staff. Since my return from France, I had been able to move around the country freely, learning a great deal about the tactics of the Viet Minh and gaining much respect for their ability.

My visits were largely to Vietnamese units fighting against the Viet Minh side by side with the French. The only way to really assess the effectiveness of a unit's ability to fight was by operating with them in the field, so I spent more time out with the troops than in my Saigon office. I discovered that our soldiers, when properly led and equipped, could hold their own with the enemy and even, on occasion, surpass their French comrades. They fought in countless actions in rice paddies, villages, mountain passes, jungles, and the plains of the high plateau. They always did their duty without complaint and I was proud of them, both as a professional military man and as one of their countrymen.

As ex-French officers directing the new Vietnamese Army, we frequently had to play the role of mediator between the two factions, sometimes not really understood by either side. We had no true integration of forces, as did from the first the Communist side, a situation greatly to their advantage. In those days, we had trouble making our policies coincide with the French and in later days the same condition occurred with the Americans. For years, however, the Communists were united, with a common ideology and continuous leadership; this was certainly one of the principal causes of our defeat.

The French commander, General Navarre sought to get the Communists out in the open so that their forces could be destroyed in conventional warfare. This was his reason for establishing the base at Dien Bien Phu on the border of Laos and North Vietnam. He thought he could trap the Viet Minh regular force, but the reverse occurred. Lacking strong air cover and in an isolated position, he was unable to match the firepower of the Viet Minh.

The French underestimated the Viet Minh ability to transport heavy equipment by foot over otherwise impassable terrain and as a result lost a campaign, which turned out to be a psychological disaster to the French people. In other areas, the French and Vietnamese National Army were in relatively good condition and were in command of the situation throughout the country. The French-armed sects (Cao Dai and Hoa Hao) had good control in the south while other forces were in command of the Central Highlands (Plateau de Bolovens, Pleiku, Kontum, Ban Me Thuot, and Dalat). From a military viewpoint we were greatly surprised when the French accepted a partition of Vietnam at the 17th parallel. They had lost a battle, but certainly not the war because of Dien Bien Phu. We could not know, of course, the extent of popular dissatisfaction with the war in France, similar in a way to what happened in 1968 in the United States after the Communists' "Tet" offensive, which was a resounding defeat for them.

Thus, an era of French dominance over Vietnam was at an end. It did not have to finish as it did but perhaps there is a lesson here, best stated by a foreigner, Frank Trager, in his book, *Why Vietnam?* as follows:

> French resistance to any progressive development for self-government and independence created the conditions for the ultimate success of the Viet-Minh and defeated the possibility of the emergence of a nationalist, anti-Communist front.

On July 7, 1954, thirteen days after the Geneva armistice, Ngo Dinh Diem returned to Saigon as Bao Dai's new premier. One year later he established the resolutely anti-Communist First Republic of Vietnam.

Ngo Dinh Nhu at a meeting of the Vietnamese Women's Solidarity Movement, Vinh Long, 1961.

President Ngo Dinh Diem welcomes old friend Lt. Gen. John W. (''Iron Mike'') O'Daniel, 1960.

CHAPTER THREE

Ngo Dinh Diem
And His Family

Montesquieu in the *Spirit of Laws* remarked shrewdly on political freedom and the behavior of men and power: "Political freedom is only found in moderate governments . . . it is there only that power is not abused; but, it is always true that any man who has power is liable to abuse it."

Those newly coming to power are frequently marked by their enthusiasm, energy, and zeal to do a better job than their predecessors. Animated by a desire to innovate and reform, they tend to denounce the weaknesses and deficiencies, real or imaginary, of these predecessors in order to prove that many things will change for the better. In these first days or months of their administrations they are frequently given a kind of "honeymoon" in which they receive a great deal of cooperation from opposing factions and from the people being governed.

It frequently follows, then, that when the honeymoon is over, they begin to receive criticism from the same people who had been ultra-cooperative. Unfortunately, if the new public officials see themselves as somewhat indispensable, or invested with special powers of intellect and judgment, they tend to resist criticism and to oust the critics, surrounding themselves with more agreeable sycophants.

Criticism may even be labeled treason, and when that happens, a climate of rebellion evolves which waits only for the right occasion to erupt. This, broadly speaking, is the way it was with the administration of Ngo Dinh Diem, beginning when he was premier in the government of Bao Dai and carrying through and ending with his final responsibility as chief of state.

47

Ngo Dinh Diem came from an old and revered family in Hue, the capital city of Central Vietnam, Annam. From his family he received an orthodox education based on the philosophical principles of Confucius. This left an indelible mark of rigorous conformism and authoritarian paternalism on his character. At times he reminded me of a mandarin of a bygone era, at other times of a priest/confessor to recalcitrant sinners. He showed great promise early, earning through hard work and successful completion of various tests the coveted rank of mandarin which qualified him for appointment to posts in the Vietnamese government. Accordingly, he was appointed as the Vietnamese chief of Phan Thiet Province. He was so successful in this position that he came to Bao Dai's attention, and the emperor, in 1933, appointed him minister of the interior in charge of reforms for Annam and Tonkin, Cochinchina being administered separately by the French as a colony. Diem was only thirty-two at this time, but his youth did not prevent him from attempting to convince the French that reforms in their system should be made. The French were unwilling to go along with him, so he resigned his appointment in 1932.

He spent the next thirteen years out of the public eye, but building for himself a solid political base among the Catholics and various non-Communist nationalist elements within Vietnam and also obtaining backing in France and the United States. Apparently Bao Dai continued to think very highly of him because when the emperor was trying to form a government after the Japanese takeover in 1945, he again asked Diem to become his premier, but the future president refused. The same thing happened in 1948 in Hong Kong, when Bao Dai was again looking for a prime minister. As I related in the last chapter, Diem did not want to take over these duties, so my boss General Xuan became the premier.

When Ngo Dinh Diem did accede to power in 1954, all who knew him had to agree that he was both an ardent patriot and a staunch defender of national independence. However, there were those in Vietnamese political circles who distrusted the new prime minister, regarding him as an intruder, since he came from Central Vietnam and had been absent from the country for a long time. But, in many minds he was the only leader available in South Vietnam whose integrity could not be assailed.

Ngo Dinh Diem was a fervent Catholic and felt divinely inspired to lead and ensure the happiness of the Vietnamese people. He stated openly that on several occasions he had been miraculously saved from destruction—once, in 1945, when he escaped arrest and imprisonment by the new Communist regime, and again in 1957 when an assassination attempt against him failed. His belief in divine protection was only enhanced when two attempted coups d'etat, in 1960 and 1962, failed.

Diem remained a bachelor, living an austere and celibate existence. He commonly worked fifteen or sixteen hours a day. His room served as his office, where he received ministers and generals, surrounded by files and telephones. He seldom left his room, having breakfast there and working until a quick lunch interrupted the routine. After an hour's rest he would resume the same strenuous pace until midnight. Instead of delegating the minutiae of his administration to loyal and trusted subordinates, he attempted to do everything himself. It was not unusual for him to summon some official during the late evening hours, or before dawn, to obtain information or settle some unimportant matter.

From his accession to power in 1954 to perhaps the middle of 1958, Diem inspired considerable respect in foreign governments throughout the world, particularly in the United States. These were his best years and he was invited to make official state visits to several countries of Southeast Asia and to the United States.

During this period, I was Chief of Staff of the Army's General Staff and in that capacity was asked to travel with President Diem as his military aide on the trip to Washington. We went on the American presidential airplane, stayed in Blair House in Washington (not far from my present restaurant), and listened as Diem addressed a joint session of Congress in English. I am told that ours was the only such visiting party of a head of state to have been met at the airport by President Eisenhower.

Diem was an extremely nervous man but he knew how to maintain a calm appearance in the presence of others or during business negotiations. He had a kind of Asiatic tranquility which masked an inner turmoil that only insiders saw. Not many people were aware of his explosive temper, but occasionally it came out in private. Once I saw him violently kick a tray of food from a servant's hands because it did not contain exactly what he wanted for lunch. Another time I saw him threaten Mrs. Nhu with an ashtray when she pressed him too far.

By placing the fidelity of his subordinates above their abilities, Diem

49

made an extremely serious error. They exploited this weakness in order to flatter him and almost deify him. A song entitled "Adoration of President Ngo" was dedicated to him. Patterned after a Communist song eulogizing President Ho in North Vietnam, it was introduced in all public services, schools, and theaters to be sung after the National Anthem and Pledge of Allegiance to the Flag.

I was present in Hue one New Year's Day when my officers and various public functionaries came to present their greetings to Diem. This song of adulation was sung to everyone's embarrassment except Diem's. His personality cult, maintained deliberately by his advisors, was poorly appreciated by the public. Modesty is a revered virtue in Vietnam, so this public relations effort to advance Diem in the eyes of the people served only to backfire on him. Ho Chi Minh, on the other hand, was genuinely popular among his people, meriting the devotion he received through long years of leadership in the struggle against the French. Diem's clumsy attempt to emulate Ho's popularity was perceived by the people and resented. I saw it at the time as a major error.

Two other criteria guided Diem in the choice or promotion of ministers and generals to high grades in his government, their place of birth and religious faith. He preferred those who were from the central region where he himself grew up, and he preferred fellow Catholics. Since his capital, Saigon, was in the southern part of the country and 90 percent of the Vietnamese people were non-Christian, a feeling of frustration and dissatisfaction gradually penetrated the entire populace.

Since he firmly believed that he was divinely inspired and, being by nature obstinate, he did not willingly accept advice and suggestions, particularly when they came from independent personalities who were not inclined to flatter him. He liked to hear only good news, rather than failures in the application of his policies and decisions. On those rare occasions when he left the presidential palace and visited the provinces, he never saw the true state of things or the wretched condition of his people.

One day Diem went to Binh Tuy, a province 50 miles north of Saigon, to inspect a "model" village. The province chief simulated fruit tree plantings along the road on which the presidential cortege passed. These freshly cut stems were equipped with branches, leaves, and even fruit. As soon as the party had passed, the rootless trees were immediately taken to

50

the dump. They had served their purpose of deceiving the president on the lack of success of this village in achieving its goals.

Little by little the original enthusiasm for his regime was replaced by open disapproval, evidenced by passive attitudes toward work or less cordial welcomes to him when he made visits to the countryside. We began to realize that the president did not possess the required ability to direct the affairs of the country, and that his supposed administrative genius was simply not present. His experiences as an official in Hue under Bao Dai did not qualify him to govern the entire country.

Adding to Diem's problems in governing the country were the deleterious effects of the members of his family: his brothers Ngo Dinh Nhu and his wife, Ngo Dinh Can, and Ngo Dinh Thuc, all of whom I had known well for years. These close relatives exerted pressures on Diem which went far beyond the normal family advice received by any official. He had a great sense of his own family hierarchy, overly trusting them and allowing them to be his sole true confidants.

I first met Nhu and his wife in 1948 in Dalat where they were living in my father's house. He let them live there because they were very poor and she was the daughter of his old friend, Tran Van Chuong. At that time, Nhu had a passion for orchids which he collected in the forest, so he transformed our courtyard into a fairyland of beautiful blooms. I renewed my acquaintance with Ngo Dinh Diem in this house and had many opportunities to talk with him. He wanted to learn as much as he could about all aspects of the country, the government, the Viet Minh, and the army. He asked very detailed and penetrating questions and was able to extract from me just about all the knowledge I had. I was greatly impressed with him, seeing him as a highly intelligent, honest, and patriotic man.

Ngo Dinh Nhu did the most damage. He set himself up as a doctrinaire for the regime. He developed a complex ideology called "Labor and Personalism," which was inspired by the personalism of Emmanuel Mounier, a French philosopher, combined with a diluted version of Marxism. It came out as a kind of paternalistic socialism, which preached respect for human dignity as a political alternative to the Communist theory of class struggle.

Two things were wrong with this approach. First, he tried to set up cells within the civil service and the army as well as at the village level to

51

promulgate his political philosophy. This did not work, because he did not have a sufficient number of cadres who understood the philosophy or who wanted to adopt the Communist method of living and working with the common people and sharing their food. And, second, this murky philosophy was very difficult to understand. When one of his cadres would arrive at a village to lecture the people about it, stay for an hour, and then leave, the only thing that was accomplished was to further confuse his listeners. This was in marked contrast to the Communists who shared the lot of the people and whose message of land reform and suppression of corruption was easily understood.

Further, Nhu committed a great mistake in trying to impose a non-Buddhist ideology upon a Buddhist majority, with the systematic use of police state methods. Two progovernment political parties, sponsored by Nhu, recruited their members mostly from the administration and the army. An information network was instituted within these two parties under the leadership of Dr. Tran Kim Tuyen. It was intended to detect the opponents and enemies of the regime and to organize counterespionage in various areas including the American community. Nhu set up a parallel financial network to administer the funds of the two political parties, but its most influential members used it to build scandalous personal fortunes. These funds came from the national treasury and were derived largely by diverting foreign aid money which came mostly from the United States. Nhu was also the supreme leader of the Republican Youth Movement, an organization of young men and women which counted more than a million members of whom more than one hundred thousand were armed. They had cells in both small country villages and the cities, and acted as Nhu's armed force internally and externally.

More political and infinitely more astute than his brother Diem, Nhu was even more arrogant, manifesting scorn toward other intellectuals, especially those from the north. This prejudice was solidly rooted in his mind and caused him to discard some very good people ready to participate in the communal work of national reconstruction. He even showed open disdain toward his youngest brother, Ngo Dinh Can. Once Nhu stated to me that Can was ignorant because he could not comprehend the dialectics of his favorite philosophy.

52

Nhu especially hated those who were associated closely with the Americans. In August 1954, Dr. Wesley Fishel, a close friend of Col. Edward Lansdale, introduced to Diem a young nationalist leader from Hanoi. Diem received this leader at the Independence Palace, offering to make him minister of information. Hours after the meeting, Nhu secretly sent word to the young nationalist, threatening to arrest him unless he withdrew from the prospective job.

Individuals in positions of authority, including the Americans, suspected Nhu of working secretly with the Communists. His mysterious hunting parties in the wooded, hilly regions were said to have been organized to conceal clandestine meetings with the Communists.

For the first time I can say that this allegation was true, on the basis of information gained from one of Nhu's close relatives. On October 23, 1963, after he learned of the Kennedy administration's plan to get rid of him politically, Ngo Dinh Nhu held a secret family meeting with his wife and their eldest son Ngo Dinh Trac, then 15. Nhu told Trac that as the eldest son he must be prepared to lead the family if something happened to him. The Nhus' eldest child was Ngo Dinh Le Thuy,* a daughter, but according to Vietnamese tradition, the family burden following the death of the father always falls on the eldest son. Nhu was afraid because of his negotiations with the Communists, which he felt would greatly displease the Americans.

Since mid-June 1963, Nhu had had clandestine contacts with Hanoi, using the French Ambassador Roger LaLouette as one of his intermediaries. He made a proposal to Hanoi to reestablish civilian postal service and trade relations between the two halves of the country. This accord could ultimately set the stage for bilateral talks between Saigon and Hanoi for a peaceful reunification of the country. Ideas like these were nothing new, but the fact that Nhu himself proposed them to the Communists is, I think, extremely significant. Diem surely knew of the proposal to which Hanoi was reasonably receptive, but Kennedy's advisors were extremely cold to the idea. They had already decided to get rid of Diem and Nhu, so negotiations with the enemy were considered out of the question.

*Later, while on exile in France with her mother, Le Thuy was killed in an automobile accident near Paris.

53

Since he was so close physically to the president at all times, helping him in his administration and preparing most of his official speeches, Nhu was regarded as the second leader in the state. Ministers, generals, and ambassadors coming back to Saigon would visit him, sometimes even before seeing the president.

As years went on, Nhu's appearance began to change. His complexion became more sallow and his condition more emaciated, with his dark eyes showing signs of a distinct physical and moral decline. He smoked heavily, using very strong cigarettes, but not opium as was rumored. His normal expression included a thin and sarcastic smile, which remained on his lips after his death.

Nhu's wife, Le Xuan, started having grand ambitions early in her life, fostered probably by the heady associations made in her mother's opulent salon in Hanoi. During the Japanese occupation and concurrent French administration, Mrs. Chuong, Le Xuan's mother, enjoyed receiving in her home both French and Japanese dignitaries as well as the elite of Vietnamese society. The future Madame Nhu learned well at her mother's knee what a happy situation the possession and use of power was and how to play the role of a great lady.

It was at one of her mother's innumerable soirées that she met a young man of good family, Ngo Dinh Nhu, who married her when she was only sixteen. She had been an indifferent student in the Lycée Albert Sauraut in Hanoi, but her new husband was able to continue her education and formed his young bride into a confident and intellectually able member of the Ngo family, able to conduct herself in any situation.

Her ambition knew no bounds, spurred greatly by jealousy of her elder sister who had made a highly successful marriage with a prominent Saigon attorney. One day in Dalat in 1949 she told me that she would eventually take the place of Bao Dai's empress and become the first lady of the land. At the time I thought she was just saying crazy things, but events proved her right and us wrong. When her bachelor brother-in-law, Diem, came to power, she formed the women's solidarity movement and in 1956 was elected to the national assembly where she energetically defended women's rights. In a short time her ambitions were realized and she became the acknowledged first lady of Vietnam.

Her women's rights movement was pushed very strongly by the

54

government, with committees established in each province throughout the country. I have no accurate figures, but would estimate that she had perhaps a million adherents in this movement.

Le Xuan was instrumental in convincing Diem to pass two laws which she thought helped defend the rights of married women. The first, which made the old practice of keeping concubines unlawful, was not especially controversial, but the second, prohibiting divorce, was very unpopular. Her motives in pushing the law against divorce were not completely pure, unfortunately. Her main desire was not religious as one might suppose, but merely to protect her sister Le Chi from being divorced by her husband, who belonged to a very wealthy family in South Vietnam, and thus preserve the family fortune.

In 1961, she asked me to study the possibility of arming some of her women members as a kind of paramilitary force that could defend itself when the men were away in the fields or in the army. The arms for these women were to be taken from excess stocks of French weapons made surplus when American items were made available to us. I made the study and she began implementing her plan, but not very much came of it.

She was an immensely attractive woman, beautiful by anybody's standards. She saw herself in heroic terms as a modern reincarnation of the two Trung sisters who headed an army that defeated the Chinese before the time of Christ. To commemorate these heroic sisters, she had a monument erected to their memory in Saigon. When we looked at the statue we found a most curious thing; the sculptor had copied Mrs. Nhu's beautiful face on each of the Trung sisters' stone faces. Just after the 1963 coup, the people of Saigon destroyed this statue.

Her influence, however, was pernicious and she became unpopular with the Vietnamese people. She participated in corruption within the government and aided her husband in his dishonest schemes. She gained much unfavorable attention during the Buddhist crisis of 1963 when she described the tortured immolation of the Venerable Thich Quang Duc as a happy "barbecue."

Mrs. Nhu had a better and more realistic sense of the materialistic side of life than either Diem or Nhu. I was present one day in 1955 when she spoke vehemently to Diem on the impossibility of engaging in practical politics without a supply of money. As a result she was given an allowance out of the national treasury to be used in her own political affairs. Part of this money she had deposited in secret accounts abroad. This illegal use of public funds was practiced by many people in high places, particularly by members of Diem's family. Strangely enough, Diem was oblivious of what was going on because he himself lived a simple and austere life.

Monies were expropriated for private use in a variety of ways. In some cases, not at all apparent to the public or even people in other high positions, it came from secret funds designed to support political parties and the National Revolutionary Movement. In other cases, secret instructions were given to the Office of Exchange to transfer local funds abroad at the official rate with special kickbacks to various officials and businessmen. Import and export licenses were sold to the highest bidder and artificial monopolies were constructed for trade in some substance in critical supply—like cinnamon. Kickbacks also occurred in contractual arrangements for various construction projects, and people were arrested and then released when the required bribe money was provided.

Next to Nhu in influence was a younger brother, Ngo Dinh Can, who was the least intellectual but had a strong personality and a sparkling wit. I first met Ngo Dinh Can in Hue in 1951 when I was Director of Security. Nhu recommended that I talk to him about setting up an intelligence network in the area consisting particularly of a number of informers. I also needed recommendations for officers to fill several important intelligence posts. Can was very helpful to me since he knew his own area so intimately. Later, of course, when I was a corps commander in that area, I saw him often on various business matters.

Can lived close to the masses, wearing the national costume with its traditional long robe. He behaved like a petty king inside his fief of Central Vietnam and held court at Hue where the officially nominated governor was a dull character who would not decide anything without his prior consent. Can and his brother Nhu frequently disagreed about political problems.

On October 30, 1963, Can told me, "Set up a coup d'etat and take me as your advisor." He set up an efficient information network which permitted him to keep Central Vietnam and the Highlands in the palm of his hand, helping him neutralize both Communist subversion and political opposition.

The other brother, Ngo Dinh Thuc, was the Roman Catholic Primate of Vietnam and Archbishop of Hue. Through Diem he extended his religious

56

influence to such an extent that the regime became intolerable to those who were not of the Catholic faith. Any effective measures to placate the Buddhists were not possible. We all believed that one of Thuc's ambitions was to be created a cardinal by the Pope.

Other family members used Thuc's special position with President Diem to obtain personal favors from him because Diem believed that he was incapable of lying. I once asked Diem why he had granted a certain privilege to Mrs. Nhu which made no sense. He responded that Thuc had vouched for her and that, after all, a bishop could never tell an untruth.

In 1954, France, through her High Commissioner for Indochina, General Paul Ely, transferred to Diem and his new government the beautiful Norodom Palace named for the ancient king of Cambodia. Ely told him that the palace was not important in itself; it was after all only a pile of stones. Its real importance was a symbol of authority of the French administration in Indochina. Diem therefore called the building Independence Palace and took up his residence therein. He moved from this building in 1962 when two dissident pilots attacked it with bombs, making a new residence with the Nhus in the Gia Long Palace about three hundred meters away. The Gia Long Palace had previously been the residence of the French governor of South Vietnam.

Construction in a strategic hamlet, Ban Me Thuot, South Vietnam, 1963.

Government indoctrination meeting in a South Vietnamese hamlet, 1963.

CHAPTER FOUR

Diem Asserts Authority

After a great deal of negotiation and American pressure, toward the end of April 1955, French troops, the last remnants of the old colonial administration, left the country. The country nevertheless was still in a state of chaos. The political-religious sects Hoa Hao and Cao Dai,* armed by the French, retained wide territorial zones under their authority. The armed river pirates, Binh Xuyen, had total control of the police in Saigon and Cholon and its suburbs, openly maintaining casinos, brothels, and opium dens which provided them with substantial revenues. In the provinces, the Viet Minh controlled many rural areas. Roads and railroads, often sabotaged by Communist guerrillas, were insecure, making food supply to Saigon and other main cities difficult. The cost of living had increased alarmingly.

By the time the French troops left, Diem began to assert his authority. He subdued the Cao Dai, Hoa Hao, and Binh Xuyen, and took command of the army which had previously been under General Nguyen Van Hinh,† but only after a struggle with Hinh for overall power. This officer, despite his brilliant capacity for organization and command, was considered too pro-French and independent for the prime minister. At the time this seemed a major error because Hinh was probably the best officer we had. If he had

*The Hoa Hao and Cao Dai were politically oriented religious sects in the areas south and west of Saigon. They had an anti-Communist bias and strongly desired to exercise personal control over their own areas. This is why the French permitted them arms and closed their eyes when they collected illegal taxes from the populace. The Hoa Hao controlled a rich rice-producing area in the Mekong Delta, while the Cao Dai lived in a region near Tay Ninh having large timber stands. Their actions against the Viet Minh prior to 1954 were to defend their own regional, religious, and cultural interests.

†Hinh returned to the French Air Force after 1954, concluding an outstanding career upon his retirement in 1971 as a major general.

remained in charge, I feel we would have had a much better chance of defeating the Communists.

Diem's early successes were due in large part to the advice and independent action of Col. Edward G. Lansdale, USAF, chief of a so-called American military mission which was really the CIA office in Saigon. At first, the American government, and especially President Eisenhower's special envoy, Gen. J. Lawton Collins, were lukewarm on Diem and had grave doubts about supporting him and his new government. Lansdale's energetic intervention finally tipped the balance and the Americans came forward solidly behind Diem.

I first met Lansdale during the French period in 1954 when he came to Vietnam to contact the Cao Dai leader, General Trinh Minh The. My first impression was that he was extremely able and courageous, well deserving the plaudits given him for his work with Magsaysay against the Communist Huks in the Philippines. At that time, he also made contact with Ngo Dinh Nhu to help him get his brother's prospective new government formed and put him in direct touch with General The.

Later, after Diem's accession to power, I remained in much the same job that I had when the French were there, so I had frequent occasion to observe Lansdale and his relationship with Diem. Our premier and later president relied heavily on Lansdale, so much so that members of his staff had orders to always put him through to Diem, night or day, whatever Diem was doing. He was a great help, but went a little far when he tried to have Diem copy Magsaysay. The two leaders were quite different personalities, so this really hurt Diem's feelings.

He pushed Diem to make his first state visit to Magsaysay in the Philippines, and I was sent on ahead to prepare the visit. Unfortunately, the meeting never took place because Magsaysay was tragically killed in an airplane crash shortly after I arrived in Manila.

Lansdale arranged for a lot of help from the Philippine government for our fledgling government. The brotherhood teams he brought in from that country were extremely effective in the medical and sanitation fields. He was a good friend to Vietnam.

Toward the end of 1955 when I did not see Lansdale by his side any more, I asked Diem the reason for it. He answered, "Lansdale is too CIA and is an encumbrance. In politics there is no room for sentiment."

60

But, despite their falling out, Lansdale's efforts certainly paid off, especially his missionary work in getting the Cao Dai General The and Ngo Dinh Nhu together. General The was persuaded to lend his support to the fledgling Diem government and became one of the active participants in the antimonarchial campaign organized by Nhu to overthrow Emperor Bao Dai in the middle of 1955. Nhu was pleased to learn that General The was a true non-Communist revolutionary. General The rallied to the government in a solemn ceremony which all the Ngo family attended.

General The soon proved his loyalty to the new government by participating in the campaign to suppress the Binh Xuyen river pirate organization. This group of totally corrupt gangsters appealed to Bao Dai who had previously promised them his protection, so the emperor summoned Diem to France with the intention of regaining his power. Diem wisely refused and instead ordered me to proceed with the army/Cao Dai coordinated operations against the Binh Xuyen. The backing of the army was vital during this crisis, but we never wavered in our support for the future president. Diem's refusal to visit Bao Dai* in France was the simple and bloodless act that "overthrew" the emperor. Diem, backed by the United States and our army, could then act independently and proceed to establish the First Republic by referendum.

In a subsequent joint operation, General The was killed while leading his troops in a courageous assault on a Binh Xuyen position. Trinh Minh The had been a highly effective guerrilla fighter against the French and was, at the time of his death, a loyal supporter of the new government.

As chief of staff, it was my duty to organize a funeral for him, which was attended by Ngo Dinh Nhu and many high officials in the government. We buried him at the Black Virgin Mountain near Tay Ninh. Nhu lost a splendid ally, and Lansdale, a loyal friend.

Among other provisions, the Geneva Accords of 1954, to which neither the French-sponsored Bao Dai government of Vietnam nor the United States were signatories, specified that a "temporary" boundary and demil-

---

*Bao Dai was on one of his frequent sojourns in France just after Dien Bien Phu and remained there even after Diem assumed his duties as premier. His trip ostensibly was to supervise and support a team from his government negotiating with the French preparatory to the start of the Geneva conference which led to the cease-fire and the partition of Vietnam.

61

itarized zone would be set up at the 17th parallel and that elections to reunify the country would be held at an early date.

At the time, the Bao Dai government through its foreign minister, Tran Van Do, stated its opposition to foreign powers like France, Britain, and the Soviet Union making such essentially political decisions as elections and national boundaries for the Vietnamese. We contended that such decisions were internal affairs to be negotiated among Vietnamese and were none of the foreigners' business. So, in an action that completely contravened these accords, Ngo Dinh Diem and his brother, Nhu, aided and abetted at every turn by the Americans, organized a national referendum in October 1955 which asked the people south of the 17th parallel whether they wanted a continuation of the Bao Dai monarchy, or a new republic headed by Diem.

These were heady times indeed for us Vietnamese. For the first time we saw a really dynamic and popular leader who would turn the anti-Communist cheek against Ho Chi Minh's forces of the north. At that time we all were behind Diem: the army, civil service, and the farmers out in the villages. This support was so complete that in the election, Diem's position carried overwhelmingly and on October 26, the First Republic was pro-claimed with Diem as the president. A constitution was promulgated concurrently and fifty-two foreign nations recognized the new republic. We even appointed an observer to represent us at the United Nations.

Later, in separate conversations with Diem and Bao Dai, I learned that letters were exchanged between the two leaders about their respective roles. Diem had volunteered to continue to serve as premier in Bao Dai's government if the emperor would return to assume more of a position of leadership to help Diem control the very touchy military and political situation in the country. Bao Dai refused to return from France, largely because of his premier's suppressive moves against the sects who had been his supporters against the French. This was especially true of the Binh Xuyen, who had supported Bao Dai financially; and he had appointed one of them Saigon's police chief.

Bao Dai knew about the upcoming referendum and could have returned to contest it, but he chose to sit on the sidelines in Cannes on the beautiful Mediterranean Sea. He told me that he could not continue being emperor for only the southern part of the country since by heredity he had to govern the entire country.

In splendid humanitarian spirit, the Diem government agreed to the resettlement in the south of almost a million refugees from the north. This enormous task was accomplished, but only after overcoming tremendous difficulties. The bulk of these refugees were Christians, fleeing the north because they feared religious persecution.

An agrarian reform plan was begun by the new administration to distribute badly needed small plots of land to peasant families. This reform seemed at first to give good results and served to rally the common people to support Diem.

The administration also made great efforts to reorganize itself. A team of experts, supervised by Dr. Wesley Fishel of Michigan State University, helped the government in this reorganization. Fishel especially concentrated on making the various elements of the Vietnamese police an effective organization, capable of maintaining control in crisis situations.

A strategic hamlet program to help pacification of the countryside and the struggle against corruption, gambling, drugs, and prostitution was a popular step taken by the president at the start of his regime.

I could see at first hand from many conversations with people at all levels of society that Diem's early actions were tremendously popular. In the army, all ranks were enthusiastic at our unified spirit after the suppression of the sects and the rallying of their members to our side. Diem's visits around the countryside made him very popular with the farmers. In Binh Dinh and Quang Nam provinces, which had long been Communist strongholds, I was told by villagers that, "In ten years of leadership by Ho Chi Minh, he never once took the trouble to visit us, but after only ten days, Ngo Dinh Diem has already come to see us and listen to our problems." The people, both in cities and hamlets, were becoming aware of Diem and liking what they saw.

Despite Ngo Dinh Diem's promising start and the initial confidence given him by most of the Vietnamese people, the situation in Vietnam began to deteriorate. Exhilarated by first successes, Diem gradually lost his modesty and clear-sightedness. His autocratic behavior, obstinate character, conceit, and strong prejudices made him impervious to the advice of strong and independent people. He listened only to those who flattered him,

63

usually cronies of members of his family in various powerful positions. We could see that nepotism would eventually undo him.

There is no denying the solid intellectual qualities of most of his family, but he granted them control of some conspicuous political and administrative functions. This was a grave mistake, ever weakening his support from the people. In ancient days, the mandarins who surrounded themselves with close relatives were universally criticized. Diem, who boasted about being a revolutionary, would have been better served if he had avoided the mistake of the ancient kings.

As an example of this undue influence on the president, one morning at about six o'clock I was summoned to his private residence in the Phu Cam section of Hue which was in the military region that I commanded. He was waiting for me in the sitting room with Archbishop Thuc by his side. As soon as the prelate saw me he abruptly asked, "Do you know that one of your colonels, Nguyen Van Hien, openly displays anti-Catholic feelings?" I responded that I knew nothing about it, but that it would surprise me and I had no reason to believe that the officer had done any such thing. This unexpected confrontation deeply hurt me since no officer of any rank should have any control over the religious convictions of his subordinates.

Apart from the privileged positions provided to various members of the Ngo family, rumors and innuendos concerning them were widespread, many of them true. All the members of Diem's family took very good care of themselves and their friends.

Mrs. Nhu, for example, built a beautiful estate and compound in Dalat as a summer residence. The building of this huge complex, consisting of tennis courts, swimming pool, and several luxurious structures, took several years and had not really been completed before the coup d'etat in 1963. But an army of architects, designers, and builders spent many months working on the construction in full view of the world. Such ostentation could not help but generate rumors and stories that spread over the whole country.

Archbishop Ngo Dinh Thuc evidently forgot his vow of poverty because he became a landholder and businessman in a big way. He bought and paid cash for three pieces of property in Saigon, the "Tax" building on Nguyen Hue Street which housed a large department store, a bookstore and print shop in the Eden Arcade patronized by many Americans, and an

64

apartment house on Tran Huong Dao Street. I learned of these transactions from the broker who handled the sale, and even saw the duplicate receipts of the cash transactions. My father, who was then ambassador to Italy, got involved with Thuc when he asked him to make deposits of illegal funds for him in Italian banks. My father was reluctant to act as Thuc's agent in this way and stated publicly that the prelate was dishonest. This got back to Diem and my father was removed from his position in five days. Diem refused to see him upon his return, despite our close family friendship, because he could not bring himself to believe that the archbishop was at all tainted with corruption.

Ngo Dinh Can lived like a king in Hue, with a luxurious villa on Thuan An beach and another in the hills outside the city in addition to his city residence. All these were built during Diem's period in office. In 1961, Can told me that if something were to happen, the various members of the family and their friends had nothing to fear, because they would be able to leave the country using five ships they owned. He said that they had about U.S. $7 million in foreign banks, so that they were well fixed monetarily. I took him seriously because I knew of the highly profitable coffee and cinnamon trade in which he had been engaged for a long time. I got the impression during this conversation that he intended to evacuate me and other such friends if conditions got very bad.

A veritable court came into being around each of these powerful characters and it was there that ministers, high-ranking officials, as well as businessmen seeking protection, recommendations, or favors circulated. Racketeers and swindlers of all types were in evidence around them and their most influential colleagues plotting unscrupulous dealings such as the financial manipulation I have already mentioned or the obtaining of unauthorized and preferential trading concessions. It is easy to see how the reputation for personal integrity that Ngo Dinh Diem had at the start gradually became tarnished because of the excesses of his family members and their friends.

Various high-ranking officials, many in the army, were bought off by the Ngo Dinh Diem regime by prompt promotions and other favors. These unpatriotic opportunists considered themselves immune from prosecution for their graft and corruption. This, of course, contributed to discrediting the regime and weakening it throughout the country.

65

Diem and his brother, Nhu, seemed to agree on only one single inflexible policy: repression of Communist infiltration. They resorted to arbitrary arrests, confinement in concentration camps for undetermined periods of time without judicial guarantees or restraints, and assassinations of people suspected of Communist leanings. Their use of Gestapo-like police raids and torture were known and decried everywhere. In the central region, the most brutal measures of repression were used with Ngo Dinh Can's assent and encouragement. Had they confined themselves to known Communists, or proven Communist sympathizers, one could understand their methods. The repression, however, spread to people who simply opposed their regime such as heads or spokesmen of other political parties and against individuals who were resisting extortion by some of the government officials. Many good men who had genuine anti-Communist feelings were driven to the National Liberation Front (NLF)* as a lesser evil than the Ngo Dinh Diem regime. In remote regions, agents of the central government committed incredible abuses and retaliated against their enemies by charging them with crimes that were entirely fabricated. Nhu and Can were in charge of the secret police who carried out these repressive measures throughout the country.

A notable instance of arbitrary arrest and torture involved the distinguished nationalist, Phan Khac Suu, later Head of State, in 1964. We released Suu from prison at the time of our overthrow of Diem. He told us an incredible story.

Although he had nothing to do with it, after the abortive coup of November 1960, he was seized by Nhu's secret police in the night, and was imprisoned in a cell, dug out like a cave under the Saigon zoo. This was a terrible place to exist, almost without air, hot and humid. Later he was

*I have used three different terms throughout this book which mean essentially the same thing: Viet Minh, Viet Cong, and National Liberation Front (NLF). The Viet Minh was the name given to the Communist insurgents during the French-Vietnamese War (1945–1954). The Diem administration changed their name to Viet Cong (Vietnamese Communists) because the previous name was one respected by many people and a more pejorative title was desired. In 1960, Hanoi organized in the south the NLF as a kind of resistance government there to attract southern nationalists who were disenchanted with Ngo Dinh Diem. This turned out to be a successful maneuver, incidentally, but as soon as they seized the entire country in 1975, they dissolved the NLF and treated many of its leaders as prisoners of war.

66

transferred to other jails, but he was tortured often. One method used was the old "Chinese water torture," where he was strapped down and a periodic drop of water was directed at his head from above. He felt himself going mad. His feet were so deteriorated from the conditions of his imprisonment that he had to have a lengthy period of medical treatment in 1964 after his release.

Another acquaintance of mine, Nguyen Van Yen, the owner of the Morin Hotel in Hue, was arrested and denounced in 1956 by Ngo Dinh Can as being pro-French. This was really a ruse to enable the government to seize the hotel. Yen stayed in prison without trial for several years. Apparently they had means of persuasion in jail, because he sold the hotel at a very low price to the Can Lao* party after his release and the government bought it back to make it into a university.

One of the greatest of all mistakes made by the Diem government commenced in June 1956. The elected chiefs of villages were replaced arbitrarily by agents appointed by the central administration. This went against the traditional autonomy of Vietnamese towns which had been scrupulously respected by even the hated French colonial administration. Diem's new policy, therefore, went directly against many centuries of tradition and was a bitter pill for the peasants working on the land or the inhabitants of the small villages in the countryside.

Another problem was that the officials appointed by the Diem government were generally not from the area being managed. For example, it was common to see a Catholic from the middle section sent to one of the predominately Buddhist southern towns as the official in charge. His customs were different from those of the villagers. He spoke a somewhat different dialect and generally held them in contempt because of their different religious practices. It was easy to see how the NLF took advantage of this situation. They were easily able to rally the villagers to their views and show themselves as saviors by assassinating village chiefs whom the villagers despised.

*Can Lao Nhan Vi Cach Mang Dang (Revolutionary Personalist Workers Party) was a semi-secret political society of Diem and Nhu. It possessed great power, indirectly controlling a private intelligence and secret police apparatus. It was organized in cells and permeated the entire governmental structure, to include the army.

Although agrarian reform was a totally justified political measure, and had a great theory backing it, its methods of application in South Vietnam generated a climate of hatred toward the government. The Diem government was persuaded by the American expert in land redistribution, Wolf Ladejinsky, that large farm holdings should be bought from individuals holding them and resold or given to homeless refugees who wanted plots of their own. My own family farm is a good example. This was a producing farm of modest size of about 2,900 acres which had been in our family for a long time and on which we employed about 400 people.

The government technique was to divide our farm into ten-acre parcels, pay us for them, and resell them to the refugees. Certainly it was correct to find some land for the Catholic people who fled from the north, but a better way was available to the government. There were extremely large tracts of land, previously untilled, in the Mekong Delta which could have been provided to these people without charge. What happened deprived the landowner of his property and put out of work the people who had been farming the land for him. So, a humanitarian gesture wound up not pleasing anybody. This gave the NLF a chance to propagandize both the fairly well-to-do landowner and the displaced workers who had become refugees in their own villages.

Another disastrous and unpopular program was carried out relative to the aboriginal minority groups in the highlands region. These Montagnard tribesmen are of different racial stock from the Vietnamese and always enjoyed an autonomous status under the French administration. They were backward people, but generally not warlike, and if left alone caused no particular trouble to any central government. No one can deny that in order to achieve the unity of the nation the territory of the highlands people had to be integrated sooner or later. If done properly, such measures could only benefit the Montagnard tribes, who had remained largely closed to progress. They lived in 1960 as they had done for centuries, under the most primitive conditions. Programs for schools, sanitation, medical care, and modern farming methods should have been introduced, with sufficient restraint and flexibility, to ensure the continued friendship of these aboriginal people. The government should have prepared them, psychologically and politically, and assured them that they would not be hurt or treated badly. No preliminary work was done, however. The government suddenly decided to create

68

centers for the Catholic refugees evacuated from North Vietnam in the Montagnard regions without consulting the chiefs of the tribes or asking their permission. Montagnard lands which had belonged to revered ancestors were distributed to these refugees, with pastures for their cattle and wood-cutting licenses for the construction of their homes. The Montagnards became hostile toward new administrators imported into the area for these and other programs, and again the NLF was able to profit by another government mistake.

But, of all errors perpetrated by the Ngo family the most serious were those pertaining to the Buddhists. This was reported widely by the press, both in Vietnam and abroad.

Considering our tradition of tolerance in religious belief, the abuses perpetrated by the Ngo family are that much more difficult to understand. This adventure in which they were recklessly involved was loaded with risks and possible repercussions. They were attacking a religious group that comprised about 80 percent of the population of the country.

The Buddhists' feelings of distress did not come from problems they were having with their Catholic neighbors. Instead, Buddhist leaders began to get more and more upset about the various injustices perpetrated by the Diem regime on all the people of South Vietnam. Younger Buddhist bonzes* picked up the struggle against all forms of oppression and injustice and many malcontents were attracted to militant bonzes like the Venerable Thich Tri Quang. They saw the Buddhist confessional organization as a force capable of resisting government pressures and suddenly the Buddhist faith became a political ally of those anti-Communists who opposed policies of the Diem government. They were able to convert thousands of people who formerly were mild Buddhists or simply sympathetic to that religion. Considerable moral as well as financial support accrued to the Institute of Teaching of the Buddhist Doctrine and to the pagodas, which became

*A bonze is a type of priest or monk, dedicated to a highly austere and celibate life. Bonzes generally are vegetarians because they refuse to enjoy the normal pleasures of life such as eating meat and raising families. They have always played an important role in politics in Vietnamese history, organizing secret meetings along with fortune tellers in their pagodas. Even Ngo Dinh Diem in his resistance activities against the French in the 1930s met a revolutionary leader in a pagoda near Hue.

69

centers of resistance against government policy. Various disparate elements rallied to the Buddhist cause: high-school and college youths, professional men, members of the press, disappointed politicians, and parliamentarians belonging to opposition parties.

As with many struggles, a single simple event brought the Buddhist crisis to the attention of the whole world. This had to do with the flying of the Buddhist flag. A presidential decree, issued in April 1963, specified that on the occasion of religious holidays the national flag must be hoisted above any religious material displayed.

The first such event occurring after this decree was the pompous celebration organized for the twenty-fifth anniversary of the episcopal ordination of Archbishop Ngo Dinh Thuc, brother of the president. During this ceremony the papal flag was displayed along with the national banner. About one month later the Buddhists celebrated the anniversary of Buddha's birth. The bonzes decided not to fly their flag in the same way that the Catholics had for Thuc's anniversary, and thus adorned their pagodas and homes with the Buddhist flag alone.

In the city of Hue, the deputy province chief ordered them to display the national flag above their multicolored Buddhist banner. They refused and to show their solidarity on the principle, they gathered in the streets for a demonstration. The assistant chief of the province, a fervent Catholic, interpreted this attitude as a challenge to the government. Acting under the advice of Archbishop Thuc, he ordered the police and the army to disperse the demonstrators, forcefully if necessary. The operation led to a tragedy, with nine dead and fourteen hospitalized.

There are false versions of the incident. The government, through Vice President Nguyen Ngoc Tho, attributed this disaster to the explosion of a grenade thrown inside the crowd by the Communists. This was palpably untrue since there were many eye-witnesses and foreign press reporters on hand who took photographs during the entire demonstration.

Despite its sinister aspect, even this issue could have been solved without too much difficulty had not Ngo Dinh Diem adopted an unbending and obstinate posture toward the Buddhists. Since the government offered no real appeasements, Buddhist protests multiplied everywhere. A demonstration organized in Hue on June 3 by various student groups was broken up by police shooting gas grenades. Some sixty seven people were badly injured in the ensuing fracas. On June 11, an old bonze, the Venerable Thich Quang Duc, sat down in a public street intersection in Saigon, sprinkled his body and clothes with gasoline, and set himself on fire. He died without crying or moving, making the populace react toward him as a martyr. As the intemperate remarks of "barbecue," by Madame Nhu were reported, this suicide aroused general indignation both in Vietnam and abroad.

To reverse this antigovernment feeling, a joint communique was agreed to by President Diem and the high Buddhist pontiff, Thich Tinh Khiet. This conciliatory step, however, was immediately overcome by the public accusation of Mr. and Mrs. Nhu that Communists had infiltrated the Buddhist movement and by other derogatory accusations.

Buddhist leaders began hunger strikes and nine other flaming suicides occurred by both male and female bonzes in Saigon and other communities. These further inflamed the local people and brought severe criticism on the government from abroad.

On July 15, the American ambassador, Frederick Nolting, suggested to Diem that he make a radio announcement granting concessions to the Buddhists. Diem simply ignored him. On July 16, I went to see Diem, since I was going to make a trip to Hue myself. I tried to make him understand that the situation in Hue was getting worse through the repressive measures undertaken by the police and army units commanded by Colonel Do Cao Tri, the new commander of the First Division. This highly efficient officer, one of our best military leaders, executed his orders with truly excessive zeal, even using dogs to chase the demonstrators.

In Hue, I found that the pagoda Tu Dam, seat of the Buddhist movement, had been encircled and deprived of water and supplies for several days. The Buddhist people in Hue, however, did their best to help the bonzes who had been cut off from all contact with the outside world, this at the risk of their own lives. I intervened as best I could to alleviate the situation.

Seeing at first hand the suffering of the poor people in the pagoda, I went to see Do Cao Tri and appealed to him as the military governor of Hue to relax the oppressive policy which was literally starving the Buddhists. I told him, as Diem's personal envoy, that he had gone too far in using dogs

71

against the demonstrators and in cutting off food to the pagoda. After our conversation, he reversed his policy and allowed food and water to be provided them and opened up the barbed wire encircling the pagoda.

Returning to Saigon on July 17, I reported to the president what I had seen and heard in Hue. I informed him that the people were very surprised at his total silence since May 8. They could not understand his indifferent attitude since he had always been most solicitous of Hue, his home town. I suggested that he make an announcement, in the language of Hue, worded in the most appeasing manner possible. Ngo Dinh Nhu supported my suggestion by telling Diem that his assistant, Cao Xuan Vy, in the Republican Youth had reported the same things and had made the same proposal.

On July 19, Diem made an announcement in the Huen dialect but it was too brief and vague. He promised to solve this incident "like a family matter" and vaguely outlined a reconciliation. If he expected this message to have a soothing effect, it was not realized.

A month later on August 21, Ngo Dinh Nhu ordered a midnight raid on the pagodas of Saigon, Hue, and other coastal province cities. In Saigon, the operations were undertaken by the special forces of the president and by units of the combat police but were blamed by Nhu on the regular army which had not participated in the operation.

More than 1,400 bonzes and other Buddhists were arrested and sent to concentration camps. This figure did not include an undetermined number of wounded and missing. Three bonzes, including the Venerable Thich Tri Quang, obtained shelter in the United States Embassy. The break between the government and the Buddhists was from then on irrevocable.

This unfortunate attack by Nhu's personal forces caused great discredit on the government of Ngo Dinh Diem. The General Assembly of the United Nations appointed a commission of delegates from seven countries to visit Vietnam and investigate the Buddhist problem. They denounced the attack and other repressive measures as serious blows to freedom of worship in Vietnam.

Vietnamese Army soldiers in forest operations in central highlands, 1962.

President Diem and Maj. Gen. Timmes inspect a Self Defense Corps unit, Kontum, 1962. Note the presence of both armed men and women.

Diem
and His Soldiers

Up to this point, I have confined myself to describing the regime of Ngo Dinh Diem from the political and sociological point of view. It is now time to consider the military situation.

Acting on my request, on October 15, 1957, President Diem appointed me to command the 1st Corps with headquarters in Hue in Central Vietnam. Prior to that time, I had been the chief of staff of the Army of Vietnam (ARVN).

In my first few months in Hue, having learned of the government's overall plans, I became quite confident about the future. I was especially pleased with the idea of cultivating new lands in Quang Tri, the scheme to develop the iron mine at Hoa My, and the program to further improve the coal mine at Nong Son. These projects would help create jobs for thousands of poor people and thus could be the first steps toward a real social revolution. I also was quite hopeful about the military situation.

Unfortunately, what seemed to be lofty aspirations on the part of the government had no real basis in fact. Government officials were not trying to better the lot of the people by administering their programs in the most efficient and honest way but, instead, were trying to consolidate their own positions, using military properties for their financial gain. I became definitely worried about the disastrous consequences if this situation was not corrected and improved.

Our adversary, the Viet Cong, had left a great number of their cadres in the south to implement their phase-to-phase secret activities, as follows:

75

Phase One:	Secret propaganda
Phase Two:	Terrorism, assassination, and sabotage
Phase Three:	Attack of remote and isolated outposts and progression to mobile warfare
Phase Four:	General offensive to overthrow the government

In Central Vietnam the Viet Cong resumed their activities in 1959 and 1960. Their propaganda leaflets appeared in many areas publicizing their terrorist and assassination activities. Their base of operations was in the Truong Son mountain chain.

The first important confrontation was the attack against Hiep Duc in Quang Nam province during the night of August 20, 1960.

Hiep Duc was an outpost in the foothills in about the center of the province in my Corps zone, established to control both a road and a river running from the coast to the mountains. We had a company of about eighty men of the regional forces there armed with light and automatic weapons and light (60-mm) mortars. The post was quite isolated and was too far away to be covered by friendly artillery fire.

The Viet Cong attacked this post from the top of the hill and in flank. At the same time, a soldier inside the camp opened a gate which allowed the enemy to infiltrate a squad of their men inside. This caused great confusion in the camp, and the defenders thought they were being attacked by at least a battalion. Actually, the Viet Cong had only about one hundred men in their attack, but they simulated greater strength by exploding a lot of firecrackers which caused the regional force unit to become greatly dispirited.

The enemy occupied the camp for a few hours, leaving before our reinforcements could get there. On the march to the camp we had to be extremely careful because we knew the Viet Cong would anticipate our reaction and perhaps try to ambush us.

The situation was not that serious, but it showed that the Viet Cong already had a real fighting force in Central Vietnam, an area long famous for its lack of Communist activity. Our government officials in Central Vietnam at that time not only did not recognize the Communist peril, but also tried to hide the facts. They even hid behind a slogan of "Communist extermination" to destroy certain nationalist elements that opposed them politically or economically.

As the 1st Corps commander in the northern part of the country, I was able to recognize at first hand the deteriorating military and political situation. In frequent visits by foot to remote outposts in my military region I had ample opportunity to talk directly with the enlisted men and officers. These visits also gave me an opportunity to be closer to the people, both in cities and rural areas, and to learn more about their problems, how they lived their lives, and what they wished for the future. The lives of the soldiers and low-ranking officers were terrible, simply because they could not make enough to live any kind of dignified existence. As a result, little towns of wretched hovels sprang up around the various posts where the troops were stationed, because a soldier did not get enough pay to allow him to maintain a house for his family in a village away from his post. This caused great problems for everyone since the nearby villages and towns were not equipped to provide such necessities as medical care and schools for this floating population. These temporary towns were also highly vulnerable to the Viet Cong who made them pay double taxes.

My heart went out to these poor people, but as a Corps Commander I had no means available to help them much. After I became Minister of Defense in 1963, I developed a plan for model cities for dependents of military personnel which included decent housing, sanitation, medical care, markets, police, and defense against Viet Cong aggression. Unfortunately, Khanh's countercoup prevented my plan from being implemented, and it was never considered by any future administration.

I began to discuss these matters with Generals Duong Van Minh (Big Minh) and Le Van Kim (my old friend), officers for whom I felt the greatest of respect and in whom I had special trust.

Big Minh was an old comrade of mine with whom I had served for many years. He was not a French citizen and therefore not an officer in the French army. His actual commission was as a Vietnamese officer serving in the French Army of Indochina. He was personally courageous and was advanced rapidly in grade during the years of the French-Vietnamese War. He was a Buddhist like myself and was born in Long An in the Mekong Delta.

At the time of the Geneva Accords, Minh was commander of the Capital Military Region which comprised Saigon and its environs. He strongly backed Ngo Dinh Diem during the struggle for power with

General Nguyen Van Hinh and was in charge of the government troops that suppressed the Binh Xuyen and Hoa Hao. Diem really appreciated Minh's loyalty and efficient service, so much so that by 1957, Minh had attained the grade of major general, second in rank to General Le Van Ty, the chief of the Joint General Staff. By this time, Minh was probably the most popular officer in the army with a wide following among both the troops and the civilian populace.

He was something of a paradox, capable of extremely decisive action at one time, and procrastinating on decisions on other occasions, to the utter consternation of his colleagues. He derived his nickname from his large physical stature, much taller and better muscled than the average Vietnamese. He excelled at sports, especially tennis and soccer. His tastes were strongly artistic, however, and he liked to collect a wide variety of orchids, tropical birds, and tropical fish. He had also managed to obtain a collection of Japanese dolls which he displayed with great pride in his home.

Diem gradually came to mistrust this early supporter and decided to deny him key positions in the army. I remember one event where, after a government victory, Minh was proclaimed as the "Hero of the Nation" by an orator. Diem and his family entourage, especially brother Nhu, took this very badly, feeling that there was not room for two heroes in the nation. So, a major army headquarters was organized called Army Field Command, with Big Minh as the commander. This highly qualified headquarters staff had no real duties, despite the fact that many of its officers were highly intelligent and well qualified. Minh's only function was that of 1st and 2nd Corps inspector. He did, however, have many opportunities to visit Hue and Da Nang where he and I could meet to discuss our country's situation.

Much of Minh's problem was Ngo Dinh Nhu's mistrust of him and the rest of the top generals in the army. I believe that Nhu was behind the decision to move Minh off to the side since I knew he disliked the popular general even when he was in favor with Diem. Minh returned this animosity from Diem's younger brother, seeing him and his beautiful wife as evil and detrimental to the president. He was very outspoken in his criticism, even to foreigners, so it is a little strange that he survived as well as he did. His overall popularity in the country saved him, I suppose.

At the start of 1960, the Viet Cong began to increase their activities throughout the country. The all-out attack against a regimental headquarters of the 12th Division fifteen miles north of Tay Ninh appeared to be the beginning of their third phase of a planned aggressive takeover. This surprise attack inflicted heavy casualties on our forces and caused people to doubt the fighting spirit of the army.

Minh and I examined carefully the military situation in light of this new Communist capability and agreed that it was our duty to present to the president the true situation that prevailed in the country. We felt that if Diem really loved the country he had to replace many politicians who had assumed military command and administrative direction of governmental functions, but who were basically incompetent. These people lacked qualifications for their positions and were making financial gain at the expense of the common people. We agreed further that if the president refused to make necessary changes in his administration we would have to overthrow his inefficient government and install other nationalist leaders more capable of dealing with the crisis.

Both of us sent reports direct to President Diem and to Ngo Dinh Nhu. We clearly pointed out errors made by the government and, at the same time, suggested corrective measures. We wanted them to take seriously our unbiased reports obtained from loyal sources in the country.

As we quickly learned, however, we were not the only members of the army considering the possibility of a coup d'etat. On November 11, 1960, Colonel Vuong Van Dong made an attempt to overthrow the government using the paratroop brigade.

On that day I was on an official mission in Saigon attending a special meeting of all corps commanders. The coup attempt happened so unexpectedly that we did not know whether it was real or was a false one planted by the government.

Dong was a former airborne officer assigned to the military staff college in Saigon. The plan for the coup was formulated in the college in conjunction with several civilian politicians. In picking the paratroops for the coup, Dong chose wisely since they were as good as any available in the army. The initial assault was successful. They surrounded the presidential palace, seized the radio station, and gained control of the Saigon police. Then they lost resolve. An American CIA agent named Miller was with Dong and Colonel Nguyen Chanh Thi, the paratroop commander, at the palace gates just before the final assault. He reckoned that the day had been won, and that Diem would soon surrender. So, he advised his Vietnamese friends to hold up the attack which could easily have defeated Diem's palace guard. Both armor and artillery were available to reduce the defenses of the palace.

Diem asked for a chance to negotiate and agreed to surrender to the insurgents, but secretly ordered the 7th Division commanded by General Tran Thien Khiem to come from the Delta to relieve him. General Nguyen Khanh also joined the defenders inside the palace grounds. By nightfall, the relieving troops arrived, and the coup was defeated. Fortunately, there was no large loss of life.

Diem's retribution came swiftly. Many of the plotters and some perfectly innocent spectators were either imprisoned or executed without trial or any kind of due process. Even though I and other generals had nothing to do with the coup, we were still suspected by the president. I was suspended from my command for two weeks while an investigation was conducted. My old comrade General Kim, commandant of our national Military Academy at Dalat, was dismissed and placed under house arrest for a long time. In his case, the coup plotters had publicly named him as the premier of the new government without taking him into their confidence.

This abortive coup should have awakened Diem and his brother to the fact that the whole country was on the verge of revolt. The American Ambassador Durbrow and General McGarr, Chief of the Military Assistance Advisory Group (MAAG), did not promote this coup, but still saw it as a good warning for Diem to start making some necessary reforms.

Sixteen months later, on February 22, 1962, two young pilots of our air force bombed and strafed Diem's palace. This building which symbolized the regime was partially ruined, but Diem and Nhu were uninjured. One pilot, Nguyen Van Cu, flew to exile in Cambodia. The second, Pham Phu Quoc, was imprisoned when his plane was shot down and landed on the Saigon River.

Even this second attempt on his life made no impression on Diem. We thought these two incidents would make him take more seriously the information we had been giving him and persuade him to make the required changes in his policy and in his administration. Instead, he attributed his delivery from danger to the workings of divine providence and became more intransigent than ever. We, therefore, became more convinced than ever that only a well-planned coup d'etat, a real revolution, could solve our country's problem.

During this period, various United States intelligence services sent agents to learn our intentions concerning a possible coup against Diem. We guarded our responses to these Americans because we did not trust United States intelligence as they had so many different operational branches and had their own jealousies and internal dissensions. We also felt that a coup against Diem should be strictly an internal affair.

The NLF which had been organized by Hanoi in 1960 was able to rally increasing adherence for its programs of subversion and eventual overthrow of the government.

Like the Viet Minh in North Vietnam in the mid-1940s, the NLF was a front organization having many non-Communist members. Under the leadership of Viet Minh cadres who had remained in the south after the 1954 Geneva agreements and some prominent Communist officials from Hanoi, the NLF succeeded in enlisting the help of progressive intellectuals, liberal bourgeois, and frustrated nationalists. These patriotic elements had been harassed previously, or jailed by President Diem's overzealous secret police. Unable to support a government that did its best to persecute them, they were forced to go over to the only other political and military movement, the NLF.

The military and political situation became more and more critical as the NLF began to occupy previously loyal regions in the Mekong Delta and the area adjacent to the Truong Son mountains in the center of the country. People in the countryside lived in constant fear, because in the daytime they were threatened and oppressed by corrupt government officials and at night they were harangued and terrorized by the NLF. Danger was always close.

To try to rescue the situation from the NLF, the government established the strategic hamlet program. In theory, this national policy was quite sound and timely because portions of the population would be regrouped and thus produce a type of desirable social revolution. In addition, a self-defense force would be established which it was hoped would protect the villagers from the Communists.

Ngo Dinh Nhu was the father of the strategic hamlet program which was patterned after a similar program of the British in Malaya in the 1950s.

All 16,000 hamlets in Vietnam were to be converted to small armed bases and a new democracy would be created from the bottom up. But, the farmers in the Mekong Delta preferred to remain on their large land holdings, refusing to be resettled forcefully. This is, of course, typical of all Vietnamese, even the present-day people who will also resist any resettlement desired by their Communist rulers.

The government, however, had a hidden motive of destroying opposing nationalist elements and consolidating its own position by placing loyal Can Lao party members in command positions from the village to province level. This program gave unscrupulous officials in rural areas the opportunity to perpetrate reprisals, embezzle funds, and oppress the people by forcing them to perform compulsory labor without pay. In order to curry favor from their superiors these scoundrels did not hesitate to make the people under them suffer. The villagers became so frustrated with their local leaders that they cooperated less and less with the government and began to tolerate the NLF more and more.

My responsibility was to maintain peace and order in the five northern provinces: Quang Tri, Thua Thien, Quang Nam, Quang Tin, and Quang Ngai. To carry out this extensive mission, I had only two divisions, about thirty thousand men, under my command dispersed throughout these provinces over thousands of square miles. We had to provide security, attack the enemy in secret hideouts, and prepare for an anticipated North Vietnamese invasion across the 17th parallel. One would think that I would have been given full control of all forces in my region and been allowed to carry out operations as I deemed necessary. This was decidedly not the case. No officials, military or civilian, were allowed to carry out any plan without the personal approval of Ngo Dinh Can, President Diem's brother and advisor in charge of Central Vietnam. This was the time, of course, before the introduction of American ground forces in large numbers, when we still had a largely Vietnamese internal fight.

Government operations against the NLF forces were being conducted against dedicated guerrillas who lived and worked with the villagers. I can remember on one such strike in Quang Nam province that a farmer came to me and openly disapproved of our actions. He said, "You came here with artillery, trucks, and well-equipped soldiers to fight against our own people.

You have plenty of supplies while we are poor and have nothing. You blame us for giving the NLF soldiers rice, but you must remember that they are living here with us, sharing our poor lot and protecting us. They are our own children and brothers and belong to our village."

All I could do was to shake my head sadly because I had no logical answer for him. Everything he said was true. The NLF never told the villagers that they were Communists, only that they were trying to help them against governmental interference in their lives.

I found in my corps area many patriotic nationalist leaders who were definitely anti-Communist but had as much trouble accepting the government programs as I did. They were civil servants, professors, and prominent businessmen who had been meeting secretly and discussing the problems of the country. Our ambitions were mutual: to build a true democratic society, improve living conditions of the people, and continue the struggle against the Communists—eventually bringing a genuine peace to the country. We met every two or three months to exchange ideas and information and, over a period of time, my plans for leading a coup d'etat against the Diem government took more concrete shape.

In mid-December 1962, I was transferred back to Saigon to become the commander of the army. This position, with its headquarters and a strength of eighty men, was newly established by presidential decree. Although bearing the title, in reality I was not allowed to command any army unit and did not have the proper authority to operate as a commander. Simultaneously, General Big Minh's field command headquarters was dissolved and he was assigned to a new job as military advisor to the president. Giving him this function was like putting him on an extended vacation because he was the advisor of nobody and had no authority or responsibility.

In my own case, I could not stand to stay inactive in Saigon. Therefore, I asked the president to let me go out and inspect field units and observe the establishment of the strategic hamlets throughout the country. He agreed, and through these visits I was able to ascertain the true state of morale in the army and what was going on in the minds of the citizenry. I tried to go to as many places as I could, from the Ben Hai River in the north to the point of Ca Mau. The more I saw, the more I realized that the situation throughout the country was even worse than I had previously thought. I was certainly

83

able to see that if the situation was not improved, the country would fall rapidly into the hands of the Communists.

After each inspection tour, I made extensive reports to the president on the local situation, with suggested measures for improvement. I told him about declining morale in the officer corps because of promotion for religious preference or party loyalty instead of ability. I made specific suggestions that various incompetent military leaders be dismissed and others advanced, but my pleas fell on deaf ears. I told him of the terrible conditions of the soldiers' families and recommended possible solutions that might help. I told him of the mistreatment of poor villagers by his corrupt officials, and suggested they be charged for their crimes and punished. Again, I was met with silence by the implacable mandarin. In addition, of course, I was also able to bring back much accurate information for our coup plot for discussions with Generals Minh and Kim.

In June 1963, Big Minh and I were sent to observe a demonstration of SEATO forces in Thailand. Here we had an opportunity to meet various foreigners and to read foreign newspapers and magazines. We discovered that world opinion was violently against the Ngo Dinh Diem government, particularly after the fiery suicide of the Buddhist bonze, Thich Quang Duc.

When we returned home at the end of June, we were surprised to see how far downhill the political situation had gone. The suicides of several Buddhists, combined with demonstrations and riots caused what I can only characterize as a boiling atmosphere with people furious all over. The turmoil existed directly in the nation's capital and in other principal cities throughout the country, but still the government did not come up with any kind of effective solution. We three, Minh, Kim, and Don, saw that every day the National Liberation Front was making further gains because of the disgust of the common people with the government. Our suggestions to President Diem and Ngo Dinh Nhu were met with vague promises or by simple silence.

We began our detailed planning for the coup at this time. We were careful not to let anyone know the name of the coup leader since we wanted to preserve absolute secrecy. Each of us tried to contact and bring several generals and colonels who had troops under their command to our way of thinking. One major principle in our planning was to keep foreigners ignorant of the coup since this was strictly a Vietnamese affair. A second objective was to achieve our goal of overthrowing President Diem with a minimum of bloodshed and disruption of our national economy. We were very aware that our success was definitely contingent on our ability to contain the NLF and improve the military and political situation. We could not succeed if any residual scars were present after we had deposed President Diem.

Gen. Le Van Ty, Chief of General Staff at change of command ceremony, 1963.

Gen. Le Van Ty, Maj. Gen. Charles Timmes, and Lt. Gen. Duong Van ("Big") Minh at meeting in 1963 (Ty is third from left.)

CHAPTER SIX

Diem Must Go

I have often thought, since the time of the overthrow of the Diem government, that one of Ngo Dinh Diem's greatest errors was to give some of his most efficient and highly regarded generals meaningless jobs. Not only did they become bitter, but they used their time to think, make plans, and perfect strategies. The inevitable result could only be the overthrow of Diem. He was as shortsighted in his dealings with Minh, Kim, and myself as he was with the farmers in the villages.

By mid-July 1963, we had completed a considerable amount of work toward Diem's overthrow. Our biggest problem, as far as the execution of the coup was concerned, was that none of us was in command of any troops. We knew we had their respect, but without some kind of formal command relationship, no orders that we would issue could be obeyed. The troops themselves were loyal to the officers commanding them. It was important, therefore, that we bring into the coup circle several troop commanders.

The first general I approached for this purpose was Major General Ton That Dinh, then 3rd Corps and 3rd Tactical Area commander, who also had full control of the forces around Saigon.

Ton That Dinh was one of our youngest generals at this time, only about thirty-seven years old. He had been a minor functionary in the police station at Dalat, but volunteered for the Vietnamese army. He was in the first class at the Military Academy in Hue at the same time as Nguyen Van Thieu. In 1950 he was sent to France for further military schooling and when he returned he was given command of a battalion while still a lieutenant. He was an excellent fighter and troop leader and was promoted to colonel in 1954. In that year I gave him command of Group Mobile 34 which afterward became one of our first divisions. He retained command of that division and later became commander of our 1st Division at Hue under my overall command.

Dinh was extremely handsome, fiery, ambitious, and flamboyant. He was an audacious troop commander, but sometimes he acted first without thinking of the consequences. Ngo Dinh Can was his champion and one day told me that he was going to recommend him to his brother for promotion to general. He wanted to know if I had any objections. I had none except for his relative youth, so in 1959 the promotion was made and he became commander of the Second Corps in Ban Me Thuot at the tender age of thirty-three.

I have read the sensational Pentagon Papers, as published in the United States, with great interest. In general, I can agree with the description of our coup as stated there, but the derogatory comments about Ton That Dinh are certainly not true. Dinh was not at all the opportunist portrayed in these writings. He was thoroughly committed to our coup from the start, having come to roughly the same conclusions I had that Diem and Nhu had to go. He did play a kind of double game with Nhu all during the month of October, but he remained loyal to us, cleverly deceiving Nhu as to his real intentions. The notion that even up to the day of the coup he had not committed himself fully is total nonsense. He and I were in constant touch during that trying period and never did his loyalty to us waver. I never had need to play on his pride, since he was as committed to the coup as I was.

I visited General Dinh in his house on a Sunday afternoon in mid-July 1963. We discussed the increasing activities of the National Liberation Front, various incidents with the Buddhists, and the overall indignation of the people against the government. I was pleased and relieved to find that he agreed totally with my ideas. He felt that it was his duty to convince the president of the truth of my arguments. From that day I began to have great confidence in General Dinh because it was evident that even though he was young and ambitious and had been very well treated by the government, he was definitely a patriot, loyal first to his country and his people. Unlike so many others in positions of responsibility he always placed the nation's interests above any of his own affairs. In making decisions, he thought first of the effect on people now living, but immediately thereafter he considered how future generations would be affected. In all our conversations, he never asked for anything for himself, only to help others or satisfy his conscience that the work at hand was to be done as well as possible. We became close friends and frequently met at his residence or in his office.

The most important point that General Dinh and I had to make to President Diem was that unless the Buddhists could be appeased, the NLF would take advantage of the situation and further exploit the population. Diem and Nhu not only rejected our proposal, but blamed the generals for being demoralized and confused in facing this difficult situation. Therefore, Nhu ordered a weekly political orientation meeting at the Joint General Staff headquarters for all principal armed service officers.

One of the recommendations I had made several times to the president was to put the army clearly in control of the military situation: to remove the office of the president from military decision making. To do this speedily, I openly advocated that a temporary condition of martial law be imposed throughout the country so that essential military actions could proceed without political interference. Suggestions like this had been resisted by Diem, so we were surprised when the government on August 20, 1963, declared martial law, directing us generals to reestablish law, order, and security throughout the nation. I was now in charge of this because the army's senior officer, Le Van Ty, was hospitalized in the United States and I had been appointed to replace him temporarily as Chief of the Joint General Staff.

But, as it turned out, we were duped by Ngo Dinh Nhu who had a most devious plan up his sleeve. Early in the evening of that same day, Nhu called a meeting of the top command concerning the suppression of the Buddhist demonstrations. We were surprised to learn that Nhu had designated only special forces and secret police under his direct command to carry out the operation. His plan was a simultaneous raid against many Buddhist pagodas, as described in the last chapter. The army as a whole was unaware of the raid except for some generals such as myself and Tran Thien Khiem, the Chief of Staff.

We stayed up all night waiting for the operation to end. At 1:30 A.M. Khiem and I visited the Xa Loi pagoda, the main resistance center of the Buddhists, to assess the situation. We were sickened at what we saw. The place was a shambles. Most monks who normally served the people at the pagoda had been arrested by the secret police on the pretext that arms were present in the building. The official report stated that three weapons were seized there, but these had actually been brought to the scene by the police. At this pagoda, Xa Loi, more than thirty people were wounded and many listed as missing.

Khiem and I were then summoned to the palace where Nhu briefed the president on the operation at 5:00 A.M. One of Diem's cabinet, Foreign Minister Vu Van Mau who later was Big Minh's premier, resigned and shaved his head to protest this assault on the pagodas.

Nhu's decision to attack the pagodas and implicate the army with myself at its temporary head turned out to be his and his brother's ultimate downfall. In giving me the position of Chief of the Joint General Staff, Nhu thought that he was safe; that I was somewhat of a "yes man." Although Nhu deeply feared the possibility of a coup, he told his closest aides that I was incapable of pulling one off. Nhu's view of me was not shared by many foreigners, especially *Newsweek* correspondent, François Sully who had been expelled from Vietnam for his truthful anti-Diem coverage.

I learned that when he heard of my new job, he told several of his colleagues in New York, "They just pulled a boner. This new command position will help General Don carry out his coup." Fortunately for us, and me, of course, nobody reported Sully's comment to Diem or Nhu.

I must admit that the operation was very successful from a military point of view. Most of the pagodas in all major cities were ransacked, with over fourteen hundred Buddhists, mostly monks, arrested. Nhu, during the period of this operation, resorted to his "divide and conquer" tactics. So that the army would be blamed for the raids, he ordered them to begin after martial law had been declared. Also, to further implicate the army, some of the policemen assigned to the operation were in uniforms of the paratroop brigade. This was a stupid maneuver, because he should have been trying to enlist our support rather than alienate us. He knew that we would have opposed his scheme to suppress the Buddhists in such a brutal manner, so he executed his unprovoked raids with his secret police and had the army take the just criticism of the citizenry for them.

I knew that the Americans were upset about the raids, so I decided to do some missionary work for the army with them. A CIA operative who was an old friend could be trusted to carry the truth back to the ambassador. This was Lt. Col. Lucien Conein, an old member of OSS who had been operating in Vietnam since about 1945, first in support of Ho Chi Minh against the Japanese, and later against Ho and the Communists as the situation became clarified.

90

Conein had had an amazing career, having enlisted in the French Foreign Legion before the United States entered World War II and then, after his country's entry, proving to be a most efficient operator against various enemies. Since he spoke fluent French, he was highly effective in his work in Vietnam. He was one American whom I could always trust to report facts accurately and keep things confidential when necessary.

So, on August 23, 1963, I called Conein and asked him to meet me at my office. When he arrived he was armed and was apprehensive that he might be falling into a trap. He knew that the situation between Diem and Ambassador Frederick Nolting was very tense because Diem had promised to be conciliatory to the Buddhists in accord with a joint communique they had issued. I explained the attack against the pagodas to Conein in detail, making certain he understood that the army had not been involved. He and the other Americans had been taken completely by surprise by Nhu's operation, so Conein was pleased to be given this timely and accurate information.

The name of the army had been sullied by this operation and those of us who had not participated in the attack on the Buddhists had to accept the recriminations and complaints of the public. We felt cheated by the government, feeling ashamed each time we put on our uniforms. Despite this ignominy we had to wait for a more favorable occasion to act.

At Big Minh's suggestion I got authority from Diem to have the generals on duty in Saigon meet with me daily to study the situation involving martial law in the country. After several discussions, we sent a proposal to Diem requesting that the martial law decree be lifted since it had been used as a subterfuge to conduct the raid against the Buddhists and had proved ineffective without wholehearted support from the rest of the government. We proposed instead that a new political concept be formulated to reorganize the government to better meet the people's needs, with the participation of a number of effective generals in positions of authority. Further, we demanded in a letter that Mr. and Mrs. Ngo Dinh Nhu should leave Vietnam. General Dinh and I delivered this petition at the Gia Long palace to President Diem on September 5. A few days later we met again with the president who refused even to entertain our proposal. He then denounced us both as men of ambition.

On our return to 3rd Corps headquarters, Dinh and I agreed that we had been used very badly by the government in this entire matter and that, along with the army, we had been exploited. We solemnly swore that very moment to overthrow Diem and Nhu as soon as possible.

The following day General Dinh went again to ask about our September 5 letter, but was unable to get any kind of satisfactory answer. Dinh was so annoyed at the president's attitude that he left Saigon and went to Dalat under the pretext of being ill. I advised him to stay in Saigon because I feared that Diem might replace him with some other general and endanger the coup.

After Dinh had left for Dalat I feared that Nhu might become suspicious. I went to see President Diem and covered for him, saying that under the stress of the past few days Dinh had become so overtired and tense that he was close to a breakdown and needed a rest in a tranquil place like Dalat. After listening to my half serious and half humorous recommendation, both Diem and Nhu burst out laughing and assigned General Tran Thien Khiem to take charge of operations in Saigon.

With Dinh's departure, I continued contacting other trustworthy officers throughout the country to enlist their support for our plot. I received encouragement from most of the key generals and colonels who were commanding troops in the vicinity of the capital, since they were as disillusioned as Dinh and myself about Diem and his government.

One of these key individuals was General Mai Huu Xuan, commandant of the Quang Trung training center. He had approximately sixteen thousand troops under his immediate command and, thanks to our routine meetings held each week in Saigon, I was able to contact him frequently. Xuan promised to support me actively when the time came for the execution of the coup.

Big Minh made contact with General Tran Thien Khiem whom Diem had appointed to take charge of operations in Saigon. We were cautious with him because he was probably the general that Diem and Nhu trusted most, since Khiem with his Seventh Division had rescued the president during the abortive coup of 1960. Minh reported to me that Khiem had agreed to participate in the coup and suggested that I meet with him for further discussion.

At our first meeting, in mid-September, Khiem agreed completely on the necessity for a change in leadership but had a separate plan for a coup, one sponsored by the American CIA operating out of the embassy. I advised him not to discuss any part of this with the Americans because this had to be a Vietnamese internal affair. He agreed to drop his plan completely and said that he was ready to cooperate with me in planning our internal Vietnamese coup.

As subsequent events proved, General Khiem was a flighty person who could not be counted on in time of trouble. We were correct in approaching him cautiously and probably should not have given him a high position in the government. As the reader will discover, Khiem turned out even worse than we dreamed as premier in later governments of Nguyen Van Thieu.

In July, I visited General Nguyen Khanh who was the commander of the 2nd Corps and 2nd Tactical Area, and another real mistake for us. In our conversation I told him about my proposal to Diem to reform his government with the inclusion of a number of generals in the new cabinet, including Khanh as one of the ministers. Upon hearing this, he became very happy and said that he fully agreed with me on our proposal.

I had known Khanh and served with him for years. He, Le Van Kim and I were aides for ex-Premier Xuan of Bao Dai's old government. Despite our close relationship, I knew that I had to be careful with him since he always had been the complete opportunist. As things turned out, Vietnam would have been better served if we had kept the entire plan secret from him and arrested him in his command post the night before the coup. We should have remembered that Khanh was the one who had made the grandstand play by rushing into the palace grounds at the time of the 1960 coup attempt, subsequently taking credit for saving Diem.

We had two additional private meetings. In mid-September he visited my residence in Cholon. He volunteered his help and support if I intended to conduct a coup d'etat. He told me that if for some reason the coup was unsuccessful, I should come to him in the 2nd Tactical Area where he would help me establish a resistance zone.

In mid-October Khanh told me that he had intended to stage a coup himself but was unsuccessful because he had discussed it with a CIA station chief Richardson, who in turn passed the information on to Ngo Dinh Nhu. I already had known this story because Nhu had told me about it. At that time I defended Khanh, blaming the affair on the Americans. Khanh later agreed to arrest any officers in his corps who, at the time of the coup, remained loyal to the president.

Khanh was one of the most talented and intelligent of the officers in on the coup plan but, unfortunately, was very inconsistent and highly deceitful. Khanh was the type of person who relied totally on the government to advance his career, while looking for any occasion to overthrow it. He would seem to side with anyone who happened to be stronger, so during our coup planning we were careful not to have him participate directly though I gave him orders to cut off all signal communications between Saigon and his infantry divisions as soon as he received news of the coup. Further, he was to declare martial law throughout his region and prohibit troop movements to Saigon. We felt we could not afford to exclude him because we thought he might reveal our plot to the president. We only informed him of the real coup a day or so in advance and did not give him any details of the plot.

Another key officer was General Do Cao Tri, commander of my old 1st Corps and the 1st Tactical Area. After he had heard my arguments concerning the necessity for a coup he readily agreed to join us. I gave him instructions, with the following code words to use as soon as the coup started: "Please apply special training measures in the camp at Phu Bai beginning at. . . ."

Colonel Do Mau was the director of the military security service. At first I did not trust him entirely because of the good opinion that Ngo Dinh Nhu had about him. He came to see me one day after the attack on the pagodas, however, expressing his great dissatisfaction with the Diem regime. I became convinced of his sincerity and permitted him to join our group.

Colonel Tran Ngoc Huyen at the Dalat Military Academy joined our plotters' ranks early in the game. Huyen was a devout Catholic and an officer highly trusted by President Diem. He was revolted by the government's treatment of the Buddhists, especially in Hue. Because of his close attachment to Diem, he made a special visit to him to try to persuade him of his errors in trying to suppress the Buddhists. This apparently angered Diem, so Huyen's intervention proved worthless, just as my own had several times before. His obvious frustration made him into one of our strongest adherents. His code word for action was: "The training program of officers, students, and helicopters has been approved. The helicopters will take off at 1:30 P.M."

In the preparation for and execution of the coup, Nguyen Cao Ky, a lieutenant colonel in the air force, was an individual that we could count on. He was chief of a transport squadron of C-47s and also in charge of an educational program on psychological warfare. The day before the coup, Ky thought that the noise made by some landing helicopters was the entrance of tanks into the air base and started to announce the coup to his students. One of his officers caught him in time, however, explaining that it was a helicopter so he immediately stopped. This was a narrow escape, of course, because his premature announcement might have led to the failure of our coup when it actually happened.

Nguyen Cao Ky was personally extremely brave and very flamboyant. He was an expert pilot, trained by the French in transport aircraft, but he was later qualified on all the planes we possessed. At the time of the coup he was only about thirty-three years of age, but had already gathered a rather large following. Something of a playboy, he wore extravagant clothes and was a striking figure in his black flight suit with his silken lavender scarf floating behind him.

So, we had our team. I knew that we could count without reservation on such stalwarts as Minh, Kim, Dinh, Mau, Xuan, and Huyen, but that we had to be extremely careful with Khiem and Khanh. How careful we should have been we were to learn later.

We finally decided on Friday, November 1, 1963, as the historic day for overthrowing Diem's despotic regime. This day had special significance in several respects. In the first place, it corresponded to September 16 of the Year of the Cat, according to the lunar calendar. That day would appeal to the Vietnamese masses because it was considered to be favorable. And, since November 1 was a Friday, we could expect both President Diem and Nhu to be present since Diem never left Saigon on Friday and Nhu would be presiding over his weekly strategic hamlet meeting. That same day was also All Saints Day for the Catholics, and civil servants had half a day off. We thought, therefore, that not many people would be aware that a coup was taking place. We decided to start the action at 1:30 P.M. because we wanted everything to be open and perfectly apparent to anyone who happened to be watching.

Our plan for the coup against Ngo Dinh Diem was simple, yet thorough. We needed to have the cooperation of, or at least no opposition from, the major troop commanders in the country to ensure that Diem could not call for help and thus escape being overthrown as he did in 1960. After lining up the major commanders, the rest followed easily. As events proved, we did our homework well.

In the first place, we wanted to get as many high-ranking officers together as possible to indicate our solidarity and also to be able to control them better in case anyone had a change of heart. So, we invited all the generals in Saigon to lunch at the Joint General Staff Officers Club at noon on November 1, except General Ton That Dinh who was in charge of the assault troops against the presidential palace. Commanders of the special forces, presidential guard, airborne brigade, and the Saigon police were to be put under arrest by 1:30 P.M. when the actual coup was to be launched.

Our contacts with most military region commanders, new navy and air force chiefs, the Dalat military academy, Nha Trang naval and air force bases, and the various school commands made it certain that Diem and Nhu would have no place to turn for help after the coup commenced. To ensure overall security in Saigon, we planned to have all key points in the city controlled by 4:00 P.M. All police stations, armed forces bases, the radio station, and the city hall were to be covered.

There were two strong points, the presidential guard compound and the presidential palace itself, which would have to be attacked swiftly and decisively. Both of these bastions were to be surrounded by armor, artillery, and infantry troops and then attacked with overwhelming force. This would resolve the issue speedily and minimize casualties. The troops to be used were the 5th Division under Colonel Nguyen Van Thieu, the marine brigade, troops from the Quang Trung training center near Saigon, and a strike force from Vung Tau (south of Saigon) of one airborne battalion, armor school units, and a regiment from the 7th Division.

Our biggest problem was to prevent reinforcement from the Fourth Corps in the Mekong Delta commanded by General Huynh Van Cao who had been very loyal to Diem. Our plan was to replace the 7th Division commander with Colonel Nguyen Huu Co who would keep it in place and isolate the 9th Division on the wrong side of the Mekong River by moving the ferries. Both the 7th and 9th Divisions were subordinate organizations in the Fourth Corps.

In order to provide for as much security as possible and prevent leaks, we purposely did not reduce the plans to writing, simply keeping the details in our minds. Since we were in close daily contact, this was possible.

After my August meeting with Lou Conein concerning the army's participation in the attacks against the pagodas, I did not see him until October 2 at Tan Son Nhut Airport. I was on my way to Nha Trang, a city on the ocean 200 miles northeast of Saigon, and was surprised when he approached me in the terminal. We chatted a little and then on the spur of the moment I suggested that he meet me later in Nha Trang.

That evening we met at my quarters there and I informed him officially that we were planning a coup against Diem for late October or early November. He asked if we needed any help from the Americans to ensure its success, but I responded in the negative. We had plenty of means at our disposal; all we needed to know was whether or not we would have the moral support of the United States government. He promised to report back to me. I told him that Big Minh would also like to see him on October 5th.

This private meeting between Conein and Minh took place as agreed on October 5. Minh's greatest worry was to ensure that we had United States support, so he put the question on the Americans' position directly to Conein. Again, Conein could not commit himself or his government directly and so agreed to report back later. Minh told Conein that three plans were being considered, including the assassination of Diem and his brother. There was a second meeting between the two on October 10 because Conein wanted to get more details on the actual plan. At that conference, Minh told him that in the future all liaison between the Americans and Vietnamese would be through me; that I would be the coup committee's spokesman.

What we did not know at this time was that an internal fight was going on in the American ranks. Ambassador Henry Cabot Lodge and Conein were definitely backing us, feeling that a change in leadership was long overdue. General Paul Harkins, Chief of MAAG, was against our coup and in favor of keeping Diem in control. John Richardson, the CIA office chief, was also pro-Diem and was keeping Ngo Dinh Nhu informed of any coup rumors being heard by the Americans. We were fortunate when Richardson was recalled to Washington on October 10. Had he been there, he could have put our plan in great jeopardy.

The British military attaché gave a party on October 22 where General Harkins drew me aside and asked me about the coup rumors he was hearing. I was noncommital, but he advised me strongly that he was against any coup we might be planning; that he certainly did not support it. He then told me that if such a coup did not succeed and if I were in any trouble that I should come to him with my wife and children and he would give me sanctuary in his residence. This was a curious thing to tell me, but I did appreciate his friendly gesture.

I was worried about the remarks Harkins made about United States support, so I telephoned Conein and asked him to visit me on October 23. Conein gave me assurance that United States support was still present and asked to be given a detailed plan for the coup. We had two meetings the next day. In the morning he told me that he had been asked to apologize to me for General Harkins and that his remarks at the British party were simply his own view and did not reflect official American policy. In our evening meeting I told him that our committee had decided not to turn over a written plan to the Americans, but that perhaps I could provide something for Ambassador Lodge's eyes a couple of days before the start of the coup.

I had a good chance to try to clarify various positions when I saw Lodge at the airport before a trip he was taking with President Diem on October 28. I drew him aside and asked him if Conein spoke for him, to which I received an affirmative reply. I told Lodge that we had to insist that the coup remain a purely Vietnamese affair. The ambassador nodded his agreement and then asked about timing. I declined to answer, telling him that we were not yet ready to divulge that information.

That same night I had a brief meeting with Conein. He offered us money and weapons, but I turned him down, saying that we still needed only courage and conviction, which we had abundantly. Conein pressed me on the date and time because Ambassador Lodge was intending to fly to Washington to report to President Kennedy on October 31. He wanted to be in Saigon when the coup occurred. I told Conein that I could not be more definite and that Lodge should stick to his plans, because if he made an abrupt change, Diem might get suspicious. Lodge could always turn around if he heard of a coup in progress. I said that I would call Conein as soon as the coup started.

On October 29, I visited General Dinh in Nha Trang for a last overall review of our plan. We returned to Saigon on the afternoon of the 30th for a meeting with Minh and Khiem at a private club in Cholon. It was here that we made our final decision on beginning the coup, dividing all our duties for the entire trying period. Dinh insisted on saving the lives of Diem and Nhu, which Khiem and I fully supported. If Dinh's forces failed in their attacks at the Cong Hoa presidential guard camp and the palace, Khiem's reserve units would be used. All four tactical areas would be put under martial law and await orders, with troop movements absolutely forbidden.

The American Admiral Felt, Commander in Chief of the Pacific, was scheduled to visit Saigon from noon, October 31, to the morning of November 1. According to his itinerary, President Diem was not scheduled for a visit from him, a rather surprising occurrence. I was afraid Diem had scheduled a surprise meeting outside the city and would not be present to receive the admiral. Therefore, I decided to contact President Diem personally and did so on the morning of October 31. He was surprised to hear that Felt was coming and said that he wanted to see him, suggesting that he would be free the morning of November 1. This meeting was later confirmed.

ARVN troops in armored personnel carrier like that in which President Diem and Ngo Dinh Nhu met their deaths.

Ngo Dinh Nhu (center left in dark suit) arrives in Cu Chi village to visit the defenses.

CHAPTER SEVEN

Our Coup Succeeds

On the morning of November 1, I met Admiral Felt at 9:15 at the Chief of the Military Assistance Command office. We talked for about half an hour. Then I agreed to see him at 11:30 at the airport where he and General Harkins would conduct a press conference. After the meeting with the press, Felt left for Hong Kong and Harkins invited me to lunch. I refused, simply saying that I had to attend to some other business, hoping that he had no hint of our plan.

When I had talked to Diem and Nhu about Admiral Felt's visit on October 31, Nhu had complained about Colonel Nguyen Huu Co. He said that Co had talked to a number of his military subordinates about a coup plot and, therefore, Nhu had ordered General Dinh to arrest him. The Chief of Province of Dinh Tuong, Lieut. Col. Nguyen Khac Binh, who later became Thieu's chief of police, had reported everything to Nhu. It was imperative, therefore, that Dinh take special care to silence any other talk on the project. Nhu's suspicions were quite disturbing because he tried to be ahead of anybody else as far as information was concerned and was always making subversive plans of his own, such as his personal contacts with the Viet Cong. For example, at a weekly meeting with the generals in mid-October he said that we ought to have a false coup d'etat one night in order to scare certain members of the administrative branch of the government. He tried to flatter us by saying that if Diem was stuck with some incompetent cabinet ministers we, the army, should work with him in this false coup to help Diem get rid of them.

Despite his physical prowess, successful army career, and great popularity among his troops, Big Minh frequently became plagued with doubts about events beyond his personal control. In particular, he started to become hesitant about our coup plan and never became entirely satisfied with our scenario almost up to the last few hours. He was afraid that the troops we had available would not be enough and was also mistrustful of some of the key figures, notably General Ton That Dinh. About midway in our planning, he proposed the idea of assassination to me in lieu of our planned overthrow of the regime. The following personal experience shows how far he had gone along this road.

After one of our weekly meetings with Nhu at Joint General Staff Headquarters in mid-October, I was asked to accompany him back to his office in the presidential palace. As he saw me stepping into Nhu's black Mercedes, Big Minh made a gesture to hold me back. Only afterward did I know that he was trying to warn me against an assassination plot that he had set up.

Under Big Minh's orders, a squad of army sharpshooters were to wait for Nhu's car at a busy intersection, one mile north of the palace, but the assassination order was countermanded at the last moment for fear that I might accidentally be killed. Later Big Minh severely reproached me for having indirectly saved Nhu from death.

On October 31 we had a stroke of luck that helped us greatly in carrying out the coup. Since Nhu was aware that a coup attempt was in the wind, he decided to try to forestall it. Fortunately for us, he picked one of our fellow plotters, General Ton That Dinh, to help carry out his scheme.

Nhu's plan was an elaborate job of play acting: he planned to stage a false coup which would send the special force troops loyal to the president out of Saigon. The "coup" would then occur, but loyal troops from the Fifth and Seventh Division were to rescue the two brothers and "restore" them to power. Dinh, of course, reported Nhu's plan to us and then began to play the role to the hilt. The forces involved consisted of about three thousand troops, with forty armored vehicles and six special forces companies. He called a meeting of these commanders and then ordered Colonel Tung, the special force leader, to move the troops out on October 29 against a supposed Viet Cong buildup. Nhu gave the name "Bravo I" to his plan so we, in a light-hearted moment decided that "Bravo II" would be a good title for our deadly serious coup.

On the evening of October 31 after having dinner at the home of Major General Weede, General Harkins's Chief of Staff, I stopped by General

102

Dinh's office at Third Corps headquarters. He was drawing up his plan of attack, along with Colonel Co, the officer whose assassination Diem had ordered Dinh to carry out. We decided to have Co go to Dinh Tuong province the next day to command the Seventh Division. When I finally left them at 12:30 A.M. I saw armored cars entering the Third Corps headquarters compound.

After another sleepless night, I called my office at 6:30 in the morning to be brought up to date on combat news throughout the country. I directed my aide to have the Officers' Club provide a food supply for a few days in case we had to be confined there for the entire coup period. At 7:30 I went to my office to prepare to meet Admiral Felt as scheduled. Before leaving I instructed my security officer to increase my escort and guard beginning at noon. A man was sent to the Quang Trung Training Center to request General Xuan to send two officers to meet General Khiem and to invite Xuan to have lunch at the Joint General Staff headquarters. I sent another man to the Thu Duc school center to have the student battalion brought to the JGS headquarters. We planned to use twenty trucks to transport the students from the school center at 1:00 P.M..

At 8:30 A.M. Dinh called and said that Khiem had just come to see him and seemed to be discouraged. Dinh urged that I should be cautious, but that I should receive him. A short time later, Khiem came to my office and reported his visit to Dinh. He told me he had put some irritating ointment in his eyes to make Dinh believe he had been crying. Khiem had suggested to Dinh that we give up the plan because he felt sorry for the president and didn't want harm to come to him. He was pleased that Dinh did not agree. Apparently both Dinh and Khiem were afraid of each other's loyalties and wanted to have some definite checks made on each other.

At 9:15 I met Admiral Felt and General Harkins at MACV headquarters. I did not want to reveal the correct coup date and time, so I invented some small talk to fill the time we had together. I told Felt that if we wanted our struggle against the Communists to be more effective we must first gain the confidence of the people. He agreed with that and we all concluded that the question of victory in Vietnam was not purely a military matter. At 9:45 I left MACV because Felt had to go to his meeting with President Diem.

At 10:00, I got back to my office and called Colonel Huyen of Dalat to give him and Colonel Nguyen Vinh Xuan of Nha Trang the date and time to

103

start the revolution in those localities. I gave orders to have combat-ready companies available to set up a defensive perimeter around the JGS headquarters beginning at 12:00 noon.

At 11:30 A.M. I went to Tan Son Nhut Airport to see Admiral Felt off. He boarded his plane after his press conference at 12:00 noon, so I returned immediately to my office where I learned that the office of the president had called me several times, reporting that Diem wanted to see the Saigon Military Commander, Major General Nguyen Van La immediately.

I called the presidential switchboard to tell them that when General La came in I would have him call the president, and told my aide to tell the president's office that La had not arrived here yet if they called back. In fact, La had been at the Officers' Club since noon. I had Colonel Do Mau, the security chief, work with Generals Kim and Chieu since he was more attuned to the political life of the republic than most of the rest of us.

At the Officers' Club, Generals Nguyen Van La, Nguyen Giac Ngo, Le Van Nghiem, Mai Huu Xuan, and Nguyen Ngoc Le were already present. Then, one by one, Generals Duong Van Minh (Big Minh), Tran Thien Khiem, Tran Van Minh (Little Minh), and Tran Tu Oai arrived.

When I met Big Minh he told me that he had ordered troops to arrive at the capital earlier than previously scheduled because pro-Nhu Navy Captain Ho Tan Quyen had been killed inadvertently and the information about the coup might already be out. By 1:30 P.M. troops from the Quang Trung Training Center had already occupied Tan Son Nhut Airport, the Joint General Staff headquarters, and the radio station. Armored units also took up defensive positions at the JGS. All the commanders of the various branches, services, and special units of the army were present because they had been invited to attend the meeting by General Khiem who kept them there. I invited all the generals at the Officers' Club to come to Khiem's office to work and had all escorts of the other generals disarmed.

All troop movements proceeded like clockwork. Commanders at the air bases, training centers, and other important installations outside Saigon reported that our objectives had been achieved without any fighting or loss of life. General Dinh called and asked me to order Colonel Bui Dinh Dam to transfer his command of the 7th Division to Colonel Co. I called Dam at My Tho in the Mekong Delta and gave him this order. Co was already present to accept the command. I also ordered Colonel Co not to let the 9th Division, commanded by pro-Nhu Colonel Bui Dzinh, move anywhere. He reported that he had brought all the ferryboats to the Saigon side of the river so the 9th Division could not possibly cross.

Captain Que, medical doctor of a marine unit, had occupied the Saigon radio station which later was reoccupied by soldiers of the presidential guard brigade. Later in the afternoon a unit from Quang Trung reinforced the marines and recaptured the station. We could not get the station to do any transmitting at this time, however, because of technical difficulties, so we used the Quang Trung radio transmitter to make necessary broadcasts.

The 1st and 2nd Tactical Areas reported that the plans were being carried out and the situation was favorable. In the 4th Tactical Area, pro-Nhu Major General Huynh Van Cao was at Ben Tre in Kien Hoa Province. When he received news of the coup, he ordered a regiment from the 9th Division to move immediately to Saigon to rescue President Diem. When they arrived at Ben Tre, however, they could not cross the river because all the boats had been ordered to the Saigon side by Colonel Co.

Troop movements to execute our plan were bringing the assault forces into place, Colonel Nguyen Van Thieu's 5th Division in from Bien Hoa, north of Saigon to positions around the palace, and the combined strike force from Vung Tau to their places at the guard's Cong Hoa camp.

Their movements to surround these installations at about 3:00 P.M. evidently alarmed President Diem because he called me half an hour later at Joint General Staff headquarters.

He was very alarmed. Suddenly he seemed to realize that we had been serious. I reminded him of our futile attempts to persuade him of the necessity of reforms. He was frightened enough to offer to listen and make any kind of public proclamation we suggested, but by then it was too late. The troops already had their marching orders. His only course now, I pointed out to him, was to surrender unconditionally and safe conduct would be provided for him and his family to leave the country.

Big Minh then spoke to him, and even more vehemently reminded him of the agonies the people had suffered because of the corrupt government, of how his family had bled the treasury dry for their personal gain, and how we had become so vulnerable to the Viet Cong.

Nobody in the room would agree to any further negotiation with Diem, and thus the telephone conversation ended.

105

At 4:00, I ordered two fighter planes from the airport to strafe the presidential guards' Cong Hoa camp to support the attacking force. At the same time, I authorized the artillery units now in position to direct their fire into the palace and the guards' camp.

At 6:00, Dinh informed me that he had released a number of students who had been arrested and jailed during the Buddhist repression period. I told him to have them brought to the JGS to visit us. When they arrived we met them at the stairs of the main building.

When the group saw us they quietly knelt down in the courtyard as a gesture of thanks for their rescue. The scene moved most of us to tears. In front of us there were the emaciated young people in their dirty clothes but, at that moment, happiness clearly showed on their faces because their hopes had finally been fulfilled. Big Minh explained to the students the progress of the coup and advised them to contribute their efforts toward the reconstruction of a strong and democratic country. They all applauded and vowed absolutely to support the Military Revolutionary Council (MRC). They were happy to return to their homes after such a long time in prison.

This evidence of public support was continuous and rather amazing to us, because even we did not anticipate the enthusiasm of the common people when they became aware that Diem and his brother were overthrown. It was the same type of enthusiasm that we had seen throughout the country when the Japanese surrendered in 1945. It was a heady thing for us to be considered heroes, especially when we compared this with the low repute we enjoyed immediately after the pagoda raids.

At 10:00 P.M. I called pro-Nhu General Huynh Van Cao of the Ninth Division at Ben Tre. He told me that he now supported the council and would be loyal to us in the future, so I ordered him to send a message expressing these sentiments.

At midnight, General Dinh reported that the Cong Hoa camp had been captured by the Vung Tau strike force under Colonel Lam Van Phat. He requested permission to allow the troops a few hours of rest so they would be able to resupply themselves. I granted this request but told him that the Gia Long Palace must be seized before dawn.

In accordance with my promise, I had called Lou Conein and invited him to join us at our headquarters early on November 1. He had been with us all along, following the situation every minute. We discussed together the drafting of a provisional constitution, which Big Minh would proclaim to the people the following morning. We agreed that Mr. Nguyen Thanh Cung, Diem's secretary general, should deliberate with us on this matter. I therefore sent a military police car to bring Mr. Cung to our headquarters.

At about 3:00 A.M. I was informed that Diem and Nhu were no longer at the Gia Long Palace so I gave orders for security personnel to search for them, not knowing whether to believe this report or not. Conein seemed to be irritated by this news, saying that Diem and Nhu must be found at any cost.

A white flag, assumed to be a surrender indication, was seen by our troops outside Diem's palace at about 5:00 A.M. on November 2. The beseiging soldiers naturally advanced in the open and the captain leading them was killed. An all-out assault was then undertaken and at about 5:45 General Dinh called to report that the palace had been captured, but that there was no trace of Diem and Nhu. Palace personnel told him that they had both escaped to Cholon during the previous night.

The news of the escape was verified by Diem's aide, Captain Tho, who called his uncle, Colonel Do Mau, to inform him that they were in Cholon. Further confirmation came in a call to me from Diem at 6:20 A.M. He told me that he knew they would have to surrender, but that he wanted it done with military honors from the troops he had commanded so long. I recounted to him the story of the treachery of the white flag at the palace, and told him that because of this, nobody was in a mood to render any kind of honors to him. I advised that his best course of action would be to leave the country and live in exile abroad, that his surrender would be unconditional, but that safety was assured for him and his family.

It was widely believed that Diem and Nhu escaped through a secret tunnel especially constructed for that purpose. This is completely erroneous since no tunnel in fact existed. They simply went down the stairs at about 8:00 P.M. to the Cong Ly Street side of the Gia Long Palace, passed by some cars parked there, and eluded the soldiers who had surrounded the grounds since late afternoon. They were accompanied by an aide, Captain Tho, and a servant.

Nhu advised that they should strike out for Cholon alone, because they would have a better chance of escaping detection that way. Diem would not permit this, however. He feared for Nhu's life if he were not there to protect

107

OUR ENDLESS WAR

him. He said to Nhu, "Come with me; alone, away from me, they will kill you." They left together in a car driven by Cao Xuan Vy, General Secretary of the Republican Youth Organization.

They first tried to get refuge in the home of Colonel Cao Van Vien, the paratroop brigade commander, but Mrs. Vien told them that her husband had been arrested and that her house was being watched. They then went to the home of a friend, a Chinese businessman in Cholon, and later proceeded to the Catholic church where they were captured. Nhu advised Diem not to surrender to our coup group, but instead to try to escape separately. Diem would not take this advice, keeping Nhu with him as he made contact with us.

Diem called again (at 6:45 A.M.) to talk to General Khiem. He told Khiem his whereabouts at the church in Cholon and asked for transportation to pick them up because he felt insecure there. At 7:00 A.M. we informed Big Minh that Diem and Nhu were at the Cha Tam Catholic Church in Cholon. Minh assigned General Xuan, Colonel Quan, Colonel Lam, Major Nghia, and Captain Nhung to pick them up. Nhung, who was Minh's bodyguard, was included at the last minute without my knowledge. They left our headquarters at about 7:30 A.M. Meanwhile, I arranged a place for them to stay. At 8:30, the convoy returned and Generals Kim and Chieu told me that the brothers had been brought back but both of them were dead. I was extremely moved by this unexpected news and asked if they had committed suicide. I was told that they had not.

At about this time, I promoted Nguyen Van Thieu and Lam Van Phat from colonel to brigadier general as a reward for their bravery and the successful action of their troops during the coup. At lunch, on November 2, I promoted Dinh to the rank of major general.

Lou Conein, representing Ambassador Lodge, called and asked for permission for a plane to land at Tan Son Nhut. He said the plane was carrying Dr. Phan Huy Quat back to Saigon from Can Tho where he had been grounded. I had to grant the permission, since all flights were banned by the coup leaders.

I learned afterward that Quat's hurried return to Saigon was linked to an American plan to make him premier of the post-coup government.

Dr. Quat, a pro-American statesman, had served as a cabinet minister

108

during Bao Dai's reign. Later in 1965, at the height of a religious and political crisis, the Americans succeeded in giving their protégé the premiership.

Conein also asked us to visit Ambassador Lodge to brief him on the current situation and our program for the future. Big Minh assigned Generals Kim and myself to meet Lodge at 4:00 P.M., November 2.

We went to the American Embassy and Lodge came out personally to greet us. He was extremely enthusiastic and congratulatory about our achievement, telling us that a full report had been made to President Kennedy. Our meeting lasted about an hour. He let us know that when the Americans learned that Diem and Nhu were dead, they had become quite confused and deeply moved. I told Lodge that I had had the same emotions and that one hour after the coup had started I had asked Conein to make an American plane available to us to fly Diem and his brother to the Philippines.

Ambassador Lodge asked that we send Nhu's children to their mother overseas, pointing out that this humane act could gain back for us sympathy from the American people.* I was happy to accede to his request. An American embassy official, Mr. Flott, later accompanied Nhu's children to Rome aboard the aircraft originally designed to carry the deposed Ngo brothers.

After the meeting, Lodge took us downstairs to see the Venerable Thich Tri Quang. I had heard a lot about this great Buddhist leader, but this was the first time I had ever met him. It was a joyous occasion for all of us present. Quang said he would select a "good and lucky day" according to the lunar calendar for his return to his pagoda and faithful followers.

After leaving Quang's room, Lodge told us that during the martial law period he had granted political asylum to three monks. In addition, the day before, an American woman, Mrs. Gregory, wife of the director of the *Times of Vietnam,* came to ask him for the same help. She was worried because she saw people looking for houses belonging to friends of the Ngos to burn them down. Since everybody knew that she was Madame Nhu's close friend, she was afraid she might be killed. Lodge requested an exit visa from the country, which I approved.

*Mrs. Nhu had gone to a conference in Belgrade on September 9, 1963, as a member of Congress. She remained abroad after the conference was over.

109

On November 3 also, Big Minh and I visited the Gia Long Palace. Almost everything inside was ruined and the building was damaged considerably. It had been bombarded by artillery fire for several hours, so fires had broken out, walls and ceilings were down, and much of the furniture was destroyed. What had been a beautiful example of French colonial architecture was now only a ruin. I ordered a team to clean up the mess and gather all papers found in the files for delivery to us. On November 4, we received the documents and some Vietnamese and United States money which had been in Diem's possession. We also received a visit from Ambassador Lodge. He asked that a Mr. Tran Quoc Buu, an internationally known member of the Labor Federation be released from arrest, a request we honored immediately.

Although the Americans made no effort to restrain us in either our coup planning or its execution, they were never really part of the plan. In the beginning, Conein offered us help on several occasions, but, faced with our firm refusals, later confined himself to the role of spectator and reporter.

Several uninformed writers have maintained that the entire thing was a CIA planned and directed plot. Nothing could be farther from the truth.

On November 10, a high CIA official met with me at Conein's house in Saigon. He asked me not to reveal to the press that, despite its intensive efforts, the CIA in Vietnam failed to obtain a copy of the coup plan before November 1.

There have also been a number of wild stories about Diem's and Nhu's deaths. Here I can report the facts of the matter for the first time.

As soon as we received precise information on their place of refuge, on November 2, Big Minh suggested that we all consult together on what should be done with them. As the first speaker, I told the council that we should detain them temporarily and then exile them abroad. Others thought that Diem alone could be allowed a safe conduct and Nhu should be retained for trial. Still others wanted to try both of them. I felt that eliminating them both from power and getting them out of the country would be enough, something like what happened to Syngman Rhee, former president of South Korea. After much conversation I thought my arguments had brought most of the officers to my side. I then left the meeting to prepare quarters for the two prisoners.

There were press accounts that the fate of Diem and Nhu was decided by a vote. The truth is that no vote was taken. Perhaps the lack of a clear decision was one of the reasons for the subsequent deaths of Diem and Nhu.

Later that morning, when the convoy arrived at the main headquarters building, I was surprised not to see any passenger cars, and grew worried about what might have happened. I met Generals Kim and Chieu and learned of the deaths of the president and his brother. I told Kim to tell the members of the press that the deaths had occurred from accidental causes and then went to General Khiem's office where Big Minh was waiting.

I demanded: "Why are they dead?"

In a rather haughty and proud tone of voice he retorted, "And what does it matter that they are dead?" Looking to the side I noticed Colonel Quan, Big Minh's assistant, lying on a table with a pale face and drawn features, apparently sick over what had happened.

At the same moment, General Xuan, our security chief who had been responsible for escorting the deposed brothers from their hideout to our headquarters, burst in. Unaware of my presence, he turned to Big Minh and uttered dryly in military fashion two words in French, "Mission Accomplie."

I then walked to the window and saw two armored cars surrounded by soldiers on the lawn downstairs. General Khiem told me that one of the vehicles contained the two bodies.

On the afternoon of November 2, the corpses were transferred to the St. Paul Clinic. The next morning Minh and I went to visit Mr. and Mrs. Tran Trung Dung at their residence. She was President Diem's niece. Minh said to her, "We are not here to present our condolences to you. We hope you will understand that their deaths occurred as an unfortunate incident during the coup d'etat. We are very sorry about this but now that it has happened there is nothing that we can do about it. We hope that you will arrange for their funerals."

On the way back to our headquarters we passed in front of the St. Paul Clinic and saw that a large crowd had gathered and was demanding that the bodies be turned over to them. We decided to tell Mr. and Mrs. Dung that Diem and Nhu should not be buried in the municipal graveyard because we feared that the excited population might exhume their bodies and profane them. The Dungs agreed, so the bodies were brought back to our

111

headquarters on the night of November 3 and were discreetly locked in a basement while waiting to be transferred to Hue, their birthplace.

After several days, we decided that the same kind of problems were present in Hue and that the only possible solution was to bury them in a vacant field inside the security fence of our headquarters. In the presence of Mr. and Mrs. Dung and a Roman Catholic priest, a proper burial ceremony took place with the most attentive care and in the strictest simplicity. I later had their graves cemented over as a kind of last tribute to them as the one-time leaders of our nation. Despite the errors and abuses they perpetrated during their rule, it was appropriate to grant them decent treatment at their deaths.

This still leaves unanswered the question of who ordered their deaths. I can state without equivocation that this was done by General Big Minh, and by him alone. I base this in part on my conversations with Minh, and on hearing General Xuan's report to Minh that his mission had been accomplished. The last-minute addition to the convoy, Captain Nhung, Minh's devoted bodyguard, is very significant since he was the only officer in the group who would carry out Minh's orders without question. In addition, I received two reports from eye-witnesses.

Colonel Quan, Big Minh's assistant, told me shortly before his death in 1967 that Diem and Nhu were killed by the two officers who had been included in the escort by Big Minh. From the turret of the armored vehicle, Colonel Nghia shot point-blank at them with his submachine gun, while Captain Nhung, who was inside the same vehicle, sprayed them with bullets before using a knife on them.

Colonel Quan's account was confirmed by General Xuan, who told me that they had loaded Diem and Nhu into the armored car, with Nghia and Nhung already in it. Xuan led the convoy in a jeep; when they arrived at the general headquarters he found both Diem and Nhu were dead.

Captain Nhung was arrested a few months after for his attempts to resist during a countercoup pulled by General Nguyen Khanh against me and other November 1 coup leaders. Khanh ordered military security to conduct an inquiry into the deaths of Diem and Nhu during which Captain Nhung confessed to the double assassination. He told the investigators that Big Minh gave the order to kill.

Believing that he would be tortured and later executed, Captain Nhung hanged himself in his cell with his own shoelaces.

Big Minh never admitted his responsibility for the double murder. Whenever the matter was raised, he would try to implicate me. During his exile in Bangkok (1965–1968), Big Minh claimed to a Catholic priest that he was in no way responsible, and advised him to get information from me.

After the deaths of Diem and Nhu, their younger brother Can took refuge among the Redemptorist Fathers in Hue. He later went to the American consulate to ask for asylum, but Ambassador Lodge decided that Can could not receive sanctuary there; instead he should be transferred directly to the new Vietnamese government.

When he arrived in Saigon, Can was delivered to us, with three conditions imposed by the Americans. First, he would have to be tried publicly according to regular procedure; second, he should not be mistreated; and third, he certainly should not be executed or otherwise punished without a proper trial. Lodge's conditions were carefully observed and Can's trial before a court in Saigon lasted several days. He was found guilty and sentenced to death by rifle fire.

Can would probably not have been executed if he had accepted a financial deal reportedly suggested by General Nguyen Khanh, who later became Vietnam's leader.

The interior minister, General Phat, told Mrs. Dung, Can's niece, that Khanh would be willing to grant the convicted prisoner complete pardon and an exit visa if Can consented to give up all his overseas bank accounts. Phat made it clear that Can's money should be transferred into Khanh's bank accounts, and that Can would be reimbursed in Vietnamese currency.

Can rejected the offer. He reasoned that the tricky Khanh would have him executed after pocketing the "ransom" money. Can was probably right. Many generals and high-ranking personalities were involved in a succession of illegal financial dealings in the late 1960s under Can's sponsorship, so it would have been to their advantage to silence Can for good.

So Can was executed. His personal fortune, deposited in foreign banks, was given by him to Catholic charities. He actually made a will, which was smuggled out of his Saigon prison cell by a visiting priest.

113

Other important relatives of the three slain brothers were abroad. Mrs. Nhu was in Los Angeles,* Archbishop Thuc in Rome, and Ambassador Ngo Dinh Luyen, the least unpopular of the Ngo family, in London.

Two interesting events occurred after the coup was over, involving Mrs. Ngo Dinh Nhu. The first was a telephone call from her in Los Angeles, put through direct to me at a meeting of the MRC on November 4. She was terribly agitated, not really believing the truth about the deaths of her husband and her brother. She berated me for conducting the coup, particularly after the army had pledged its support to Diem after the raid on the pagodas on August 20.

I responded that many events had happened since that day, and that the demands for Diem's removal had escalated daily, both within the army and the civilian populace. She responded that the only agitation seemed to be coming from young people, from riffraff as she called them.

Then she took a different tack, telling me she wanted to return to Vietnam to take charge of her private belongings contained in the presidential palace. I told her she could not return, and that all her things had either been destroyed, stolen, or confiscated. She then inquired about her three children, her brother, and her brother-in-law, Ngo Dinh Can.

I informed her that her brother was safe in Saigon, Can was still in Hue, and that her children were on their way to Rome by special American plane.

This conversation was probably overheard by many operators in the telephone office, because the director had closed off all incoming circuits to ensure good reception at my end.

The second interesting event was when I learned that Mrs. Nhu and her husband had devised a bloodless coup against Diem in which they had planned to seize power from him. But someone in Nhu's entourage broke the news to Diem, so he spent a lot of time in Nhu's office continuously checking on what he was doing. I had known that something strange was happening about a month before our coup because all the pictures of Diem which had adorned the palace walls were taken down, ostensibly for cleaning.

After our coup, in going through Nhu's file cabinet, I found a letter written by his wife from abroad asking how his own coup plan against Diem

*Mrs. Nhu later rejoined her children in Rome.

114

was coming. As it happened, poor Diem had everyone plotting against him, his top generals, the Americans, and even his own brother.

Immediately after the success of the coup d'etat, a provisional constitutional charter was proclaimed. It provided for General Big Minh to be the chairman of the MRC, which was composed of twelve generals, and for a civilian cabinet of fifteen ministers to be headed by a prime minister who would be responsible to the MRC and to Minh as head of state. This was appropriate because Minh was our leader and known by all as the hero of the coup. Mr. Nguyen Ngoc Tho, former vice president of the republic under the Diem regime was appointed prime minister. He was chosen because of his long administrative experience which would help to smooth this transition phase. In addition, he was a long-time friend of Big Minh and we felt we could trust him.

Having promoted the coup, we were well aware of the difficulties that always follow a sudden change of regime. We understood that this provisional government structure should be replaced as soon as a definitive constitution could be promulgated. Another closely related problem involved our decision to purge the administration and the army of elements we knew to be inept, despotic, or corrupt. We expected a certain breakdown in the functioning of the administration because of this, but thought that the good psychological effect on the people and the purifying influence of new officials would more than overcome any disruptions.

Students, priests, and those politically opposed to the previous government were immediately released from prison and instructions were issued prohibiting arbitrary arrest and confinement. Freedom of the press and of religious belief were solemnly proclaimed and welcomed with enthusiasm. Hard labor in the rural areas was abolished in connection with the strategic hamlet program, and we attempted to obtain support for our new government from the religious sects Hoa Hao and Cao Dai.

The economic and financial situation was disturbing, however, because American aid had been temporarily suspended during the months preceding the coup. Further, the Tho cabinet was having difficulty since its members could not agree with each other. Part of the problem was that Tho, the former vice president under Diem, was inflexible and narrow in his policies. He was a superb administrator, which we needed sorely, but could not act

115

with the speed and revolutionary zeal required to be a truly effective premier in a government like ours. Proposals requiring prompt attention would be pigeonholed, awaiting the type of routine protocol he had learned in the old administration. Xuan, who was in charge of the capital region, Dinh, minister of the interior, and I, as minister of defense, were having trouble working with him on solutions to numerous problems within our jurisdictions. Things got to such a state that Dinh and I decided to resign in December. Big Minh, however, persuaded us to stay on our jobs during this hectic period.

On January 23, 1964, during a meeting of the MRC, we deliberated about a replacement for Tho. Many names were suggested, including Generals Chieu, Khiem, Thieu, and myself. When my name was called Minh looked at me sympathetically and smiled. I think he wanted to make me understand that I was too gentle and sentimental and that consequently I should not try to be a politician. I suggested that he combine the functions of chairman of the MRC and that of prime minister and run the whole show. He answered that he was not yet ready to take this upon himself.

Toward the end of January, after a series of contacts with many political, religious, and military leaders, I had been able to plan out the main orientation of our revolutionary program. On January 27, I gave my reform program to Big Minh and Khiem for further submission to the government. It suggested many radical changes, political, economic, social, and cultural, and handed power over to a new revolutionary cabinet under a different prime minister. Especially important were the roles to be entrusted to the youth of the nation for the realization of our revolutionary goals.

I knew that if the war were to be won against the Communists military measures alone would not suffice. Our struggle against the NLF had to be waged with political, economic, cultural, and social considerations as well. The NLF strategy had been to occupy and control the countryside and turn it into a springboard for advancing to the cities. We, therefore, had to make our presence felt in the same rural areas, winning the people's support, seducing them away from Communist influences, and enlisting their participation in a full-scale struggle. My concept was that the war in Vietnam was between two factions of Vietnamese, so it should have been settled between ourselves by all means available. Aid obtained from our Free World friends should have been confined to moral, technical, and

116

material support. Our national policy should have been geared toward solving simultaneously the two overall goals of winning the support of the population and then annihilating the enemy's armed forces.

We also wanted to show the people that we meant what we said, that we truly intended to do away with graft and corruption and special privileges for the governors. I proposed to my colleagues that we lead austere lives, turn in the official limousines so prized by the Diem administration, and sell off the luxurious homes maintained at the expense of the common people. We had to get ourselves used to the idea that we had to get closer to the people, living our lives more like them.

In our military mission we needed to destroy the enemy's secret bases, prevent infiltration of men, weapons, equipment, and supplies, and neutralize his units. Local organizations such as the civil guard and the police were to be responsible for law and order within the local areas. Their purpose was to protect the villages and the people living in them from the political and military cadres of the NLF. In areas that were so rugged that our troops would have unusual difficulty conducting normal military operations, we might have had to request air support such as helicopter transport from our allies.

In winning the support of the populace, we had to remove the insidious influence of the NLF from the villages. This had to be the principal object of the war, with all necessary resources utilized for this purpose. We had to help the people develop their individual capabilities and get them to understand their political rights and enjoy them. To achieve this they needed a great number of well-trained and sympathetic local officials capable of replacing the Communist cadres who had been working with them. Once the people in the countryside, who were 80 percent of our overall population, were won over to the national cause, the NLF could no longer be sustained because it would have lost its main source of support.

I still believe that these objectives were obtainable because the NLF had not yet achieved such power in the countryside as to deny us access to the populace. It is good to remember that no large-scale infiltration of North Vietnamese regular units had yet occurred so that we were faced only by the irregular cadres. The principle we wanted to follow in pacifying the countryside was that of an "oil spot" spreading out from a safe area, making it larger and larger as we gradually made whole provinces secure. Even-

117

tually these spots would meet and after a certain time full sections of the country would be thoroughly under government control. Then we would go on to destroy enemy secret bases that had been set up and interrupt the infiltration routes, such as the Ho Chi Minh trail. After all this had been accomplished, we might feel secure enough to contemplate active operations against the North in order to try to unify the national territory.

These plans would, I believe, have permitted our government to secure the countryside and make South Vietnam a safer and better place to live. We had our chance. We had seized power and had the overwhelming mass of the people with us. We were inexperienced, but this probably was in itself something of an advantage. We certainly did not want to continue the sins of the past.

But, our hopes and aspirations were not to be realized. How could I believe that January 29 was to be the last day of the Military Revolutionary Council and my participation in it? How could I have predicted the events of the next few hours and the strange adventures that would involve me in the next few months?

Inshore patrol craft, Cua Lon River, South Vietnam.

CHAPTER EIGHT

Nguyen Khanh:

Invitation to Chaos

January 29, 1964, dawned bright and cloudless, promising to be hot and sultry. No rain was expected, of course, since this was a day at the start of our dry season, but I would have preferred a cooling shower rather than the storm that was to break on me that night.

The day was spent doing routine things, morning and afternoon at my office, lunch with the military attachés of the foreign embassies, and a visit to the Directory of Social Affairs. My day was completed at about 8:00 P.M., so I returned to my home for dinner and finally to bed for a good night's sleep. I was content that a good day's work had been done and was in excellent spirits for the events of the next day.

During the three months after the overthrow of Diem, a relaxed atmosphere gradually came over the entire country. We were inspired by the spontaneous outburst of friendship toward us and the national solidarity that was evident throughout the country. So, as well as liberating political prisoners, students, and monks imprisoned during the Buddhist crisis, we decided to repatriate opponents of the Diem government who were in exile abroad. The latter group included General Nguyen Van Vy and Lieutenant Colonel Tran Dinh Lan, who had been driven into exile in France in 1955.

There was nothing surprising about our permitting General Vy to return to the country. His brilliant military qualifications and broad experience would be welcome in any army. As for Lieutenant Colonel Lan, suspected of having close connections with French intelligence, the Military Council at first refused to let him return, but finally reversed its decision after General Vy's formal commitment to vouch for him.

121

We also permitted the promoters of the unsuccessful coup in 1960, Colonels Thi and Dong, Major Lieu, and Lieutenant Hanh, to return. Lieutenant Quoc who bombed the Independence Palace in 1962 with another air force officer, Nguyen Van Cu, was released from prison. Cu returned from self-exile in Cambodia. Another prominent expatriate, General Duong Van Duc, asked for and was granted permission to return to Vietnam from France.

It was the repatriation of these officers from abroad that was used as the excuse for deposing us in the countercoup by General Nguyen Khanh. We were described as having neutralist tendencies and, therefore, of being incapable of fully directing the war.

At about 3:00 A.M. on January 30, 1964, I was awakened by the loud jangling of the telephone. It was Captain Khan, my aide, telling me that my residence was surrounded by soldiers trying to force entry into the house. He reported that they were from the Vietnamese Civil Guard. I ordered him not to fire on them but to have them enter and explain to me their purpose. I got up, washed and dressed, and then telephoned General Le Van Kim. He told me that his house was also encircled by soldiers. When I called the Minister of Interior, General Ton That Dinh, he was surprised at the news and suggested that he come over and find out what the soldiers were trying to do. I then received a call from General Vy telling me that the Civil Guard had just burst into his residence, arrested Lieutenant Colonel Lan, and disarmed the guards. I quickly briefed him on what was happening at my home and expressed my horror and chagrin at these sudden events.

I questioned the lieutenant commanding the invading troops and was told that he had received orders from General Big Minh to bring his men to reinforce my personal guard. I called Minh who told me that some of our junior officers were trying to do something ridiculous and that we would discuss it all in a little while at headquarters. I learned in a few minutes, however, from General Dinh that Generals Khanh and Khiem were promoting a coup.

Shortly thereafter, Major Tiep, commander of the Combat Police, arrived to tell me that my presence was desired at General Staff Headquarters. We proceeded in his car and on my way I noted that General Minh's residence was also surrounded by armored vehicles and soldiers. When we arrived there, Tiep walked in by himself, leaving me in the car. He returned and told me that the president of the council was now at the airborne brigade headquarters and that he was to drive me there.

At the airborne brigade I was put in a room in the barracks where, in a neighboring room, I saw General Mai Huu Xuan. It was apparent at this point that we were under arrest. At 8:00 A.M. General Dinh was placed in a room next door, and at 9:00 General Kim was led into another. This meant that four of the principal directors of the coup d'etat were now prisoners of the younger officers who had staged a countercoup.

I noted Colonel Nguyen Chanh Thi in the courtyard and asked that he be brought to see me. I demanded to know from him why we had been incarcerated like common criminals and he told me that he was simply carrying out orders. He informed me that in a few minutes General Khanh would be here to see me.

That same day, at 2:00 P.M., we were moved from the airborne brigade area, taken to Tan Son Nhut Airport and loaded into awaiting aircraft. I remember that on the steps of the plane Dinh suddenly turned to Colonel Thi and said, "The earth is round—we'll meet again someday."

We were taken first to Da Nang in the north and then to My Khe beach. The seas were heavy and it was very cold. We had been so abruptly taken into captivity that none of us had brought any winter clothing. We asked our guards to buy us some sweaters and other necessities.

That night I had considerable trouble sleeping, reconstructing, as I was, the events since that morning. I tormented myself with thoughts of what this day would mean to the future of the country. I could see only dire events in the future because one thing that the nation could not stand was a family fight while the Communists were standing by ready to devour us all. The next day we learned that a Revolutionary Council of the Armed Forces had been formed with General Nguyen Khanh as its president.

We spent three weeks in total isolation at this place, deprived of all contact with the outside. We had no newspapers, magazines, or even radios. To make our captivity somewhat more tolerable, we established a program of daily activities which consisted of a session of physical exercises, conducted by General Xuan in the early morning, discussions of political, social, and military topics from 9:00 A.M. to 11:00 A.M., followed by lunch,

123

other study and discussion periods, dinner, and finally bedtime at 9:00 p.m.

While alone, I was given to long and searching reexaminations of my career and the events of the last few days. I bitterly regretted that after having been instrumental in the downfall of a dictatorial regime and then having been in power only a couple of months, my usefulness to the country had been so suddenly and inopportunely interrupted.

On February 9, 1964, General Nguyen Khanh surprised us by inviting us to meet with him at navy headquarters in Da Nang. He received us one by one, beginning with a forty-five minute conversation with Dinh. I was next, with my interview lasting an hour and a half. Xuan and Kim saw him next, spending thirty and forty minutes, respectively, with him.

Khanh told us that we had been deposed and brought here under arrest because we had been accused of promoting a neutralist policy. I asked for the evidence against us and he responded that it had to do with the repatriation of General Vy and Lieutenant Colonel Lan. I demanded to know what the return to Vietnam of these two officers had to do with our supposed neutralism. Khanh responded that he had evidence that Lan was bringing in money for the purpose of buying partisans for his cause and further, that he had been moving actively in political parties in France as well as in Vietnam.

I told Khanh that he was completely wrong on that score, that Lan was totally without funds when he arrived home and that I had to lend him some cash so that he could get a few personal items. Khanh angrily said, "If we can't find any proof to substantiate our allegations of neutralism, we will make some up. That won't be too hard to do."

He then added that he had, in effect, saved our lives by taking us into custody. (I learned later that this was literally correct.) He indicated that even now, if he wanted, he could have us killed without any trouble. I responded that if he thought we were in the wrong the lawful thing would be to bring us before some court where we could answer our accusers.

Khanh said that confidentially he didn't believe that Dinh or I were neutralists, but that our private lives were not looked upon favorably by some of our colleagues because we were pleasure-seekers. I asked him how being a pleasure-seeker had anything to do with neutrality. He gave no satisfactory answer.

Khanh questioned me in some detail about the deaths of Diem and Nhu and told me that he was acting as Chief of Staff of the Army as well as President of the Revolutionary Council of the Armed Forces. He told me that although he had these functions, his own powers were limited because he had joined the conspiracy at the very last minute.

We were returned to our billet and after supper received a visit from Khanh. He was in a bragging and jovial mood and spent some time with us. After he left, we compared our separate interviews with him. We decided that his obvious goal was to sow dissension and doubt among us. He told lies to each of us to try to turn us against each other.

The soldiers assigned to guard us in our little prison were extremely kind and generous. In their hearts they probably thought we were the innocent victims of a fraudulent scheme and, as a result, they were respectfully devoted to our care. The cook especially was a marvel, ingeniously creating a variety of succulent dishes which we enjoyed thoroughly.

One week after Tet, on Feburary 20, Major Luyen came to get General Dinh, saying that they were to leave My Khe immediately. We all congratulated him, thinking he had been freed and was now authorized to return to Saigon. But the truth, as we were to learn, was something quite different. The next morning the same thing was repeated with me. The airplane that I thought was taking me to Saigon landed instead at Dalat. I was taken to Palace No. 1, the summer home of ex-President Diem, located in a woody area, where I was settled into a ground floor room with three Security Force officers as guards. It was more comfortable here than at My Khe, but separated from my companions in misfortune I became even more depressed. The palace was too big and isolated for me. I was overwhelmed by the hugh empty buildings and the forest growing above me. Here, however, I was provided with enough newspapers and magazines and even a radio to keep me up to date on world and national events. Generals Oai, Tri, and Nghiem came to see me once in a while. From them I was able to discover, little by little, what had happened on January 30. I also learned that Dinh was not in Saigon but at Pleiku. On March 6, Khanh came to visit me to tell me that he realized that the four of us had done nothing really bad, politically speaking. He asked me to be patient for a while. I suggested to

125

him that I would be safer if I could move from this dismal building and live somewhere else, perhaps my own house in Dalat, which had the advantage of looking like everyone else's house. He went along with my idea.

I felt much better in my new surroundings as it seemed to me to be the first step on the way to regaining my freedom. In accordance with tradition, I ceremonially requested the blessings of the gods and my ancestors before taking up residence once again. The next day, my brother-in-law General Kim was allowed to come live with me. We were very happy to see each other again and had much to discuss about the events that had happened since our separation at My Khe. In his spare time, Kim practiced cooking, one of his numerous hobbies.

Our detention in Dalat was not an especially happy one, but I do remember one thing that happened that had us, as well as the rest of the country, laughing until tears came to our eyes. This had to do with a visit from American Secretary of Defense McNamara to Khanh in March, 1964.

Khanh and members of his cabinet met the taciturn Secretary at Ton Son Nhut and made an effusive welcoming speech to him in English. McNamara naturally gave a warm return speech, ending with the phrase, "You have the best leader possible in General Nguyen Khanh. Long Live Vietnam!"

This was an excellent thing to say, except that he tried to say the "Long live" part in Vietnamese. The translation is "Muon Nam" which literally means, "one thousand years" in English. McNamara tried valiantly to say his lines, but gave the wrong inflection to the Vietnamese words and wound up saying literally, "Vietnam, go to sleep." It would have been a better joke on us if McNamara had really meant what he actually said.

On April 4, Khanh told me that security was too loose at my house so Kim and I would have to be reinstalled at Presidential Palace No. 1. We spent many hours in political, philosophical, and religious discussions and took long walks on the grounds of this stately house. We received daily reports on the conduct of the war through the press and radio and it seemed to us that the military situation was getting even more desperate. We became exasperated sitting there doing nothing while we might have been helping in the war effort.

On May 28, Dinh and Xuan were brought to Dalat to appear with Kim and me before a council of high-ranking officers sitting as a special tribunal

DALAT, 14 SEPT 1964

Generals Kim, Dinh, Don, Vy, and Xuan in house arrest in Dalat, 1964.

to judge our cases. The hearing was set for that night in the presence of the Chief of State, Big Minh. At 1:00 A.M. I was asked to come into a room where this court of officer judges was waiting for me in armchairs. All the faces I saw were those of childhood friends, schoolmates, fellow officers, and sworn members of the coup plot, men who I had worked with and who had worked for me for my entire adult life. I felt it ironic that I now had to appear before them as an accused prisoner. General Khanh presided over the hearing and began a five-and-one-half hour series of questions, none of which were related to the accusation of neutralism that had been raised against us. Dinh appeared before I did and was interrogated for one hour. After my session came the turns of Kim for two hours and Xuan for one hour. The questions they asked us seem especially irrelevant now in retrospect after so many years. They covered many areas they knew as well as I, such as the details of the coup, the American attitude, why we had reunited Mrs. Nhu's

127

children with her, and what happened to Diem and Nhu. They also asked many questions about our private lives.

Deliberations of the court lasted until 4 P.M., when we were led back into the meeting room to hear the verdict. Khanh asked us, on behalf of the entire group, not to take vengeance on anyone when we once again began serving in the army. Then they all gathered around to congratulate us. Our full liberty was restored but Khanh advised us to remain in Dalat a while before returning to Saigon. I picked up my belongings from Palace No. 1 and returned to my own house in Dalat where my family, who had been living in Saigon, would come and join me the first thing in the morning.

This military tribunal found us guilty of lax morality, insufficient qualifications for command, and a lack of a clear political concept. For these supposed offenses, General Vy was given a reprimand, I was suspended from command functions for one and a half years, Dinh for one year, Xuan for two years, and Kim for six years. Khanh told us that since we had been deprived of command functions we would be attached to the office of the prime minister with duties to include research and planning. He promised to have offices set up so that we could come to Saigon to work.

Things did not turn out exactly like this, however. On May 30 General Oai, commander of the Military Academy at Dalat, passed on to us instructions from Khanh that Generals Don, Xuan, Dinh, and Kim were not to leave Dalat without the express consent of the prime minister. We reported this decision to Big Minh, who was still in Dalat, but he told us he knew nothing about this or the motives behind it. In a sense we were back where we had started, in a kind of arrest, but with more freedom than before since we were allowed to go around the city of Dalat rather than being confined in a single building.

We assumed that some difficulty must have arisen between the Revolutionary Council of the Armed Forces and the pro-Khanh Dai Viet party following the publication of the verdict. A friend from Saigon told me that Dr. Nguyen Ton Hoan, a Southern Dai Viet party leader and deputy prime minister, was said to have been opposed to our return for fear that we would make damaging statements about the false accusations brought against us.

The generally pro-American Dai Viet party had been on the Vietnamese political scene since about 1941. However, due to factional fights

128

and regional rivalries, this great nationalist party failed to accomplish much of what it sought to do.

The party experienced its first major shakeup in 1946 to 1947, when many of its most effective leaders were executed or imprisoned by the Viet Minh. In the 1950s, a Dai Viet group, usually referred to as the "Mandarin Faction," since it was made up almost entirely of former ranking civil servants and French-trained intellectuals, succeeded in controlling the administration and police of Vietnam's northern provinces.

Partition caused by the Geneva agreements of 1954 deprived this mandarin faction of territorial control. As refugees, they came down to the south where they became split into smaller groups. They did, however, have a close association with the United States, and so were able to influence the country's politics. Two of their most articulate leaders were Dr. Phan Huy Quat, who became prime minister in 1965, and Dr. Dang Van Sung, also a newspaper publisher, who was elected a senator on my slate in 1967.

Another faction, the Southern Dai Viet, or New Dai Viet, was a tightly knit organization, oriented more to the South, and tended to be more pro-French than pro-American. Its leaders were Dr. Nguyen Ton Hoan, who became deputy prime minister under General Khanh, and Professor Nguyen Ngoc Huy, an advisor to President Thieu. Thieu himself was also a member of the Southern Dai Viet. It was the Southern Dai Viet faction that helped General Khanh pull the countercoup against us.

The third faction, calling itself the Revolutionary Dai Viet, was led by Professor Ha Thuc Ky. Ky's group, which was popular in two provinces south of the DMZ, cooperated with General Khanh's government and afterward had a short political honeymoon with President Nguyen Van Thieu.

The fourth faction, the Orthodox Dai Viet, was represented by the late Tran Van Xuan, a peasant leader from the South, Mrs. Ca Te, a respected seventy-two year old revolutionist from the North, and Professor Bui Anh Tuan.

In my political career, I enjoyed friendly cooperation from both the Mandarin and Orthodox Factions.

Khanh set us to work as a committee, under my direction, to formulate a constitution for the new regime. The committee consisted of four of us

129

generals, Dinh, Kim, Xuan, and me, Ambassador Tran Chanh Thanh, and Nguyen Thanh Cung, the former secretary general to President Diem. We finished our work near the end of June. The constitution we formulated was based on the French constitution of 1958 and provided for a legislature, a judiciary, and an executive with appropriate administrative agencies. The chief of state would be known as the president and he would designate a prime minister to form the government. The government would answer to the president who would himself answer to the people. This charter differed radically from the one later proclaimed by Khanh since our plan had been conceived in accordance with the democratic principles that had inspired the November 1 Revolution. Khanh insisted on absolute priority for the army for the simplistic reason that since the army had overthrown Diem, it had the right and authority to concentrate all power in its hands.

By this time, the titular head of state, Big Minh, was only a figurehead. Real power came into the hands of General Khiem, Chief of the General Staff and Commander-in-Chief of the Armed Forces, and General Khanh, President of the Revolutionary Council of the Armed Forces, and Prime Minister. A serious disagreement was recorded between Big Minh and Khanh, giving rise to reports of another coup d'etat.

At the end of July 1964, Khanh came to Dalat to advise us to accept positions of liaison officers with the American military academies. Then he changed his mind and suggested that (accompanied by our families) we go to the United States to take public administration courses. He would arrange the necessary funding with the American authorities. We replied that the government was free to do whatever it deemed proper with regard to us but we would never, on our own accord, request assignment outside the country. We discovered that Khanh was afraid that if we were released from our place of detention we might again become allied with Big Minh.

At other meetings in August and September he kept after us to leave the country for various kinds of foreign assignments. Finally, on September 5 a plane was sent to pick up Dinh, Xuan, and me to take us to Vung Tau, a seaside resort to meet Khanh. He received us for dinner and discussed national affairs which, according to him, were changing rapidly and unpredictably. He then proposed that we return to Saigon to assist him. He offered me the position of Deputy Minister of National Defense, with Dinh as Minister of Youth; Kim and Xuan would be given responsibilities at

General Staff Headquarters. He then launched a violent tirade against Big Minh, saying that he was the real cause of our troubles. As for Khiem, Khanh indicated that he would soon lose command of the army because he no longer had its confidence because of his obvious attachment to Minh.

We were subsequently informed that Khanh had lost credit with the Catholics and had to seek Buddhist support, which explained his abrupt reversal of policy toward us. On September 9, Big Minh called Kim and told us to get ready to reenter Saigon very soon. Shortly thereafter, Khanh telephoned to tell us to wait.

With the end of our captivity in sight we enthusiastically prepared for our return to Saigon, eager to get to work again. We were ready and waiting at the airport at 9:15 on September 13, but 10 minutes before it was time to take off General Vy hurried up, bringing word from Khanh to turn back. We found him in Palace No. 2. He revealed that a coup was in progress and I suggested that he talk to Big Minh in Saigon. I telephoned Minh for him and while he was on the telephone, Khanh suggested that Minh take over control of the city. Minh declined that responsibility and invited Khanh to come back and handle it himself. I suggested to Minh that, under the circumstances, he should perhaps join us in the safety of Dalat while awaiting restoration of order in Saigon. He replied that it was impossible for him to leave because of the state of confusion and turmoil.

Around noon, on the radio from Saigon, we heard the harsh voice of General Lam Van Phat, Interior Minister. He was reading an acrimonious declaration by the Popular Military Committee for National Salvation. Khanh visibly paled on hearing this declaration. He cursed Phat with the most vulgar insults. He suspected that General Ky of the Air Force was in with Phat and that he would send planes up here to bomb Dalat. Becoming more and more panicked, he hastily evacuated his family, packing them off to seek refuge at General Tri's house. Then he ordered the installation of antiaircraft batteries at Palace No. 2.

General Ky, in Saigon, tried to persuade Khanh to return but Khanh remained in Dalat to have a discussion with representatives of the American ambassador, Mr. William Sullivan and General Richard Stilwell. This meeting agitated him because the Americans were checking the balance of forces and pressing him for the establishment of a civilian government to better inspire popular support.

131

We wondered at the time why Khanh did not want to return to Saigon but it soon became clear why he had chosen to remain in Dalat. The coup, such as it was, had been mounted by Khanh himself to oust his irksome rivals, Minh and Khiem, and to place on the promoters of the coup the responsibility for having forced us into detention. The plotters were upset, however, by the unforseen intrusion of General Phat on the scene. Phat, having learned the truth, then denounced Khanh over the radio. He then, in turn, was routed by government forces.

As an aftermath of the coup Khanh was able to consolidate his position by removing some of Khiem's followers whom he did not trust. He seemed determined to depose Khiem, blaming it on the "Young Turks"* group of generals and colonels.

Khanh, at this time, was in a terribly confused state saying one day that we all should leave the country and the next that we were needed in Saigon because our expertise was required to handle difficult and delicate jobs. On September 24, Khanh had a new story for us. He told Dinh and me that we would be reinstated in the government in Saigon soon. About a week later he went back on his word again, now blaming the Americans for the change in our status. I could not further contain my irritation, so I said, "One day it is the Dai Viet party keeping us out of the army, yesterday you told us it was the Young Turks who opposed us, today you dredge up the Americans—what will it be tomorrow—who is our next enemy?" We then parted company. The next day Dinh appeared at my house to announce that Khanh had just told him that he alone would return to Saigon and that no one would oppose him.

On October 13, Khanh telephoned me to tell me that he had appointed General Ngo Dzu to develop with us some new army personnel regulations. We got right down to work and made rapid progress. One point, however, caused considerable discussion, that of retiring all generals with twenty-five years of active duty. Khanh's ulterior motive was easy to see. In assigning

---

*"Young Turks" was a name popularly given to a group of youthful senior officers who managed to seize power in Vietnam in 1965 and generally keep in control of the government for the next ten years. They included Generals Nguyen Van Thieu, Nguyen Cao Ky, Nguyen Chanh Thi, Nguyen Huu Co, Nguyen Bao Tri, Le Nguyen Khang, Cao Van Vien, Nguyen Duc Thang, and Admiral Chung Tan Cang.

to us the mission of establishing retirement criteria, he could then apply these regulations against us without fear since we had written the rules ourselves.

On October 18, Khanh visited us in Dalat and stated that he was appointing me to be his assistant for military instruction, Dinh, his advisor for military operations, and Xuan, assistant for the military intelligence service. It was decided to leave Kim in Dalat as the overall supervisor of the Military Academy and the Command and General Staff College. It surprised us after all this that finally we were to be returned to Saigon on October 20. After landing at Saigon we contacted Khanh for instructions and had dinner with Big Minh.

We now had ample opportunity to look into the real reasons for our overthrow and subsequent detention at Dalat. It became an amazing history as we put the pieces together.

Our problems apparently started with American Secretary of Defense McNamara during his visit to Saigon on December 20, 1963. I met the secretary who was coming from Paris. He coldly shook hands and did not utter a word, trying to avoid looking directly at me. I was puzzled at his attitude, but supposed that he might have been displeased at the double murder of Diem and Nhu, like many Americans.

We had two meetings with McNamara and his party, both in the afternoon. Virtually our entire government was present at the first, all the generals and cabinet officials, while most of the American team was on hand. Kim briefed the group on the political situation, I covered the military outlook, and Dr. Oanh presented economic factors.

At the subsequent executive type meeting with the leaders of our Military Council, McNamara was accompanied by Ambassador Lodge and CIA Director McCone. The Vietnamese side included Big Minh, Premier Tho, Kim, and myself. After introductions, McNamara stared at us sitting together and said, "Who is the boss here?"

We replied with courteous smiles. Minh, of course, should have seized this opportunity and responded, "Me. I am." Instead he looked around at the rest of us and said nothing. This made a bad impression on McNamara and the other Americans. McNamara was critical of our method of operation, feeling for one thing that we were each trying to do too much. For example, I was Minister of Defense and also Army Chief. These were

133

only temporary arrangements, but we could not convince the hostile secretary.

Later I learned that McNamara had been upset over a lack of coordination between the American Embassy and ourselves. In this he was absolutely correct, and the culprit was Big Minh. Our titular Head of State could not be bothered to have frequent meetings with Ambassador Lodge as he should have, so gradually the gulf began to widen between the two governments. As a result, the Americans were becoming less and less informed and Lodge was getting frustrated. He asked me on several occasions to try to get Big Minh moving, but my entreaties to my rather lazy friend were ignored.

During the month of January 1964, there had been vehement criticism of Prime Minister Tho in the press. At the same time, a group of politicians and people of great prestige from the Mandarin Faction of the Dai Viet Party were backing General Le Van Kim to lead a new cabinet. They believed him to have the intellectual and ethical qualities required to be an effective premier. The partisans of the Southern Faction of the Dai Viet, however, feared that if Kim came to power their political organization would suffer. Kim was noted for his strict integrity and his reputation for never having taken a bribe. They wanted to act quickly, therefore, to prevent this plan and to hasten the repatriation from France of Dr. Nguyen Ton Hoan, their leader, and to push his candidacy for the office of premier. They knew General Khiem bore a grudge toward me so they exploited him in staging the countercoup to remove us from power. The New Dai Viet officers also managed to enlist the aid of General Nguyen Van Thieu, Commander of the 5th Division and a close friend of Khiem. They used the return from France of General Vy and Major Lan to label us as neutralists as a kind of justification for their action. Nguyen Khanh, although a last-minute addition to the plot, seized for himself the lion's share of the spoils, thanks to his devious game with Khiem and the New Dai Viet officers.

This business of neutralism which Khanh used as his excuse began as a theory of Charles de Gaulle of France who thought at about this period that South Vietnam should become a neutral nation, nonaligned with any particular great power. I am not sure of his actual motives, but the idea was a pretty good one, if it could have been implemented.

134

In January 1964, I took a military delegation to Bangkok, Thailand, at the invitation of the Thai Army. In the party were Ton That Dinh and Nguyen Cao Ky who actually piloted the airplane. At the airport there I was asked by a reporter what I thought of de Gaulle's idea. I responded that it seemed to have merit, providing North Vietnam would also become neutralized and stop trying to conquer us.

Adding this statement to our rather open social associations with our French friends and our repatriations of the exiled Vietnamese officers who had been residing in France probably formed the case against us. But, since this was all there was, no reasonable man would have let himself be convinced of our guilt by this flimsy evidence. And, the truth of the matter was that we had done nothing disloyal, or even contrary, to American interests.

Khanh especially misrepresented us to the Americans, telling Ambassador Lodge that he had staged the coup to prevent us from declaring Vietnam a nonaligned nation. Khanh offered to give Lodge documents that would prove the truth of his assertions, but never produced them. I believe, however, that General Harkins was not ignorant of the plan to depose us. Harkins failed to warn us in time or to discourage the others from carrying out the coup. The Americans were thus faced with a *fait accompli*. Lodge, who warned the State Department in Washington about the coup, received instructions to remain strictly apart from it and make sure that the Americans' neutral attitude was well known. He also was apparently instructed to ensure that Duong Van Minh was to continue as Head of State even though he was simply a figurehead.

Our return to duty was quite brief, lasting only a couple of weeks. The first important event occurred on November 1, the celebration of the first anniversary of the coup that overthrew the regime of Ngo Dinh Diem. The entire population participated in this observance, from the cities to the most isolated villages.

A civilian cabinet had just been formed with Tran Van Huong replacing Nguyen Khanh as prime minister. Khanh had become Commander in Chief of the Army and Phan Khac Suu was made Head of State in place of Big Minh, who had exiled himself to Thailand. Khanh, demonstrating his independence and probably also his defiance in the face of recent changes in the government, refused to accompany the Head of State in inspecting the troops. He delegated that task to me, preferring to watch from the dais.

All along the parade route, the tightly packed crowds greeted Suu and me with prolonged hearty applause as we stood side by side in the presidential car.

Suu, a French-trained engineer, was known for his patriotic activities against the French colonists. He was one of the two opposition candidates elected by the people to the National Assembly as a challenge to President Diem's authoritarian regime.

As soon as the ceremony was over Kim, Dinh, Xuan, and I were literally enveloped in a sympathetic mass of people, a large number of whom were young university and high-school students. They came to express their happiness to see us once again free among them after ten months of unjust captivity.

We quickly perceived that our new jobs had been given us reluctantly by Khanh; that they possessed no substance whatsoever. This was borne out when in Nha Trang on military business on December 19, Khanh called me asking me to meet him with Kim and Xuan in Dalat. As soon as we arrived, he began a vituperative condemnation of the High National Council, a newly formed legislative and consultative body.

He stated that the High National Council was composed of Minh's cronies who systematically opposed every decision he made. He was in combat uniform. He said he was going to return to Saigon to call the Armed Forces Council into session and cause either a coup d'etat or arrest all the "reactionaries" of the High National Council. He did the latter. He then played his final card: he advised us to submit our requests for voluntary retirement from the army; and we would then be named to various ambassadorial posts such as Kim to Morocco and myself to the Philippines.

We responded without hesitation that we would continue as we had previously and make no such requests. He was free to make any decision he wanted but that he would never get our willing agreement, much less a written request from us to carry out his desires.

On December 28, 1964, Xuan and I were over at Kim's house in Dalat having a fine dinner cooked personally by our host and making some

136

personal plans. Our plotting this time had no political connotations. Instead, we were getting ready to become businessmen, and at this meeting we were doing preliminary work toward setting up an import-export business.

Khanh had also been invited because he had indicated that he might want to become associated with us. He apparently felt we had a good thing going, because he brought his share of the partnership, one million piasters, which he tried to give us that night. We decided to keep the business to ourselves and therefore refused this money.

Khanh was pleased that our future activities would be confined to the business world and would not compete with him in any way. It was better to have us as business partners than as political enemies. Perhaps even then he realized that his prospects might be more uncertain than ours, if he continued to spread his temperamental mumbo-jumbo on the political scene.

The tense atmosphere in Saigon after Khanh's arrest of the High Councillors prevented our leaving Dalat at that time. Four or five days later we received a message telling us we would be allowed to come back to Saigon. We returned to set up and start running our new business which we called DOXUKI, an acronym formed from our three names: Don, Xuan, and Kim. As it turned out, I proved a very bad businessman and Xuan wanted to work at something else, so Kim continued the firm and made it quite successful. When I ran for Senator in 1967, I became a silent partner.

About mid-January 1965, I visited Prime Minister Huong to whom I submitted a request for authorization to establish our import-export firm. We had a long and extremely cordial talk. He was sorry about our leaving the army and related that Khanh had made the decision in a session at his Armed Forces Council. The supposed decree ordering our retirement was brought before the Head of State, Phan Khac Suu, by General Khanh. Suu, supported by the High National Council, refused to sign it, feeling that the army already was suffering from a pitiful lack of competent leaders. This affair was a good example of Khanh's friction with the Head of State and the High National Council. Huong believed that the various antigovernment demonstrations were being orchestrated by Khanh who hoped to satisfy his limitless ambition by fomenting an atmosphere of revolt.

Huong's overthrow came about on January 27, 1965, when Khanh, in the name of the Armed Forces Council, proclaimed a vote of no confidence in the government. Courting the Americans, he finally wound up with Dr.

137

Phan Huy Quat to form a new government, with Suu reinstated as Head of State.

After Khanh's overthrow of Premier Huong's government and the installation of the more pro-United States Quat government, he became more and more unstable. I suppose he was getting alarmed about his own status and, because of the treachery he had exhibited toward everyone who had trusted him previously, he feared that he would probably get the same treatment from others. He knew that there were other ambitious men around who would like to seize power and authority in the same callous way he had, so he had good reason to be afraid for his skin.

The United States, Khanh's protector, showed signs of abandoning him toward the end of 1964. In November of that year, the most serious rift between Ambassador Maxwell Taylor and Khanh developed at a dinner given by General Westmoreland* at his Saigon residence.

Taylor, one of America's greatest and most respected soldiers, was ordered by Washington to caution the ruling "Young Turks" against pulling coups, countercoups, and other shows of force in Saigon.

At this dinner, we were sitting around Westmoreland's long table enjoying a lavish dinner when Taylor in a pointed way explained to the group his thoughts on using the army for political purposes. He directed his remarks at Khanh and Nguyen Cao Ky, stressing that there had been too much instability and what the United States desired above all else was a stable Vietnamese government which could achieve the national objectives of both our countries. He made it clear in a rather condescending way that the United States was losing its patience at so many coups and other changes in our political framework. To me, he sounded like a schoolmaster lecturing a class of errant students.

Taylor was a splendid soldier, to be sure, but tended to be a little too blunt and forthright to function as a diplomat. I cannot tell, of course, but United States interests at that time might have been better served by the infinitely more suave and practical diplomat, Henry Cabot Lodge.

Despite Taylor's recommendations, General Khanh launched a new

*General William C. Westmoreland replaced General Harkins as Chief of the American Military Assistance Command (new name for MAAG) about six months before this dinner.

coup a few weeks later, arresting journalists, politicians, and members of the High Council, a non-elected legislative body widely regarded as the last connection between constitutional democracy and military dictatorship.

This, of course, displeased Taylor greatly so he asked that a delegation of "Young Turks" come to see him on December 20 about Khanh's latest adventure. Present were Generals Ky, Thieu, and Thi, and Admiral Cang for the Vietnamese, with Taylor and his deputy, U. Alexis Johnson, for the Americans.

After a brief exchange of greetings, Taylor launched into a scathing denunciation of the four young Vietnamese in blunt, soldierly language. He reminded them of his warning at Westmoreland's dinner, but despite this they had made a "real mess" of things. Much palaver ensued with Taylor attacking and the Turks defending, but nothing really was accomplished except to bring Unites States-Vietnamese relations almost to the breaking point.

Taylor also lodged a furious protest with Khanh the next day. "You understand English, do you?" he told Khanh over the phone. "That night, at Westmoreland's house, I made it clear to all of you that the United States is no longer willing to tolerate any attempts to destablize the situation."

Pretending that he did not grasp Taylor's meaning, Khanh requested the American ambassador to repeat his words. The popular American soldier, who was a symbol of uprightness, could not know that his angry speech was secretly recorded by the astute Khanh. I learned of this personally from Khanh who told me the whole story at Dalat later.

With this evidence, Khanh publicly denounced Ambassador Taylor for political interference. And at the same time he mounted a virulent press and radio campaign against the American envoy.

In late December 1964, Khanh was informed by his intelligence aides that a United States-sponsored coup against him was in the works. Promptly Khanh switched sides, desperately but deliberately attempting to curry favor with the NLF.

He ordered the release of the wife of Huynh Tan Phat, the number one Communist leader of the predominantly non-Communist NLF. Khanh then sent Phat a secret letter, proposing his collaboration. On January 28, 1965, Phat forwarded a vaguely worded reply which Khanh showed me, praising him for his "indomitable spirit in the face of repression by imperialism and

139

colonialism." Phat also invited Khanh and his friends to come and join them if the troubles they were having with the Americans persisted.

Khanh's conflict with Ambassador Taylor presented the Young Turks with a real problem, because they knew they could not govern for long without American aid and support. As a result, they gradually lost confidence in Khanh and started looking for other solutions to the dilemma of how to direct government operations.

A close friend informed me that a coup against Khanh was imminent, led by Nguyen Van Kiem, a patriotic Catholic professor, and General Lam Van Phat. Unfortunately for their plans, they could not resolve certain differences quickly enough, so missed arresting Khanh at both his office and his home. Some high comedy then occurred, with the plotters and their troops chasing Khanh in his car with a military policeman all over Saigon like Keystone Cops.

Khanh finally arrived at Tan Son Nhut Airport trying to find General Ky. He met Ky driving a jeep and Ky gestured to him to follow him. They went to Ky's C-47 transport, climbed in, and taxied out on the runway. Ky then, without asking for flight clearance, immediately took off as the coup group's armored vehicles entered the field, and flew his trembling passenger to Vung Tao where he left him.

Khanh then found another plane and flew all over Vietnam trying to drum up support. Frustrated by all this he finally wound up in Dalat on February 22, 1965, when he came to see me and told me the whole funny story. He now wanted to get to Saigon without being detected because by this time the Young Turks had met and decided to oppose him and his recent savior. Ky had fighter planes up to apprehend him if he took to the air again.

The fat, brash Khanh proposed to me that he might succeed in going by car to Saigon. I responded that if he did he had better shave the small tuft of hair he insisted on wearing which was not a real beard at all. This was a joke that related to an ancient tale of an old Chinese general who, after losing a battle, found himself alone on the battlefield surrounded by enemy soldiers. He first discarded his identifying purple cloak and then hacked off his equally obvious long beard, leaving a little tuft of hair like Khanh's. The enemy soldiers then went looking for a man with a "half beard," but he eventually escaped by hiding it with a flag. His hairy adornment was almost his downfall, however.

Khanh was amused by my story but finally disclosed that the Americans were coming to get him and return him safely to Saigon. At this point, of course, Khanh knew that he was finished and had agreed to be an Ambassador at Large. The Young Turks had met, decided to dismiss him, and decided to keep him out of future trouble by sending him abroad.

He told me in a mood of complete candor, "I've already spread my share of mud around this country. I think the time has come for me to cause a sensation or two on the world political stage, just for fun." This gives an idea of how rational his thought processes were in these last days.

Khanh returned to see me the next day, apologized for all the grief he had caused, and told me of a private dossier he had amassed about the countercoup of January 1964. He gave me the name of an assistant who had orders to turn it over to me, so at last I had the material I needed to prove our complete innocence of the charges that had been placed against us.

This strange man who had been able to hoodwink so many otherwise intelligent people left Vietnam, never to return, on Feburary 25, 1965. They had quite a ceremony for him at Ton Son Nhut and, before his flight left, he made a great theatrical gesture by scooping up some dirt near to the runway to take away with him as some soil of the native land he loved so much.

Khanh's departure did not bring stability, however. The Armed Forces Council, whose strong men were Generals Thieu, Co, and Ky of the Air Force, had not thought far enough ahead to the effective forming of a sound national government. All they managed to do was get rid of Khanh. Our poor country suffered under indecisive leadership until June, when the young generals were able to consolidate enough power to seize control of the government.

Another sorry chapter in the history of our divided country thus ends. The reader can only imagine what might have been possible had the leadership that overthrew Ngo Dinh Diem been allowed to continue in power for the months during which Nguyen Khanh served us so badly.

American armored personnel carrier in river-crossing operation.

CHAPTER NINE

"Bring Soldiers,

and More Soldiers"

Long before most United States citizens had ever heard of my beautiful little country, there was one famous American soldier who had given long and patient study to Vietnam. This was Douglas MacArthur who probably knew as much as any man then alive about how to fight a war in Asia.

At a dinner given by General LeClerc in Saigon in 1946 where I was the only Vietnamese present, we were told of his memorable experience when he witnessed the Japanese surrender to the Allies aboard the battleship *Missouri* in August 1945. Part of the story LeClerc told that night over fine cigars and good French wine seems current today after all that has happened.

As LeClerc was about to leave the *Missouri,* MacArthur asked him to stay and talk with him awhile. The great general shifted his corncob pipe and said, "General LeClerc, you have just been named as the new Commander in Chief of French forces in Indochina. Please accept this advice: if you expect to succeed in overcoming the resistance of your enemy there, bring soldiers, and then more soldiers, and after that still more soldiers. But, even after all the soldiers you can spare are there, you probably still will not succeed."

After dinner, LeClerc directed a remark at me which has proved to be very true. He said, "You alone, you Vietnamese, are the ones who can win your independence." He alone, among the French of his generation, really understood our situation. Much later, after a torrent of French blood had fertilized our land, the Americans came to us with the best intentions possible and only succeeded in adding fresh American blood to the French.

143

Up to now in this narrative I have covered our struggle through 1964 without saying much about the involvement of the United States government, its political and military advisors, combat troops sent to our country, and the actual combat in an attempt to prevent takeover by the Communists. I will not attempt a documented history of American involvement because this is covered better in many publications such as the *Pentagon Papers* or *Fire in the Lake* by Frances Fitzgerald, or *Summons of the Trumpet* by Dave Palmer. What I will try to relate is what this American involvement meant to a Vietnamese and why things never came out in the way planned by the Americans. They failed to accomplish their objectives because they could not really understand us as Vietnamese. We are not French, Japanese, Chinese, Koreans, or Americans. We simply are Vietnamese with our own 4,000-year history with its peculiar customs, traditions, and culture.

Most people are unaware that American policies for Indochina began to be formulated during the presidency of Franklin D. Roosevelt in 1940. From then to the end of the Second World War, American policy was ambivalent, reaffirming France's right to exist and maintain her colonial possessions on our land while, at the same time, favoring the principle of self-determination for all people as stated in the Atlantic Charter. Roosevelt's anticolonial sentiments were well known throughout the world.

In the case of Indochina, Roosevelt proposed in March 1943 that after the war a type of trusteeship be instituted to administer the country. This was discussed at the Cairo and Teheran conferences where it was endorsed by Stalin and Chiang Kai-shek, while Churchill temporized, fearing, I suppose, problems for his own government. After all, the British were in no mood at that time to discuss the dismantling of their colonial empire which would have been a logical second step after doing the same to France's.

Both the Roosevelt and Truman administrations offered practically no help to France in restoring her sovereignty in Indochina. On the contrary, after the Allied victory over Japan and the Viet Minh takeover in Hanoi and Saigon, the first American missions* were sent to Vietnam to contact not the French, but Ho Chi Minh.

*These missions included teams led by Major Patti and two State Department officers, Moffat and Landon. Finally, a liaison staff headed by General Philip E. Gallagher was established.

144

There was considerable contact between the Office of Strategic Services personnel operating out of China and the Viet Minh during the last years of World War II because Ho's followers were offering the most effective resistance to the Japanese. A group of OSS officers was dropped into the Viet Minh-held areas to help Vo Nguyen Giap form the nucleus of an army, and these same Americans were seen parading with Viet Minh units when they triumphantly entered Hanoi in August 1945.

Through the OSS, Ho Chi Minh who superbly played his role of a non-Communist leader expressed his desire to meet with a qualified representative of General de Gaulle to discuss the political future of Vietnam. Accordingly, Jean Sainteny, who represented Free France in south China, was authorized by de Gaulle to contact Ho. A first Sainteny-Ho meeting was scheduled for the first week of August 1945, but the Frenchman could not make it because of bad weather and the confused situation relating to the Japanese surrender.

Finally, Sainteny flew to Hanoi accompanied by OSS Major Patti, on August 22, 1945. For the French, the results were far from encouraging since Ho Chi Minh had formed a semblance of a provisional government, which included no pro-French personalities, and which vowed to settle for no less than independence.

A highly placed French intelligence agent told me that this first Ho government was set up with advice from his OSS ally. Being the shrewd politician he was, Ho succeeded in playing the French against the Americans in order to get the best deal he could.

The American OSS agent who later was to play such a major role in our coup d'etat against Ngo Dinh Diem came on the Vietnamese scene at this same time. Lucien Conein was then a young French-speaking captain who was also on the plane carrying Sainteny to Hanoi. Conein was married to an Eurasian and had been representing the OSS with a French guerrilla unit operating in China.

Another American, very important to Vietnam, also made his entrance at about this time. Ho Chi Minh arranged to have Bao Dai meet an American whom he described as influential to the emperor. His invitation served a two-pronged purpose for Ho. He wanted to convince Bao Dai that he enjoyed American backing, and second, he wanted the American to believe that Bao Dai fully supported his administration. The "influential"

145

American was none other than Edward G. Lansdale, fresh from OSS exploits during the war; this was before his success in helping Ramon Magsaysay in the Philippines.

From 1946 to 1949, the United States observed a policy of neutrality in the war between France and the Viet Minh. This hands-off policy was partially caused by an abrupt end to the honeymoon between the OSS and Ho, who was tardily identified by the Americans as a seasoned Communist leader. Moreover, the United States was fully preoccupied with its own involvement in Europe, and the emergence of Mao's China.

Gradually and cautiously, however, the United States began to swing over into the French camp as, for example, when the Americans recognized the French-supported Bao Dai government on February 2, 1950. The Korean War was, of course, a real turning point because Truman saw a parallel between the Communist involvement in Korea and the Viet Minh in Vietnam. The "Cold War" was definitely shaping world events, and the French struggle in Indochina began to be seen as a defense of the Free World against the Communist menace.

On December 23, 1950, a mutual defense and assistance treaty was signed linking the United States, France, Vietnam, Cambodia, and Laos. It provided indirect military aid to the Indochinese countries on the premise that Communism was being resisted there. American belief in the "Domino theory" was so strong and suspicion of Communists so widespread that the French definitely looked like the side to back in Vietnam. Communist conquest of any country on the periphery of China was seen as inimicable to the overall security of the United States.

Unfortunately, the cooperation between the two Western allies did not last long in Indochina. In 1954, France's appeal for aid cut no ice with Washington. As a result, its army was routed by the Viet Minh at Dien Bien Phu, in North Vietnam. One year later, in 1955, the United States helped Ngo Dinh Diem expel France from South Vietnam. And while the United States embarked upon a large-scale war against the Communists in Vietnam, France came out in favor of a nonaligned Indochina to be free from American influence.

In their quest for independence and freedom, the Vietnamese nationalists had to cope with a greater problem, first with the French and later with

146

the Americans. Neither of these Western powers had the same motivation for conducting a war against the Communists as did the Vietnamese nationalists. Our motive for fighting was to establish a truly free republic, based on democratic principles and guaranteeing peace and a traditional Vietnamese life to our people.

The French never fought for the good of the Vietnamese. Instead, they attempted to ensure continued control over what had been a lucrative colony. Their motives were largely commercial, as with any colonists, and did not really involve containment of the Communists, a more laudatory goal. The Americans, on the other hand, sought to keep Indochina and especially Vietnam out of the Communist sphere of influence as part of a global plan to contain the Red menace. While one can appreciate their desire to keep the world in relative balance, a Vietnamese could hardly enjoy his role in such a master strategy. American policy was not the humanitarian one of keeping Vietnam free for the sake of the Vietnamese. Instead, the United States showed herself capable of going to almost any length to keep Vietnam from going behind the Bamboo Curtain, even if it practically destroyed the country.

I believed in 1946, as I believe now, that what we had was an internal fight among several factions of Vietnamese, one that was supported lavishly by the Communist superpowers, Soviet Russia and China. I feel that with economic and material support from the West we could have either defeated the other side or come to some kind of natural accommodation with them to the benefit of all Vietnamese. We could have used some advisors to show us how to use the new weaponry, and perhaps some air missions from time to time, but by and large, we should have fought our civil war as Vietnamese against Vietnamese without foreign intervention, just as North and South did in the great American Civil War.

Vietnamese disagreement with organization and tactics did not begin with the start of American aid in 1954. In fact, from the early beginnings of our national army in 1950, we and the French were working at cross-purposes. Particularly at the start of the French-Viet Minh War, French formations were based on time-honored Western military thought, organizations superbly suited for fighting in Europe but not capable of effectively engaging the will-of-the-wisp Viet Minh. My boss, General Hinh, planned for an army composed of light battalions of infantry, supported by a

147

minimum of heavy equipment, commanded by Vietnamese officers, and capable of living and fighting in the same terrain as the guerrillas. This highly mobile army would not be roadbound, or encumbered by heavy trucks, tanks, and other impedimenta. He finally persuaded the French of the wisdom of his views and 120 light battalions of about 600 men under Vietnamese command were authorized during 1953. We cannot tell today how these units would have performed in a protracted war because Dien Bien Phu interfered.

The Geneva Accords resulted in a withdrawal of both French military support and influence from Vietnam to be replaced gradually by American versions. We Vietnamese felt that we had learned many lessons from the French military experience since we had fought side-by-side with them for some seven years against the elusive Viet Minh. We were quite sure that our army must avoid the pitfalls experienced by the French, that it must be capable of meeting our guerrilla adversary on common ground. We must be capable of going anywhere the enemy was operating, living among the people as he was doing, and depriving him of the support afforded him in the countryside. If the "army were the fish, and the people the sea," we had to operate in such a way as to deny him access to the people. We therefore continued to advocate strongly our previous concept of light infantry battalions backed by light and fast supporting troops.

In November 1954, a joint planning session was held between ourselves and the new American Military Assistance Advisory Group (MAAG). Principals on our side were General Nguyen Van Vy, who had just replaced General Hinh, and myself as Chief of Staff; senior Americans at the conference were General John (Iron Mike) O'Daniel, chief of MAAG, and his Chief of Staff, Colonel William Rosson.

We presented our proposal for the creation of mobile groups formed from the already existing battalions organized under the French, with organic artillery, armor, and ancillary support troops such as signals and engineers. Artillery batteries would be equipped only with the light and mobile 105-mm howitzer, while armor units would be primarily reconnaissance units using at the most jeeps and armored cars. The infantry battalions comprising the main combat force would be recruited from local areas and remain there with both an anti-guerrilla and civic action mission. These local troops would be the protectors of the villagers and their friends and neighbors, having family ties to the populace. In addition, underground guerrilla forces in the Highlands would be established to choke off possible Communist infiltration from Laos and Cambodia. We felt we already had enough high-level staff personnel available, trained both by combat and in French schools.

Our arguments unfortunately fell on deaf ears. The Americans evidently put us in the same mold as the Koreans whose army they had organized and trained, and they seemed to think that our country was similar to the Korean peninsula. They believed, I suppose, that what would work for Korea would certainly work for Vietnam. Again, unfortunately, they could not have been farther wrong. Korea is different and Koreans are not Vietnamese. Further, the type of war just concluded by division of that country at the 38th parallel was totally dissimilar to ours in Vietnam. The Americans were organized to fight a war in which there are well-defined front lines with relatively secure rear areas against an enemy, and where the overwhelming fire superiority of American weapons could bring decisive results. Korea is suited to this type of war and thus the decision to create a Korean army that more or less mirror-imaged the American was a good one. Such was not the case in Vietnam.

Nevertheless, O'Daniel insisted that our existing light formations be reorganized into light divisions as in the Korean model. These American-type organizations would be backed up by mobile support units. He also passed on to us the State Department's decision that the numbers supported would be cut to about 90,000 men from 270,000 despite the fact that the Communists could count on more than 450,000 in the entire country. It took a personal appeal from Ngo Dinh Diem to President Eisenhower to get a compromise figure of 150,000.

The biggest problem, of course, was organization of the forces. Although we tried to use the most effective arguments possible based on personal experience in our own country, we could not sway the well-meaning but stubborn O'Daniel. He and Rosson explained that in order to receive American logistical support, our major units had to be organized like American divisions. According to them, the Americans could not tailor logistics units, especially for supporting the type of forces we advocated, because of their structural incompatibility with U.S. divisions. Another reason specified was that American advisors would be ineffective if they

149

tried to work with unfamiliar units organized under a different doctrine than the one they had learned in service schools.

There was a great preoccupation on the part of the Americans which persisted for years that the chief danger to South Vietnam was an overt invasion from the North. In that case, American plans were to send their own combat divisions in to help us repel the attack, so I suppose they were afraid that the units of the two armies could not fight effectively together unless they had the same basic organization; again, a lesson learned from Korea which did not apply to Vietnam. In fact, the real threat from the Communist side was at village level in the form of the highly disciplined guerrilla units which maintained control over whole sections of the country where cumbersome conventional units could not operate effectively. The French had already proved this to us. We wondered why we had to repeat the mistake for the Americans.

O'Daniel's views prevailed, of course, and we were forced to adopt an organizational concept much against our own better judgment. To conform to the American blueprint, we had to send officers and enlisted specialists to the United States for intensive courses of study in their methods; and in the process we were to forget as far as possible the lessons learned with the French. The entire process was naturally cumbersome since long distances had to be traveled and another foreign language had to be mastered in order to understand the instruction in America.

President Diem faced a dilemma. Should he buckle under to American pressure in order to get American aid, or should he refuse to adopt their program and thus lose the assistance? Although the other side was receiving aid with few operational strings from the Communist bloc, Diem had little choice but to take the American aid with its obvious and unpalatable conditions.

From that day on until 1973, the conduct of the war was dictated by American policy. In early 1969, heading a delegation of my fellow members of the National Assembly, our Congress, I asked the then Chief of the General Staff Cao Van Vien exactly what was his military doctrine. He responded, *"As long as the conduct of the war remains an American responsibility, we have no doctrine of our own."*

After 1973 until the final fall in 1975, we had to continue the war, but under the most unfavorable of national and international conditions. On a

150

strictly military level, the residual impact of the former organizational framework had not really disappeared. It certainly weighed in the balance as one of the primary causes of ultimate disaster.

So, United States aid began to filter to the newly organized Vietnamese army, organized into ten divisions* and comprising 150,000 men. To administer the military aid a double-headed organization under control of the Chief, MAAG, was established. The Geneva Accords permitted a military presence of 342 men, the number of American soldiers left in Vietnam at the time of the signing of the protocols. This number, of course, proved highly inadequate since it had to serve also as cover for other organizations like Colonel Lansdale's CIA team† of subversive specialists, so a separate and similarly sized logistics advisory staff was built. This bore the title of Temporary Equipment Recovery Mission (TERM) and had as an excuse for existence the identification, recovery, and rehabilitation of military equipment scattered over South Vietnam during the French-Viet Minh War. Its real mission was, of course, instruction for us on the equipment being provided under the terms of the Military Assistance Program (MAP) and advice on training, organizing, and operating the new logistics units. The other MAAG officers had two general types of mission, both concerned with combat training and operations. The first was to operate as advisors down to regimental level in the Army of Vietnam (ARVN), and the other was to act as advisors living and working with province chiefs (also in command of corresponding military sectors) and being as useful as possible, as the individual situation required. Other American personnel operated in Saigon, administering the MAAG and doing general war planning with our own General Staff officers.

From 1954 until they left in 1973, the effectiveness of the American advisors was marginal at best. This was not because of a lack of zeal, intelligence, or professionalism. In fact, MAAG personnel were chosen with great care and only officers of the best reputation were sent for this duty.

---

*There were four field divisions of about 8,000 men and six light divisions having only 5,000. In addition thousands of combat, logistical, and administrative support troops were authorized.

†Lansdale's team, called the "Saigon Military Mission," started in June 1954 and consisted of about ten officers highly trained in paramilitary and unconventional intelligence affairs.

151

The problem involved the length of tour: MAAG personnel generally spent only a year in Vietnam, so they could hardly be expected to surmount a great number of obstacles liberally strewn in their advisory path. There was, of course, the obvious language barrier. It is hard to get really close to individuals if there is not direct, face-to-face, private conversation. Some Americans spoke French, but these were in the minority, and talking in Vietnamese was generally out of the question. As a result, interpreters of varied quality had to be present at all conversations, with a resulting loss of real communication. Gradually, we Vietnamese learned English, but even this posed a problem. The Americans tended to have greater confidence in those of us who spoke good English, hardly a qualification for military command or denoting special ability, courage, or integrity.

As far as advice was concerned, we had already been at war for several years against the same enemy, and did not really need to be told how to conduct operations by well-meaning men who knew all about war in Europe and Korea, but had never before been faced with guerrillas. We did, of course, need training on how to use and repair the strange equipment being provided, but this did not take a massive commitment of Americans.

Another separate part of overall assistance to Vietnam, which did not include the armed forces, was the work done by Professor Wesley R. Fishel of Michigan State University and his advisory team to help the Vietnamese government reform and redesign its civilian apparatus. Part of this work involved the national police and the civil guard, a paramilitary organization designed to keep order in the countryside and protect the people from attacks by the guerrillas. It must be remembered that in the early days the main mission of the army was to be prepared to repel an overt invasion from the North.

The idea in theory may have had some merit, but in practice was a total fiasco. The civil guard was unable to really defend itself or the villagers it was organized to serve because its organization did not give it enough strength to operate separately. It had different weapons, different tactics, and different equipment from the army, so could not communicate readily with an adjacent army unit since its radios would not net with ours when it needed reinforcement, which was often. As a result, the NLF could attack with impunity a civil guard post in an outlying area secure in the knowledge

BRING SOLDIERS, AND MORE SOLDIERS"

that an army unit a few miles away would be totally unaware of what was occurring. The result was that there could be no feeling of security engendered in the minds of the farmers and villagers, and they thus rallied to the Communist side in ever-increasing numbers.

The reason for this confused situation was twofold. First, the two programs had separate funding from the American side; one part administered the support of the armed forces and the other aided the civilian side of government. The second reason came from Ngo Dinh Diem's mistrust of the army and his desire not to concentrate too much power in a single agency.

Diem and his two brothers had difficulty in infiltrating their political cadres into the ranks of the army, since at that time, we were a relatively unpolitical group. The civil guard, on the other hand, was placed under the direct command of province chiefs who were political appointees of the president, and fellow Can Lao party members. Had these officials been elected directly by the people, things might not have been so bad, but as it was, their orientation was directly aimed at the central administration. Diem wanted the civil guard to be his own political tool as a countervailing force against the army if necessary.

This political mission might have worked if it had been administered honestly, but this simply did not occur. Province chiefs used the civil guard soldiers to harvest coffee, plant rice on large holdings owned by the party, catch fish with party boats, and otherwise perform work totally unrelated to their assigned job as defenders of the people. In fact, they even took a lead from their masters and started to extort money and goods from the farmers they were supposed to be defending.

In visiting civil guard posts in my corps area, I would find only about one-third of the authorized strength on duty at any given time. One-third would be off working at their homes or their businesses (part of their pay would be kept by the province or district chief), and the remaining third would be working directly on party business, as described above.

Obviously, their morale was at a terribly low level. This was compounded by the fact that all their equipment was inferior to that supplied the army. The Viet Cong knew all this, of course, and was able to exploit their advantage by attacking individual civil guard posts when they knew they

153

had a preponderance of strength. This happened many times in my corps area, but my soldiers could never reinforce these posts in time to prevent a Communist victory.

One of my first decrees after the November 1963 coup which overthrew Diem was to place the civil guard and all other such forces under army control so that our common fight could be waged on a properly coordinated basis. By this time, of course, much ground had been lost forever.

I will not try to cover the stationing of American forces in Vietnam since others have already provided an ample supply of words on the subject. But, starting with Kennedy's introduction of American support troops such as aviation companies, the character of the Vietnamese war changed. With the addition of each American, we Vietnamese lost more and more ability to direct the conduct of the war. Until the Americans pulled out in 1973, the war progressively was waged with American direction and tactics and for American objectives. At the peak of the American involvement, more than 500,000 soldiers, sailors, and airmen were operating in and around our country. They were amply provided with the most sophisticated modern weaponry and a fantastically expensive logistics support system, a formidable fighting force indeed.

Their war was not, however, fought on purely military considerations. The overall American commander was never permitted sufficient freedom to fight his war to a satisfactory conclusion, since both the domestic and international politics of the United States were of greater importance than military victory.

I do not mean that the conflict had to be escalated to the point of using nuclear weapons, because even if a political decision of that magnitude had been made, there were never suitable targets for such weapons. What I am saying is that the pouring of more and more men into the country without some clearly defined plan for military victory was a useless endeavor. Operations for the greater part were conducted against NLF units within the boundaries of our country south of the 17th parallel. Except for some small-scale clandestine work, American and Vietnamese major units never hit the Communist sanctuaries in Cambodia, Laos, and North Vietnam itself. It was only very late in the game that President Nixon authorized a couple of incursions into Cambodia and Laos, but by this time many valuable chances had been lost.

154

We Vietnamese had trouble understanding why this vast and highly competent force did not come in and really get down to the business of winning the war. It seemed to serve as more of an instrument of intimidation and reinforcement of policy than as a genuine war machine. The powerful air and naval forces were never used to their full potential since air strikes could never be extended beyond predetermined and preannounced limits of time and territory. The "computer strategy" of Secretary of Defense Robert McNamara ended as a semifailure, because it robbed the bombing of its element of surprise and lessened its effectiveness. The Communists were able to anticipate American bombing raids and have their missiles and other antiaircraft defenses ready to take a heavy toll of American planes. So deadly was this fire that pilots often missed their targets altogether, dropping their bombs outside the target area and thus causing terrible loss of civilian life and destruction of property and installations of no particular strategic or tactical value. Protests and condemnations of this type of bombing from Vietnam, the United States, and elsewhere increased pressure for de-escalation and compromise, to the enemy's advantage. It appeared to us that military decisions, properly the job of local commanders, were being made in Washington by politicians who could not hope to understand the complexities of this strange type of war.

In Vietnam, the American commander had a hopeless task since he had two contradictory missions to perform, one to make war on the enemy force and the other to pacify the countryside from enemy subversion. His strategy and tactics could not be standard and wound up not being appropriate to either mission.

Generally, air raids were preferred over ground combat, so most ground actions were fought by Vietnamese troops. Operations ordinarily were not carried out jointly; the too-limited participation of Vietnamese troops in American operations greatly decreased their impact. The all-important counterguerrilla campaign could not ever be waged effectively by the Americans. They needed relatively large bodies of enemy troops to engage in conventional warfare. In guerrilla warfare, where there are no lines or rear areas and where the enemy is everywhere, a strong national army is required, possessing several key attributes: the same language and customs as the people, familiarity with the land and climate, the ability to adapt readily to local conditions, and above all the ability to gain ready

155

information from its own countrymen. American troops, in spite of their technical superiority and their abundance of arms and material, could never gain these attributes, never be assimilated into the local population. We kept proposing to reorganize our army so as to combat the Communists on their own terms, but the Americans kept refusing to consider our arguments.

During the time of the big American buildup, Vietnamese forces were not used on important missions. I suppose that it was quite natural for American officers to depend on their troops for military actions they thought to be critical, but in so doing they caused Vietnamese morale to be lowered. What we did not need was the American army to be fighting "their" war, while we were attempting to fight "ours." Such a disunified approach never won a war anywhere. With the conditions we were operating under, no further buildup of American forces was required. They probably had more than they needed. What was required was true Vietnamese participation in all phases of planning and operations.

In effect, we were fighting at least two separate wars against a common enemy, one of the real reasons for our common military defeat. We should have had a single allied command charged with detailed coordination of all forces, as in the Korean War. Had this occurred, incompetent leaders, both Vietnamese and American, could have been identified and eliminated, confusion avoided, and disagreements minimized. Supplies would have arrived where intended and in proper quantity, corruption could have been detected and suppressed, tactical support such as air operations would have been better coordinated, and tragic errors involving needless loss of life could have been avoided. As it was, objectives were incompletely coordinated and defined and resulting operations lacked the proper follow-through for success.

One of the most highly publicized consequences of a lack of a single allied command was the revolting massacre of the civilian population of Son My in Quang Ngai province, known as My Lai by the American forces.

This action occurred on March 16, 1968, when American troops under command of Captain Ernest Medina and Lieutenant William Calley executed a large number of unarmed civilians while on an operation against NLF forces. More than a year later this tragedy was disclosed by the American press, and disgust at the senseless act swept the world. The stories that were printed and described in gory detail on millions of television sets were especially horrifying because the victims were largely old men, women, and children.

In Vietnam, there was no immediate large public outcry at this outrage, largely because our people had been quite accustomed to such wanton destruction of life. This was only one of many similar cases where innocent people were killed during a long war going back to 1940. Both sides were guilty of this kind of conduct, but none of the incidents had received as much publicity as My Lai. When our people saw the news of this terrible event in American magazines like *Time* and *Newsweek* which were sold openly on the street, their moral indignation was aroused at what had happened.

As chairman of the Defense Committee of the Senate, I conducted a thorough on-the-scene investigation of the incident and presented a report to the Senate on January 7, 1970. My report pretty much confirmed the concurrent American investigation of the tragedy, but more clearly established that Lieutenant Calley, the commander on the spot, performed his executions at the express direction of Captain Medina. The exact number of civilian victims could not be determined, but our best estimate was 117 dead, not the 22 that Calley was accused of murdering.

Like the American high command, the Vietnamese government did its best to cover up the entire incident by falsifying reports at both local or high-command level, or at least to play down the seriousness of the affair. The real responsibility lies not with the Medinas and Calleys, however, but with the highest leaders. The policies they deliberately established led to a division of the war effort where, to the Americans, all Vietnamese looked like the enemy. I put most of the blame on the President of Vietnam, Nguyen Van Thieu, because he unreasonably accepted American concepts and because he jealously guarded his own position by not insisting upon a unified command. This separation of command caused many military defeats and led to such atrocities as the slaughter at Son My.

Another regrettable condition that prevented real unity of purpose was obsessive American mistrust of the Vietnamese army and unjustified fear that we might some day attack North Vietnam. For this reason we were never provided with the latest weapons normally issued to American forces, despite the fact that our common enemy received the best the Communist arsenals could procure. By the time the Americans were ready to leave, however, enormous quantities of all manner of heavy equipment were being

157

poured into Vietnam in an effort finally to "Vietnamese" the war; all of this without adequate planning or time for us to assimilate it. It was a question of too much, too late.

Despite the lack of a unified command structure between the American and Vietnamese armed forces, our relations with our American advisors were generally quite good. Individual Americans accepted us and tried hard to help us as much as they could. In 1968, for example, I observed a platoon of Vietnamese soldiers operating in Quang Tri province near a similar sized unit of Americans. Relations were excellent between the two, with the Americans sharing food and other supplies with their Vietnamese friends. While I was observing them, the Vietnamese were having trouble with a Viet Cong strong point, so the American lieutenant called in an artillery barrage to help them. They saw a common enemy and reacted to it as soldiers always do.

On another similar occasion a Vietnamese soldier was wounded so seriously that he could not be evacuated from the battlefield by conventional means. Again, the Americans at this local level came to the rescue by calling for a helicopter pickup. In twenty minutes a helicopter came in and was able to save the wounded man's life by flying him to a hospital a good distance away.

This spirit of cooperation did not always work at the higher levels, however. This was especially true when a Vietnamese colonel or general was incompetent or corrupt. He naturally did not want his counterpart to discover this and report the fact. My countryman would plead that he was having a personality clash with his advisor or that there was some misunderstanding between them, hoping the American would be replaced with a less perceptive officer. Generally, the American high command complied, and many really effective officers were relieved from their jobs to the detriment of their careers.

During my own period of active duty in the army, I was associated with several highly competent American advisors. We were able to work together with perfect respect and in a friendly, professional manner. I think the reason for this was that we were both eager to learn from the other, so we had no reason to have "personality clashes."

Another American program that was begun with great fanfare and showed definite progress again suffered from a lack of overall coordination between the two powers. This was the Phoenix program, named after the traditional Vietnamese bird of peace. It was run by the CIA under the overall direction of Ambassador Robert W. Komer, a special assistant to President Johnson. Its purpose was to centralize intelligence gathering within the Vietnamese government and to carry out an effective antisubversive campaign throughout the country. Training centers were established to produce 5,500 skilled men for the insertion of 59-man teams into 93 villages every 15 weeks. These personnel were supposed to identify NLF political and other subversive agents and to capture them.

On the American side, the program came under the Military Assistance Command, Vietnam (MACV) where close coordination was effected between the CIA and military personnel operating in the program. The Vietnamese agents trained for this role and equipped with modern light arms were answerable not to the Defense Department, but to the Ministry of Rural Development under an honest general, Nguyen Duc Thang. Their budget support was also different, coming neither from the normal AID funds used to support the Vietnamese Armed Forces nor from those that supported the administrative branch of the government; money for Phoenix was obtained from the embassy itself and was administered separately.

Actual direction of the Phoenix program came under the Americans, with only nominal interest directed toward it by Thang's ministry. This was not Thang's fault, since loyalty here tended to follow the money flow. In any event it was ill coordinated both between Americans and Vietnamese and also within the Vietnamese government.

Eventually, the entire rural area was covered by these agents dressed in traditional Vietnamese peasant clothing; they were represented in some 300 villages in the country. Unfortunately not all the agents were honest and dedicated patriots and there were not enough Americans to keep track of them. So, we again saw another group of oppressive governmental cadres, mistreating the poor people and using their positions to extort from them.

Another well-considered scheme thus failed, mired in the rich mud of my country's farming areas. It was something that looked good on paper and on which untold hours of valuable time was spent. But, in the end there were more NLF cadres than before it started. It was an expensive failure.

One real Communist victory was achieved over the American soldiers with little expense and effort. The NLF caused cheap drugs to be supplied to

159

the American units wherever they happened to be in the country. I used to see teams of young attractive girls with baskets of cold drinks or cigarettes for sale to the soldiers. You would find them everywhere you found the American forces. The naturally bored soldiers would be attracted to these pretty girls and their cold drinks. Unfortunately for them, the girls also supplied them with marijuana and heroin of exceptional quality. Use of these drugs had a deleterious effect on the American fighting men and on the abilities of entire units to perform effectively. The drug trade was so extensive that the United States high command had to establish drug detoxification centers both in Vietnam and the United States to try to alleviate the problem. This psychological weapon of war was most effectively used by the Communists, but the blame for it was never given the publicity it deserved.

I have already alluded to the American dependence on air power, a situation that is quite understandable when one considers the main threat perceived by United States planners to which its armed forces must respond, namely direct aggression by the Soviet Union in Europe. In Vietnam, the reliance on air power included the ever-present helicopters, marvelous devices which, to a rich and technically proficient nation like the United States, became an integral part of transport and firepower. Following the American lead, when we Vietnamese were sent into an operation, we frequently were transported there by helicopter carrier while helicopter gunships flew ahead to cover the objective, except that after a period of time we became unduly dependent on them for everything. It really was too rich for our blood, in a land where one usually walks from one place to another, carrying one's goods by backpack. The NLF, our adversary, performed all his supply and tactical operations by using foot traffic. Until practically the end of the war he never exposed his trucks, tanks, and artillery to counterfire. He kept things simple; we should have too. Helicopters were provided to Vietnamese generals to help them get rapidly from place to place. This they could do, but in so doing they saw their own troops on the ground less and less and thus failed to understand their oftentimes wretched condition.

And, one last problem was the American presence in such great numbers. The country could not absorb so many foreigners and so many

American dollars without very bad effects on the entire fiscal and moral fabric of the country. The ready supply of money produced terrible inflation, adding immeasurably to the woe of the common people. Some opportunists, particularly in large cities, were able to enrich themselves, but the general effect was certainly negative.

There was a nagging problem that marred United States-Vietnamese relations from the beginning to end. This problem was traced back to America's unwillingness to depart from conventional views and methods when dealing with an unconventional situation like that in Vietnam.

In 1973, I invited Mr. Whitehouse, United States deputy ambassador, to have a luncheon meeting with two "nonaligned" politicians in Saigon. The luncheon was an attempt of our political group to talk the Americans into dropping President Thieu and endorsing a coalition government with the NLF. The real issue was, however, not raised at the meeting because the American diplomat disappointed us at the start.

When asked about the advisability of the United States helping the Vietnamese army set up model farms, Whitehouse said: "The United States helps the Vietnamese Army fight against the Communists. It does not help you till the fields and milk the cows."

It was very difficult for us to try to explain to our mentor and great ally that tilling the fields and milking the cows is also an effective way of fighting Communism.

In this spirit, Vietnam's Army Saving Bank (ASB), one of our best initiatives, was summarily killed by the American Aid Mission in Vietnam.

Plans for the ASB were drawn up in 1964 after careful study of similar organizations existing in Taiwan, Thailand, and South Korea. With the accord of President Thieu and other top generals, Vietnam's ASB was finally established in 1969 under the direction of two honest generals, Le Van Kim and Nguyen Van Vy.

The concept was a simple one. Each month, 100 Vietnamese piasters (an equivalent of about twenty-five cents) were withheld from the pay of more than one million troops and deposited in the bank. Interest and other profits coming from commercial loan ventures were designed to finance programs of military pensions, retirement benefits, and postwar demobilization, rehabilitation, and relocation. The ASB grew quickly and was initially

161

quite successful, expanding into other vital areas of Vietnam's private sector, including transportation, construction, food processing, and insurance.

Threatened by ASB inroads, the private sector, which had been dominated for years by foreign nationals and corrupt Vietnamese officials, launched an anti-ASB campaign. Their move was unfortunately helped by the U.S. Embassy, the Pentagon, and the U.S. Congress who strongly believed that, like their American counterparts, Vietnamese private firms should control the nation's economy and that the Vietnamese army should not be allowed to make money.

Under the pretext of "corruption" an inquiry was conducted and, although no major evidence was found, the ASB was ordered to cease all its activities.

Ly Long Than, the most powerful Chinese in Vietnam, and also one of the wealthiest Chinese in the world, reportedly engineered the anti-ASB plot. President Thieu, who helped promote ASB, reversed his own decision. He could not afford the luxury of displeasing the United States. One Thieu aide told me that Ly Long Than secretly served as financial advisor to both President Thieu's and Premier Khiem's families.

The final word of this chapter concerns the United States Ambassador to the Republic of Vietnam, Henry Cabot Lodge. Of all the American ambassadors serving our country, he was the most effective.

Lodge may have been appointed by President Kennedy to gain bipartisan political support for the Vietnamese war effort. Certainly as a Republican in a highly important post in a Democratic administration, that effect was achieved. But Lodge was much more than this. He was efficient and friendly, attributes we greatly respected. We badly needed a real American politician in that job, one who would be able to understand our viewpoints and persuade us of his own and his government's. Lodge was extremely easy to approach. He spoke excellent French and was able to communicate directly with us on a man-to-man basis. He was at home both out in the countryside looking at a farmer's rice fields or discussing day-to-day business with a village official and in meetings with the president or premier on matters of the gravest importance. He was always available to members of the government to go to some outlying place to observe something we thought important. He wanted to meet with us frequently and get information at first hand, not depend on reports and statistics.

As I indicated before, Ambassador Lodge was extremely impressed by the conduct of the coup operations that overthrew Ngo Dinh Diem. I believe we enjoyed his confidence and he tried very hard to work closely with us in solving our common problems. He knew that we generals were weak in political matters and thought he could help us by meeting with us frequently and thus letting us profit from his vast experience. He likened us to General Eisenhower just after the start of his presidency, feeling that generals can learn politics too.

Unfortunately, Kim and I could not get Big Minh to hold these meetings with Lodge. In the three-month period that we were in power, there was only one such meeting held and that was in November. Lodge kept repeating this suggestion on other occasions such as when we took him to the Cao Dai's temple in Tay Ninh and on other trips to Nha Trang, Long An, Dalat, and Qui Nhon where we were enthusiastically received by the people. On one of these visits, Lodge suggested that Minh not appear in his military cap when talking to the people because they needed to see his face.

Had Big Minh not been so lazy and kept in as close touch with Lodge as he could have, I do not believe the Nguyen Khanh countercoup in 1964 could have occurred. This, then, could certainly have been one of the other causes of defeat, because that year, before the massive United States military intervention, victory was still within our grasp.

But, the United States did intervene massively and remained as a great military presence until 1973. When the time came for them to start the withdrawal of their forces in 1970, this was done in accord with a unilateral American plan without detailed consultation with Thieu's government. Instead, the withdrawal was accomplished too quickly, to meet the political objectives of the Nixon administration, while forgetting the needs of the fighting front.

By the time the last American unit had left, the South Vietnamese army was still inadequately equipped and had not yet been trained thoroughly on the equipment newly arrived. In particular, the air force and navy were not at all ready to assume the support missions so ably performed previously by their United States counterparts.

As I shall describe in later chapters, in early 1975 the South Vietnamese found themselves lacking in almost all aspects of war-making power, while

163

their opponents were extremely well-equipped with the latest materiel the Communist bloc could lavish on them. This could be considered one of the major reasons for the final defeat and has been an instructive lesson for the nations of the free world.

This may have helped the Carter administration in formulating its plans for disengagement in Korea. In the first place, the withdrawal of American ground forces is to be accomplished over a period of five years while the South Koreans gradually shoulder the complete load. Second, strong air and naval forces will be available to South Korea to help repel any invasion from the north. I think this plan has an excellent chance of success, particularly when one considers the fact that the two Koreas are not now at war and that South Korea is in excellent condition economically.

164

Vietnamese President Nguyen Van Thieu.

CHAPTER TEN

Thieu: Transition

To Disaster

During his several terms and forms of office in 1964 and 1965, Nguyen Khanh was strongly supported by the United States, and in particular by its ambassador, Maxwell Taylor. He also had the allegiance of many internal Vietnamese factions, the army itself, the Buddhists, and the Catholics. Khanh's problem was that he could not seem to confine himself to governing the country. Instead, he let his personal ambition gain the upper hand and by using one faction against the other sought to consolidate power for its own sake. In the time he managed to divide everyone, to the country's detriment: the military, politicians, religious leaders, and finally the Americans in Saigon. Initially he was greatly trusted by Secretary of Defense Robert McNamara, who later became disappointed in his lack of leadership.

When he overthrew our 1963 government, Khanh's backing came from a group of youthful officers called the "Young Turks." Many of these young generals were promoted by Khanh in return for their support. They were said to be a fresh replacement for us "old" officers who had been deposed. Out of this group came the top leadership of our government for the next ten years, Nguyen Van Thieu and Nguyen Cao Ky.

Knowing that the Americans were losing confidence in him, Khanh sought to open clandestine negotiations with and to gain support from the NLF. This proved to be his ultimate downfall because when the Americans became aware of it they undoubtedly felt that he was about to lead both Vietnam and the United States into a type of negotiated settlement possibly favorable to the Communists. At just this time, of course, the United States administration was preparing itself for military intervention; so, Khanh had to go.

Government of the country was left rather up in the air between Khanh's removal on February 21, 1965, and the accession to power of the first Thieu-Ky government, June 19, 1965. Thieu and Ky were elected to their respective positions as head of state (president) and premier by the senior ten generals of the Young Turks. Ky as premier possessed the power within the government, but, like Thieu, he was young and without experience in politics. The real power, of course, remained with the army, backed by the Americans.

Just before their assumption of power, Thieu and Ky required the outgoing head of state, Phan Khac Suu, to sign a decree that forced all generals with over twenty-five years of service to retire from the army. This meant that Big Minh, Le Van Kim, and I were now out of the army and not able to interfere in any way with them. It was not so much that they were afraid of us, but that according to their new roles, the most senior officer in the army would be head of state. Since Minh was in self-imposed exile in Bangkok, I would have to be named to the top job, evidently an unthinkable event for them. It was at about this point that I decided on politics as a second career for myself.

Shortly after his accession to power, Ky issued a report covering a very attractive government program consisting of twenty-six points, a virtual social revolution. I was excited at this new program and followed its progress carefully. It was called a "Government for Poor People" and would, if properly carried out, have meant a whole new order for society. Many reforms were to be implemented, but unfortunately Ky was unable to carry out what he announced.

Among other things, Ky tried to prevent any illicit traffic in rice and unlawful possession of foreign currency and to suppress the black market. Another big program was to finally achieve pacification throughout the countryside. To help accomplish this, the new American ambassador, Lodge,* brought in an old friend of ours, Edward Lansdale, with rank of minister in the embassy.

Lansdale was to work with Bui Diem, our secretary of state under Ky's government. He went to work with characteristic vigor, but found that his old friend Bui Diem was so busy sorting out the routine aspects of this job

*Mr. Lodge returned to replace General Taylor in July 1965.

168

that he had little time to devote to "pacification." I saw Lansdale a lot while he was on this tour, and he was a most frustrated man.

So, through government incompetence and lack of American understanding of how to proceed, Ky's excellent program never really amounted to anything. It probably was too ambitious. Had he confined himself to only three or four top priority reforms and really emphasized them, some ground might have been gained. But Ky was lazy, like Big Minh, and could not stay away from his cockfighting and his nightly games of Mah-Jongg.

Corrupt entrepreneurs took every opportunity to take advantage of the common people to make themselves rich, bribing government officials when necessary to circumvent price controls. For example, a rice broker would buy and put into storage a large amount of rice at harvest time which he would hold in his warehouse until the price would rise. Then he would sell it at a profit at about the time of the next harvest and buy another large quantity from the farmers at a still lower price. The people in the cities were not hurt too much by this manipulation, but the farmers were squeezed terribly. These "rice kings," probably fewer than a dozen in number, of course made huge fortunes. The original Chinese rice merchants maintained a more-or-less honest trade, but in later years some Vietnamese also started dealing in rice, seeing opportunities for large profits.

The black market was another way that corrupt people could make huge profits at the expense of the economy. Many illegal practices came into being; just about any way to make a dishonest piaster was tried at one time or another. One way was with chemical fertilizer that was imported in large amounts into the country. This was especially damaging to the farmers because through judicious use of such fertilizer, two or three crops could be harvested in a single year.

Fertilizer sent to Vietnam under agreements with the Americans would be diverted into black market channels where it would be stored and finally sold at greatly inflated prices to farmers who should have been getting it free or at a very low price. There were no effective government controls over the importation and distribution of fertilizer, so many people lined their pockets at the expense of the poor farmer, helping to further discredit the government. As a matter of fact, President Thieu's own brother-in-law was one of these black-marketeers in fertilizer. The revelation of this caused a big scandal and was a severe embarrassment to Thieu's government; it was even reported in the government-controlled newspapers and was denounced in the Senate. Thieu, however, protected his relative.

Corruption in government was not a monopoly of the South Vietnamese government during the Thieu-Ky years. It has been present in one form or another throughout recorded history. Certainly it was present in Vietnam under the French and again during the reign of Ngo Dinh Diem. The problem for Thieu was the tremendous increase that occurred during his time in office. Virtually everyone who was able took advantage of his position and engaged in profiteering. Even this would not have been so bad if they had reinvested their funds within the country, because then the economy would have been stimulated and the common people helped. Instead, these vultures transferred many millions of dollars out of the country to private accounts in foreign countries like Switzerland and France.

In time, corruption extended to almost everyone in the country. Within the hierarchy of the government, most officials were touched in one way or another. Within the structure, payoffs were made according to an individual's position, the greatest amounts to the highest ranking. The importers bribed officials to let them conduct both honest and dishonest business. And finally, the consumers themselves participated in the corruption because they paid for both necessities and luxuries above the government-regulated prices. The enemy finally became the greatest profiteer, actively engaging in and encouraging our people to even greater excesses. The NLF needed money to buy various things for their soldiers and political cadres, such as rice and other foodstuffs, medicine, and even arms and equipment not supplied by the Communist bloc.

They did this in two ways. One was simply to tax the people living in their areas, business people and others as well. The other was to deal directly with the profiteers within South Vietnamese society.

A wood cutter near Tay Ninh on the Cambodian border was allowed to stay in business by the NLF because he paid them U.S. dollars for the privilege. This practice was condoned because his wood was needed in other places throughout the country, and the enemy profited. They were thus able to obtain currency, both dollars and piasters, which could be smuggled out of the country or used directly to buy whatever they needed. It seems absurd

170

that some Vietnamese official whose duty it was to prosecute the war against the NLF was indirectly supplying their needs, but such definitely was the case.

Another large source of black market suppliers was the American Post Exchange. As the American military buildup expanded, so correspondingly did the huge PX support for the troops all through the country. Many of the goods destined for the American soldier never reached their destination. Americans have told me that whenever they couldn't find an item in the PX, they could purchase it openly on the streets in Saigon or Qui Nhon. Some big operators even published catalogues listing the PX goods for sale. If you wanted a Sony tape recorder, for example, you simply picked it out of the catalogue and told the seller where and when you wanted it delivered. He would then pick it up from his warehouse in its original carton, seals unbroken, and exchange it with yours for, of course, an inflated price in piasters.

A big economic problem plaguing the Thieu government after the departure of the Americans was a spiraling inflation which most affected the people on fixed incomes such as civil servants and soldiers. A sergeant with a family might make 10,000 piasters a month, amounting to perhaps $50.00 buying power. Rice to feed his family would take this entire amount, leaving nothing for other necessities, so he would have to look to other methods for additional funds. If he could, he would try to get other work, or perhaps he would join the black marketeers. In any event his lot was a truly unhappy one.

While the Americans were still in Vietnam, there was a ready supply of American dollars to shore up the economy. When this monetary base dried up, the government had to print more and more piasters to finance budgetary deficits and the rate of inflation really accelerated.

All this burgeoning graft and corruption did not go unchallenged, particularly in one quarter, that of our ethical and moral guides, the Buddhist bonzes. Again the antigovernment leader was Thich Tri Quang who played such an important role in the fall of Ngo Dinh Diem. He did not trust Thieu who was a Catholic, nor Ky whom he considered incompetent.

Thich Tri Quang happened to come from the same village in Central Vietnam that earlier had produced Ngo Dinh Diem and the skilled Communist military leader, Vo Nguyen Giap. Although fairly youthful (42 in 1965), he had a great following among our country's Buddhists from 1963 to 1966, especially among the youth.

Quang was in opposition to all regimes from Diem's on, so he was incorrectly characterized as a Communist by all of them. About the only senior official he trusted in government was the First Corps commander, General Nguyen Chanh Thi.

In my opinion, Thieu had considerable ability and was a hard worker, but too inflexible in his attitude toward Communists. The idea of making contact with a Communist was so abhorrent to him that he even lost chances to negotiate with perfectly loyal nationalists because they seemed to favor a leftist position.

Ky was as lazy as Thieu was industrious and was not at all ready to be premier of a sovereign nation. He told me at about this time, "I took this job because nobody else wanted it. I don't know anything about governing a country. I've never had any experience in civilian government. I've been in military service all my life."

Ky tried to make up in bluster what he lacked in ability. When he first came to power, he had the army erect five poles with sandbags behind them in a very prominent place near the Saigon market and railway station. He told me that he intended these for public executions of five "enemies of the state." I told him, "This might be a good idea if you pick the right men. The people have been waiting for such strong medicine for a long time. Be sure you include at least one corrupt businessman, a public servant who has been taking bribes, a crooked army officer, a province chief who exploits the people, and some official who has been dealing traitorously with the Communists."

This grandstand play came to nothing and the poles were used to shoot a single Chinese businessman, Ta Vinh, and a couple of Viet Cong who had been under a death sentence for a long time.

The Buddhists organized many demonstrations in Saigon with the help of Colonel Pham Van Lieu, the chief of police, and in Da Nang with the help of General Nguyen Chanh Thi, Commander of the 1st Corps. They were demanding more privileges for their religion and adoption of a new constitution.

I met with Thich Tri Quang several times. He was more of a

172

revolutionary leader than a priest, so he wanted me to organize a coup to overthrow Thieu and Ky. This, of course, I could not consider because I had no power base, being already retired from the army. He thought there was a possibility that the 1st Corps under General Thi would follow us, but the idea lacked practicality. Then a strange thing occurred.

Thich Tri Quang did not have total leadership over all the Buddhists. In fact they were rather deeply divided themselves. Another bonze, Thich Tam Chau, a fanatic anti-Communist and a northerner like Ky, had a great deal of influence and was quite active. Chau joined forces with Ky against his fellow monk, Thich Tri Quang. Feeling abandoned, Quang went to Hue where he organized resistance, and then to Da Nang in April 1966 to do the same.

Ky sent General Ton That Dinh to take command of this area instead of General Thi and asked me to go there as a delegate of the government, but before I arrived a large demonstration took place in May. Ky sent troops there using American aircraft to retake control of Da Nang and Hue. In the ensuing battle hundreds of Buddhists were killed after several days of fighting. As a further result of this action there were over 6,000 desertions from the 1st Corps and the corps troops became completely disorganized. This, of course, made the NLF very happy and confused our American allies.

After this episode, Ky organized an election to provide an assembly that would have the objective of drafting a new constitution for 1967. This new charter had some strange provisions, one of which effectively pre- vented me from becoming a candidate for the presidency of the Republic since it provided that a candidate had to be of Vietnamese birth. The previous Diem constitution only provided that a candidate had to be a Vietnamese citizen who had lived in the country for ten years. Since I had been born in France, this left me out of the running. Many rumors were being circulated that I should be entered in this forthcoming election, so I think I would have had a good chance for victory.

I felt that I would have been an effective candidate because I was backed rather solidly by the Buddhist activists and continued to be popular in the army. Many people still remembered my role in overthrowing Ngo Dinh Diem and felt sorry for me because of my treatment at the hands of the Young Turks in 1964. When I ran for senator, my candidacy gained the

173

greatest number of votes in the entire country, and since we all were running at large, I believe this to be indicative of my popularity.

Both Thieu and Ky were presidential candidates in September 1967, but it was decided by a secret military committee above the constitution that Thieu would run for president and Ky for vice president. The election was to be entirely free and open, so several candidates emerged. The Americans watched the entire political campaign closely and enlisted their Phoenix pacification program personnel to help get out the vote, preferably for some other candidate than Thieu. One of these was the obscure Saigon lawyer, Truong Dinh Dzu, who ran on a peace campaign. Dzu had been in prison previously under the Diem regime and was released at the time of our coup in 1963. The American sub-rosa campaign for Dzu bore fruit, however, and surprised all of us since he was the runner-up to Thieu who won with only about 35 percent of the vote. This was enough and Thieu and Ky proceeded to form what we called the Second Republic. They chose Nguyen Van Loc, a pro-Ky attorney as their premier. I must add in passing that I was elected to our senate in this same election.

Since there was definite friction at this time between Thieu and Ky, Loc had to be very flexible in performing his functions. He tried without success to reorganize the new government, but he was suspected by Thieu as being Ky's man. Both Thieu and Ky wanted power, but Thieu had seized it, and there was not much that Ky could do about it. Another big problem to face Loc was the Communist Tet offensive of February 1968 which was one of the turning points of the war.

I will not cover this enemy action in any detail because other books cover it so well, notably Don Oberdorfer's *Tet*. We all know how the Communists, taking advantage of the Tet holiday and the cease-fire previously agreed on, launched simultaneous surprise attacks against literally all the cities south of the 17th parallel. This was to be the start of a general uprising where the people, longing for a chance to overthrow the government and end the war, would do just that. What occurred was exactly the reverse. In not one city in South Vietnam did the people go over to the side of the NLF. Instead, they did everything possible to help both the Vietnamese and American armies expel the attackers.

The Communists in their ambitious attacks gained tactical surprise and were successful initially in their military objectives. They were not as successful as they might have been, however, because many NLF cadres inside the various cities whose mission it was to guide them either did not meet them at prearranged times and places or were unfamiliar with the city streets and thus got the attackers lost. This is what happened in Dalat where I and my family had gone to celebrate the Tet holidays.

The first attack there was on an American airfield nearby where the Viet Cong cut the barbed wire and entered with explosives. Normally, the guards would have opened fire and prevented destruction of the aircraft, but a truce had been proclaimed throughout the country and they felt they had to go to higher headquarters to report and get instructions.

A similar thing happened at Vietnamese General Staff Headquarters near Tan Son Nhut airport. The Viet Cong infiltrated the compound and approached some guards and yelled at them, "A coup is in progress, and we are taking over." This had happened so many times before that the guards smiled and admitted them, whereupon the Communists shot them, gaining control of part of our headquarters compound.

They also infiltrated the American headquarters compound nearby, but a Military Police jeep on patrol came by. They stupidly opened fire on the MPs, alerting the Americans. Had they managed to penetrate the operations center which was their objective, they might have been able to paralyze the whole direction of the war.

The hero of the day was our flamboyant vice president, Nguyen Cao Ky, who went on public radio to warn the army and the people that these were true Viet Cong attacks, not any kind of coup. His decisive action served to rally the people to resist the Communist aggression.

Thousands of words have been written to the effect that the Tet offensive was a success for the Communists. In fact, it was both a political and military defeat. They took a political beating because of the failure of the populace to side with them, and a military drubbing because of the terrible slaughter inflicted on them, as many as 60,000 troops lost. Their initial tactical success could not be sustained because the people did not rally to them.

I suppose one can congratulate them for planning and executing such a vast and initially successful military operation, but this is poor recompense

175

for the thousands of casualties they suffered at our hands. This was one of the times in the entire history of the war when they were so hurt that the initiative passed to us.

The big defeat that hit our side was psychological, not in Vietnam, but back in the United States. For years, American politicians had told the people that victory was just around the corner, or that a light was beginning to gleam in the tunnel. "How," the American public asked itself, "could the Communists mount such an attack if overall victory is at hand?" From that moment on, despite the obvious military and political reverse of Tet, the heart went out of the American war effort, and the United States government began its disengagement policy.

After the Tet offensive, Nguyen Cao Ky gradually lost power, much like American vice presidents, but remained in the government. Several of his key supporters had been killed in a Communist raid on Saigon during the Tet fighting, and other events transpired which Thieu was able to exploit. His first act was to replace Loc with one of the organization's candidates for president, Tran Van Huong, an honest, aging, and ineffective nationalist. Huong had previously been in the resistance movement against the French, so his appointment seemed a kind of gesture at the time of the newly convened peace talks in Paris between Washington and Hanoi.

Finally, in 1969, Thieu appointed as premier General Tran Thien Khiem who had been abroad performing ambassadorial duties (a kind of exile) from 1964 to 1968. Khiem as premier also performed the duties of minister of interior and picked up the function of defense minister in 1970. He kept all these functions until the fall of the Thieu government in 1975.

Thieu trusted this pro-American general because he was quiet and never made any public declarations. He also trusted the chief of the General Staff, General Cao Van Vien, one of Khiem's close friends, for the same reason that he trusted Khiem: neither was apt to try to overthrow him in a coup. He knew that both were capable of such action if the Americans dictated it, but he felt secure with his American support which persisted until the end.

The overall administration of the country was performed in these days in a terribly routine way. One day early in 1969, during a lunch with Thieu and Khiem, I suggested to them that what might be necessary for the good of the country was a kind of benevolent dictatorship. I thought that the rules of democracy were not very feasible while our country was engaged in a life-or-death struggle. Perhaps such a dictatorship to save the nation, but not to keep them personally in power, might prove effective. Thieu and Khiem smiled at me and said enigmatically, "Don't worry. Just wait and you will see."

What we saw instead of a vigorous dictatorship was what I called "semi-dictatorship." Thieu seemed to work very hard while Khiem and Vien worked routine hours in their ivory towers and pondered the state of the economy while preserving the status quo. They only began to show more vigor when the Americans cut assistance to Vietnam and they had to get other Free World governments to provide direct aid and make investments in our country.

Thieu's biggest problem in trying to govern the nation was his inflexible anti-Communism and his seemingly built-in instinct to take personal offense at well-meant suggestions. He failed to see how constructive criticism could serve to point out errors for correction which would help the overall situation. His choices of men to fill high government posts were often based on the wrong criteria, thus excluding the most honest and capable. If this description of Thieu's administration sounds like my previous views on Ngo Dinh Diem's, this is exactly what I mean to convey.

I think it is appropriate at this time to explain my political activities and what I was trying to achieve through them. As I explained in a previous chapter, when I saw my military career coming to an end during the last few months of Nguyen Khanh's erratic reign, Kim, Xuan, and I organized an import-export business called DOXUKI. Events quickly proved that Xuan and I were not cut out to be businessmen, so he bowed out and I became a silent partner, leaving Kim to run the business, which he did successfully until 1975.

I am not sure exactly what pushed me toward politics; maybe the urgings of many friends; maybe a chance to further serve the country in a new way; and probably a desire to be a little in the limelight. In any event, I decided to run for the Senate as a candidate at large and won a seat in the 1967 election.

Two patriotic organizations were behind me in my political career: Former Students of High Schools of the Saigon-Delta area of which organization I was chairman, keeping this job from 1965 through 1967; and the Freedom Fighters Association where I was also chairman, from 1966 to 1975. This latter group was composed largely of military veterans, but there were also a number of members who were nationalist civilians. Neither of these organizations was a true political party, and they were both resolutely anti-Communist, but not necessarily pro-government.

During the two weeks directly after the Tet offensive, President Thieu absented himself rather mysteriously from his duties, so vice presdient Nguyen Cao Ky took over leadership of the government. He presided each morning at cabinet meetings, with Nguyen Van Loc as prime minister. Ky made a very intelligent move, which unified all of us in government, by inviting many of us legislators, politicians, and military leaders to these cabinet meetings. Having everyone together in the room, with unity clearly showing, Ky was able to make well-informed and rapid decisions to combat the attacking Viet Cong and eliminate the gains they made in the cities.

At one meeting Ky said to the group, "What we need is for one of you with an already good support base like General Don to come up with a unified political group to support the army and the government."

I responded, "That sounds like a wonderful idea, Mr. Vice President, and I think I can do it if the government doesn't interfere with our meetings and rallies. But, if we get harrassed by the police, trying to do this would be worse than useless."

Ky nodded that he understood and said, "You have our blessing. Get your organization started and we'll assure you of governmental support."

So, using my high school youth group and the Freedom Fighters, I contacted a broad spectrum of political activists from all over the country, whose only criterion for membership was that they be non-Communists. We had a first, highly charged meeting in the Academic Music College in Saigon on February 19, 1968, while Viet Cong terrorists were still occupying part of the city. The meeting was highly controversial since so many different political faiths were present, but all in all I would say that it was a successful beginning. I had a very tight budget, but we were able to get transportation from the army and thus had good attendance. We decided to call ourselves the "Popular Front for National Survival."

We had a second larger meeting a short time later on March 10 when I was elected chairman of this party at Rex Theater. Since Ky had supported us in this endeavor, President Thieu was not very happy, so he organized a countergroup called the "Free Democratic Force" which became active on March 30.

Our organization did well, while Thieu's really never got a large following. For a while we tried an alliance with the Free Democratic Force, but this proved quite useless, so I wound up on my own, continuing to lead my popular front.

In the next couple of years I made my position well known through addresses delivered to several audiences. My first important speech was on October 30, 1969, at a commemorative ceremony of the revolution of November 1, 1963. I think the following excerpts show clearly that a different path of action was available to the Vietnamese people and our allies which could well have produced a different result than the fall of our nation to the Communists in 1975. There was still time.

I stated that one of the reasons for the coup against Ngo Dinh Diem in 1963 had to do with our conviction that a Western type of army could not defeat the stealthy guerrillas. I went on,

> We are equally convinced that a corrupt and unjust society, where the rich exploit the poor, where the means of production are in the hands of a minority of foreigners and privileged persons, where the Civil Service Administration is sluggish and decrepit, where the economic, financial and educational systems are unsound or obsolete—such a society will not have a ghost of a chance of surviving the powerful story of the class struggle.

I told the large audience that, in spite of the lack of good faith evidenced by the Communists at the Paris peace talks and the fact that every succeeding government since our overthrow in January 1964 has gone down the same dead-ended road of "unchanged and unconditional alliance with the Western powers," we need not despair. I pointed out that the concept of the Free World is simply a vague association to be modified according to national interests.

> England supports South Vietnam, but at the same time she seeks closer ties with Communist China, a prime mover in the war. France maintains relations with China and Russia at

179

the same time. The United States, the most anti-Communist of countries, is not consistent in its policy; the Truman government inveighed against "the Red menace" and yet forbade General MacArthur to pursue the enemy across the Yalu River in Korea; the Eisenhower government promoted the policy of "containment" of communism but failed to intervene at Dien Bien Phu, leaving the Viet Minh to consolidate their Democratic Republic of North Vietnam and thereby to plunge 30 million innocent people into a bloody fratricidal war unlike any in history; the Kennedy government, in spite of its slogan extolling the "New Frontier," abandoned its nationalist allies in Cuba; and in the U.S., champions and protectors of the Free World, stood by and let tragedy end the Hungarian rebellion.

By tradition we are a fixedly loyal people, and we will never forget the debt we owe the United States for its important contribution in men and money. But through our experience of a thousand years of Chinese domination and a hundred years of French domination, we have become distrustful. China and Russia provide North Vietnam with aid as a master to a slave and yet the North has its own arms factories, an arsenal of modern weapons for its army of "liberation" and a leading role at the Paris talks. As for the South, the U.S. proclaimed that it would assist us on an equal and unselfish basis—but we had no munitions factory and only weapons left over from World War II to defend ourselves against the AK-47 sub-machine guns used by the Communists during the Tet offensive of 1968. In Paris, South Vietnam played second fiddle to its ally, the United States.

I expressed my view forcefully, however, that Americans and other countries in the Free World were not to blame alone for our present deplorable situation; that we Vietnamese had been principally at fault for not seeking to stand on our own feet. But, we now had a chance to take hold of the situation, reevaluate our position, redistribute the wealth of our country for the good of the majority, and establish a regime of progressive

180

socialism, and thus remove ourselves from the "international power game" we were in.

I told them that the so-called "Vietnamization" of the war effort as dictated by the Americans was no panacea in itself; that to "Vietnamize" haphazardly was like "walking blindfolded through a minefield." I went on,

> There is but one way to "Vietnamize." That is to create a Third Force to bring peace without international power-bargaining, to rehabilitate the nation, to develop the country through a vast and truly profound Progressive Socialist revolution.

> A grave illness demands a strong medicine. In this hour of crisis, we cannot afford the illusion of halfway measures. Instead we must commit ourselves without hesitation to the Revolution. To win international support, to secure the existence of Vietnam as a nation, we must radically change our foreign policy. To recapture the people's trust, to prepare for the political fight once peace is restored, the following four objectives must be realized within a period of three to six months:

> 1. Abolish all unpopular tax laws, security measures and political or military regulations.

> 2. Raise as high as possible the standard of living for soldiers, minor government officials, farmers, laborers, and small businessmen through tax exemptions or reductions and through a program of supply and distribution of essential products by the government.

> 3. Lower the standard of living for the rich by imposing a system of progressive taxation, by encouraging the people to denounce fiscal fraud, and by confiscation of dishonestly acquired property.

> 4. Apply a policy of extreme austerity, starting at the top; severely punish any corruption; eliminate waste in the civil service and in the Army.

181

> In refusing the Communists' offer of a coalition government, we cannot expect the NLF to lay down its weapons and participate in elections directly or indirectly controlled by the Free World powers. All one-way policies must be revised to allow inclusion of every political tendency, from extreme left to extreme right. The Army of the Republic must be changed into an army of the People in which the forces of both sides will be assimilated after the departure of Communist and Free World influences.
>
> After the war, political trends will lead to the formation of three pressure groups: one pro-Free World, one pro-Communist and one favoring what we call a policy of "National Survival." I am persuaded that this Third Force will be the strongest, the most numerous, and the decisive element in determining the future of South Vietnam, with an effective guarantee by the world powers . . . .

This speech, was delivered before a large crowd including the local and foreign press, diplomats, members of various political parties, and Thieu's police. In addition, it was sent to the foreign offices of many countries in the Free World and created a rather large stir at the time. In general, it received local approval, but greatly displeased both the Americans and President Thieu.

I still feel that our views on that day were correct, appropriate, and timely. If only someone had listened to us that day!

My next important public address was on May 2, 1970, as Chairman of the Central Committee for the Congress of the Popular Front for National Survival. In the speech I took the line that our party was again taking the lead in the political struggle. I explained that the war had been going on for many years as a confrontation between major powers, with the Vietnamese being used by both sides; that the war had become a "whip of oppression" used by minorities on both sides, North and South, to keep the common people in bondage. I added,

> The road to saving the nation is none but that of settling the war and uprooting all social injustices. If we continue that dialogue of the deaf in Paris, if we pursue a policy of blind

182

alliance with a single world bloc, and I address this comment to North as well as South Vietnam, we only prolong the murderous conflict. As for social injustice, it is a serious sickness and its cure demands strong remedies.

I made a strong appeal for stringent governmental reforms, pointing out again that a third path leading to national survival certainly existed which would accrue to the benefit of the great mass of the Vietnamese people. I conceded that there were within the NLF a number of loyal, nationalist countrymen "not yet unalterably dyed in Communist red" to whom such a third path would appeal. I talked as follows about where the majority stood,

> It is easy to understand the failure of the Communists in their offensive on Tet Mau Than: they did not have the support of the majority of the people. And yet, even with the seemingly overpowering support of American arms and money, the Saigon government is incapable of defeating the Communists. These failures leave no doubt that the Thieu regime, like the NLF, like Hanoi, is only representative of a minority.

I then made the point that one of the leading reasons that the NLF was able to attract the common people was that each succeeding government since 1954 had been "blindly and unconditionally bound to Western powers," relying on the power of the dollar to save us and forgetting that success in a war like this depends on grass-roots support of the people. I pointed out that a third path to national survival need not be neutralist; this is an ambiguous term used by politicans and governments as they wish. Rather, I stated that our third path could be neither victory nor defeat, simply an ending of this war and a movement to a peacetime national prosperity through a stable central government where today's minority pro-American and pro-Communist factions would be on its extremities.

I went on to further explode the myth of "Vietnamization," showing it for exactly what it was, a way for the United States to pull out with a nebulous plan and uncertain support. I stated that this was playing into the Communists' hands.

> The Communists are patiently waiting out the game of Western democracy. They know the Americans will lose patience—they have in fact already begun to do so. Gradually they will withdraw their soldiers; for a while they may keep up their assistance, but how much? and until when? The future of American help is a big question mark. And one day the Communists will know it is time to strike the winning blow. Until then the bullets will continue to fly, Vietnamese will keep on dying.

Through this speech, we of the Popular Front declared a progressive and reform-minded platform of political opposition. Three others were prime movers in our Front: Professor Bui Anh Tuan, Professor Nguyen Xuan Oanh, and Dr. Tran Van Du. Our basic policy was nonalignment with the superpowers on both sides, in the interest of preserving Vietnamese sovereignity.

We did not stand for a coalition government, sharing rule between non-Communist nationalists and the National Liberation Front. Instead, our program was designed to appeal to the non-Communist moderates in the NLF who at this time after the debacle and failure of their Tet offensive seemed to be in a state of open friction with Hanoi. Such a logical coalition of South Vietnamese could have produced a situation of equilibrium, with reforms instituted to help and protect the common people but, of course, in basic accord with our program, not that of the Communists. We felt that we could produce a viable economy, living as one of the many nonaligned countries, receiving aid as necessary from both the Western and Communist superpowers.

I had been given some very pertinent advice by a group of influential Asian diplomats in Washington, D.C., counsel that is relevant to currently emerging countries of the world and equally so to the Vietnam of today. I would like to repeat it here for politicians of this world to ponder and perhaps apply to their own situations:

> —No unqualified alliances with either bloc.
> —Preservation of national identity, avoiding the debasement of national culture through systematic indoctrination,
> —Each nation beginning its own revolution toward an

184

intrinsically native socialism, without having to rely on outside directives or conform to a doctrine conceived by foreign minds, in other times or in political, social, and economic contexts.

—Refrain from ostracizing any particular social class (in other words, allowing no dictatorship by any class or party through elimination of the others).

—Refrain from instituting any personality cults, making a place of honor for all great historical figures from the earliest times to the present, for all the heroes of the nation regardless of their political affiliations.

—In contrast, excluding the cult of all foreign political leaders or ideologues, French, German, American, Russian, British, or Chinese, to avoid confusing the people and thus causing them to forget their origins, their ancestors, or their national heroes.

Kissinger, Presidential Assistant for National Security Affairs and special envoy in peace negotiations.

CHAPTER ELEVEN

Kissinger

Negotiations

At the outset of their discussions of Vietnam, Richard Nixon and Henry Kissinger came to the understanding that the nationalist regime in Saigon and its allies, the United States included, could not win the war against the Communists. Therefore, the newly elected president and his Special Assistant for National Security Affairs decided to direct their efforts to a new policy which Nixon imaginatively christened "winning the peace." This elegant play on words had a certain pleasing rhetoric, but was in reality meaningless. In war, one does not "win the peace" unless he emerges the victor, weapons in hand. Otherwise, he can expect nothing better than to submit to the conditions of the peace as dictated by the enemy.

Such an attitude is, admittedly, defeatist, but it was reinforced by the isolationist tendencies of the majority of United States congressmen and their too-accommodating attitude toward the Communist bloc countries. The violent antiwar protests of a leftist minority, scattered around the country but centered in Washington D.C. and on college campuses, added to the pressures on a government already inclined to withdraw from the "hornet's nest" of Vietnam.

All this, plus his campaign promises, led Nixon to emphasize negotiation rather than military operations. A few sporadic escalations of too short duration served simply as a means of intimidation to stimulate the continuation of the peace talks.

The Communists knew this only too well. The state of international tension and the internal situation of the United States persuaded them that no American president would unleash American military might to crush a tiny country like Vietnam. The use of "the carrot and the stick" tactic was too obvious to really frighten them. Very astutely, they even played along with the game and turned it to their advantage, profiting from the lulls in fighting, when the Nixon administration wanted at any cost to negotiate, to prepare themselves for fresh acts of aggression. They deliberately dragged out the discussions around the conference table, confusing the situation and presenting demands they knew in advance to be unacceptable. And to exacerbate American impatience, they proclaimed their unshakable determination to carry on the war for ten, twenty, or even thirty years or until victory finally was theirs. In the end they had the best of the fight, not because they were the strongest, but merely because they were the toughest and most persevering.

In the area of negotiations Nixon accorded more power to Kissinger than to the State Department. Assured of such authority, unique for his comparative position in the government, the distinguished professor from Harvard directed and executed a secret diplomacy, a somewhat cynical corollary to the open, official diplomacy exercised at the level of the Ministries of Foreign Affairs and the quadripartite conference in Paris.

Nixon and Kissinger judged it necessary to have the cooperation of Communist China and the Soviet Union to quickly wrap up the negotiations with North Vietnam, since those two powers were the source of most of her combat supplies, economic and monetary aid, and political and ideological support. The new Nixon administration believed that other major world problems beyond the Vietnam affair, could also not be regulated without the participation of the two Communist superpowers. Unfortunately these diplomatic jousting matches went on without heed for the interests of the South Vietnamese, who were not consulted beforehand and were presented, late in the game, with a *fait accompli.*

In 1965, Kissinger was a prominent professor at Harvard University, liked and respected by many politicians, but especially by Governor Nelson Rockefeller of New York. Rockefeller recommended him strongly to President Johnson who used him extensively as a consultant on foreign affairs.

The learned Dr. Kissinger visited our country in 1965 and 1966 on fact-finding tours for Johnson and the American State Department. The fundamental Vietnamese policy drawn up by Kissinger resulted from these two visits. They were of relatively short duration, and he returned to

188

Washington on both occasions with quite sour views of us. He was disappointed at the lack of political acumen in the ranks of the Young Turks, a not too surprising fact when one considers their age and what they had been doing all their lives.

He unfortunately missed talking to the experienced non-Communist political leaders who might have been able to show him a different viewpoint from what he received from Thieu and Ky. He did try through Tran Van Tuyen, a well-known Saigon lawyer and politician, to see me, but I was in Dalat at that time and so the proposed interview did not take place. Had I known what an important personage the future Secretary of State was, I would have taken the first plane to Saigon to see him. But, in 1965, I lumped him with the other professors who were at that time coming in droves to Saigon for various kinds of research.

Another missed meeting between Kissinger and me occurred in Paris in 1972. Our mutual friend Jean Sainteny, who knew me well and was well-acquainted with the ideas of my political party, felt that an exchange of viewpoints between the two of us could be useful and instructive because I could have given him better information on our situation than he had available through his own sources. However, Kissinger backed out.

A highly placed intelligence source told me that at the time he was already deeply involved in secret talks with Hanoi and that he did not care to consider other alternatives contrary to his plans. In response to Sainteny's initiative, Kissinger said, "We know who General Don is and we know what he wants." That was a regrettable attitude because I could have provided opinions he did not have: from the representatives of various social levels, and from a large portion of the intellectual elite, as well as from the political leaders of South Vietnam. Ardent patriots, unbiased and nonpartisan, they were ready in that crucial period of our history to work toward reconciliation, harmony, and reconstruction of the country with the nationalist, nonextremist elements of the National Liberation Front. They were prepared to offer solutions that were not only acceptable but beneficial to all parties concerned. Unhappily, their ideas never received a proper hearing or correct interpretation by those in power or by their Washington spokesmen.

The type of secret diplomacy practiced by Kissinger first saw light during the Johnson era, in an early attempt to contact Hanoi secretly in

1967, although the real negotiations did not begin until 1969. Two French-men acted as go-betweens in the incident, Herbert Marcovich, a microbiologist whom Kissinger had met at an international scientific congress, and Raymond Aubrac, an old friend of Ho Chi Minh. In the course of an impromptu journey to Hanoi in July 1967, they made known to Prime Minister Pham Van Dong a proposal made by Kissinger in the name of President Johnson. It encouraged direct talks between the Americans and the North Vietnamese, stipulating a halt to American bombing north of the 17th parallel and the concurrent suspension of shipments of men, arms, and munitions from Hanoi to the Communist insurgents in South Vietnam. Pham Van Dong insisted on an unconditional halt to American air raids and the unilateral retreat of United States troops. An impasse was reached. Kissinger could not even gain an interview with Mai Van Bo, North Vietnamese delegate to Paris, in spite of the urgings of Marcovich and Aubrac.

After the psychological shock of the Tet offensive in February 1968, President Johnson and his government started to lose their enthusiasm for prosecuting the war, despite the severe military and political defeat suffered by the NLF and Hanoi. He reduced the bombing of North Vietnam and relieved General Westmoreland of his command of American troops in the South. He also announced his intention not to seek reelection to the American presidency. All these moves were to be seen by the Communists as a prelude to meeting together to discuss peace and ending the war. Finally on April 3, 1968, Hanoi agreed to negotiate and the talks began in Paris on May 13. Special Ambassador Harriman headed the U.S. delegation while Xuan Thuy represented North Vietnam.

Nothing useful occurred during these bilateral discussions and the respective positions of the parties remained unchanged. A similar situation occurred during the quadripartite talks that succeeded the United States-North Vietnamese discussions on January 25, 1969. Henry Cabot Lodge replaced Harriman after President Nixon's inauguration.

Speaking for the American delegation on February 26, Lodge called for restoration of the demilitarized zone (DMZ); reciprocal withdrawal of all foreign troops from the territory of South Vietnam; immediate liberation of prisoners by both sides; peace extending not only throughout South

Vietnam, but also to Cambodia, Laos, and the whole of Southeast Asia.

Speaking for the South Vietnamese delegation, Pham Dang Lam favored restoration of the DMZ; retreat from the South of North Vietnamese invasion forces; talks between Hanoi and Saigon on future economic and cultural relations; acceptance of the political opposition of the NLF, but within the framework of the constitution of the Republic of South Vietnam and on condition that the NLF renounce the use of force and Communist ideology. Lam also proposed that members of families separated by the partition of Vietnam be permitted to exchange mail and to visit one another occasionally.

Hanoi's delegation, represented by Xuan Thuy, and the NLF, represented by Tran Buu Khiem, called for unilateral withdrawal of American troops and of all forces allied to the Saigon regime; regulation of the internal affairs of South Vietnam according to the political program of the NLF, without foreign interference; formation of a cabinet whose aim would be "restoration of the peace."

The weekly sessions dragged on and frequently degenerated into barren polemics or sharp, bitter invective, especially on the Communist side. The conference started off on a frustrating note, with interminable arguments over the shape of the conference table. This seemed pointless to most foreigners, but in fact, the arguments centered around a matter of principle of capital importance, the validity of the political stature of the participating delegations, their powers and their representativeness. Logically, the two chief delegations could be none other than the ones from the North and the South. The American delegation, representing an allied country, could sit only as an adjunct to the Saigon group. By the same token, the NLF could only be a part of Hanoi's delegation. Saigon finally had to accept, under duress, the arrangement of parties around the four-sided conference table, not the logical two-sided table with Vietnamese facing each other and foreign powers attending as observers.

The complications that later arose derived largely from this irrational quadripartite composition and from the preponderant role played in the course of the debates by the Americans and the North Vietnamese. From their mutual acceptance of their function as "leaders" at the official conference table, they were led to undertake secret, bilateral talks. Thus, even before Kissinger's direct intervention, Lodge had already held eleven meetings in private with Xuan Thuy. They were not revealed until much later, in a national address by President Nixon.

Before beginning a more extensive examination of the secret American-Vietnamese negotiations carried on by Henry Kissinger, first with Xuan Thuy, then with Le Duc Tho, it is appropriate to sketch briefly the successive phases of the diplomatic triangle (Washington-Peking-Moscow) under the Nixon Administration, commencing early in 1969.

Its source of inspiration was the policy of the balance of power between the United States, Soviet Russia, and Communist China. These three nations, without voicing it too loudly, were doing their best to avoid the risks of nuclear confrontation. The most conspicuous indication of this was the care taken by the U.S. Air Force to spare the supply routes and logistical bases furnishing Russian and Chinese support to the army of North Vietnam.

President Nixon wanted to exploit the Soviet-Chinese tension born of their ideological discord, their squabbling over leadership of the Communist bloc, and their border disputes. The task of the Americans was, therefore, to show the USSR and Mao's China that each had a need to "make up" with the United States and thereby maintain the equilibrium of world forces. The American position was to act as a catalyst between the two Communist giants.

Psychologically speaking, the surest road to success in this triangular diplomacy lay in first reestablishing relations with China and making the most of her deep but unavowed aspirations to emerge from her isolation and take a seat in the international arena. So China must have been very pleased by the approaches of the Americans and the proposed thawing of relations between the two countries.

After some initial contacts with China between 1955 and 1969, a series of positive moves ensued, highlighted by Kissinger's surprise visit to Peking on July 9 to 11, 1971, and Nixon's visit on February 21 to 28, 1972.

Their discussions with Mao Tse-tung and Chou En-lai about the great problems of the world and Asia finally focused on one preoccupying subject, the war in Vietnam. The United States was counting on mainland China's cooperation in bringing it to a settlement. Chou's trip to Hanoi in April 1972 to reassure the North Vietnamese ally of the real intentions of the United States confirmed the promises of Chinese cooperation.

Renewed contact with the USSR got under way with a continuing series of interviews between Kissinger and Anatoly Dobrynin, Russian ambassador to Washington. They were leading up to a planned Soviet-American summit conference aimed at resolving the problems peculiar to the two superpowers.

Kissinger's April 19, 1972, trip to Moscow, then the Nixon-Brezhnev summit meetings, May 22–29, 1972, marked the essential steps in the Washington-Moscow rapprochements. The deliberations in Moscow covered a wide field: nuclear arms limitation, European security, NATO and the Warsaw Pact, the Berlin Pact, the Middle East and Arab-Israeli conflicts, trade and credit, scientific and technological cooperation, and obviously, the war in Vietnam.

Russian help in putting a rapid end to the Vietnam affair was asked. This meant a reduction in their military aid to the North Vietnamese and advising them to relax their attitude at the conference table in Paris. Although Brezhnev promised Soviet cooperation in this regard, he was a wily diplomat. He kept his future options open and justified his position to American and world opinion by declaring to Nixon and Kissinger that beyond certain limits he could no longer intercede because North Vietnam was a "free and sovereign" nation.

I was in a particularly advantageous position for a balanced, overall view of Kissinger's secret negotiations with Xuan Thuy and Le Duc Tho. My official functions and political activities required many contacts and assignments abroad. Additional information had been provided me by several high-ranking sources, Vietnamese and Western alike. One of these sources was Hoang Duc Nha, cousin and special advisor to Nguyen Van Thieu, while another was my old friend Jean Sainteny who acted as a contact between the Americans and North Vietnamese. Deeply involved in the talks with Kissinger and General Alexander Haig which shortly preceded the signing of the Paris Accords of January 27, 1973, Nha gave me an insight in depth into their substance, their evolution, and their outcome.

Four aspects are particularly important in the study of secret negotiations between the Americans and the North Vietnamese: their length, rhythm, and interruptions; the gradual increase in American concessions to Hanoi's demands; the chaotic end of the secret negotiations; and the irrationality of certain clauses in the Paris agreement.

The secret American-North Vietnamese negotiations stretched over a period of more than four years, from April 4, 1969, to January 13, 1973.

The duration of the secret talks and the long interruptions show that they unfolded under distressing and laborious conditions, due partly to the profound differences between the negotiators and partly to disruption by acts of aggression or reprisal.

Kissinger earned himself a world wide reputation for his cleverness in veiling his discreet encounters. He frequently threw the newshounds off the scent, leaving puzzled newspaper and television writers, cameramen, and interviewers behind. The surprise visits to China and Russia, his abrupt departures from Washington, his unexpected comings and goings in London, Islamabad, Paris and the Parisian suburbs (Choisy-le-Roy, Gif-sur-Yvette, Neuilly-sur-Seine) all combined to help him acquire some interesting nicknames. In Saigon, the local press gave him two quite suggestive and colorful ones: "the Midnight Diplomat" and "the King of Camouflage."

His first conversation with Xuan Thuy was arranged for April 4, 1969, at the private home of Jean Sainteny, who had lent his good offices to the previous transmission of a personal message from Nixon to Ho Chi Minh. I learned of it accidentally as I was passing through Paris in September 1969.

At a lunch given by Sainteny for me and his old Indochina comrade Colonel Demaison, our host inadvertently spoke of his "friends" Kissinger and Xuan Thuy, without, however, letting slip any reference to their ultra-secret meeting. That did not prevent my seeing through his reference and suspecting the reason for his earlier rejection of my invitation to lunch in Washington. In all probability he was anxious to avoid compromising contacts with personalities from Saigon.

Kissinger had some good ideas at first, suggesting to Nixon a new format which he hoped would pull the Paris negotiations out of their state of stagnation. To begin with, Hanoi and Washington would be involved only in discussions of military problems, leaving the settling of political concerns to Saigon and the National Liberation Front. An international conference would be convened to enforce the accords, when worked out, and a multination force functioning in the field and endowed with sufficient men and equipment to ensure respect for the cease-fire would be established. Lodge was instructed to completely divorce military questions from political ones.

Unfortunately, these initial objectives were subsequently abandoned, due in part to North Vietnam's fixed propensity to couple military and political issues, and in part to American impatience to be done with the whole Vietnam business. Greater and greater appeasements to the Communists resulted, with a deplorable infringement by the United States of the sovereign rights of South Vietnam.

Military concessions were concerned primarily with the withdrawing or restationing of foreign troops in South Vietnam by the United States and North Vietnam, the cessation or suspension of combat operations, and finally the cease-fire. The halts in bombing of the North, called on several occasions by the American command with the purpose of encouraging a more accommodating attitude on the part of the enemy, produced no lasting or reliable effects.

The greatest concession made by the United States had to do with the withdrawal of American troops without a similar removal of Hanoi's soldiers from the South. The Johnson administration opted for removal of United States forces six months after North Vietnamese soldiers had returned north. At the start, Nixon spoke of a mutual and simultaneous pullout of forces, but later modified his stand, permitting Hanoi's troops to stay in place after American troops had departed.

The cease-fire agreement that would have made the greatest sense from both the South Vietnamese and American viewpoint, if the latter really wanted to preserve us as an independent nation, was to regroup the forces of both sides out of the combat areas and develop demilitarized zones. This was carried out in most of Vietnam after the 1954 Geneva Accords. The same stipulation produced an effective truce after the Arab-Israeli War of October 1973.

What occurred was a cease-fire in place, rather like a policeman interrupting a robber holding up a candy store. Under the principle agreed to by the United States, the law enforcement officer would leave the robber pointing his weapon at the frightened store owner instead of hauling him off to jail in handcuffs.

195

I had, of course, no direct role in any negotiations. My work consisted of behind-the-scenes meetings with people we thought could help us, such as Jean Sainteny, French Foreign Minister Schuman, and Deputy Minister Froment-Morice, an expert in Asian affairs. I tried to sell these distinguished French diplomats on our proposal for limited demilitarized zones, but even though they appeared to agree with me, they had no success in convincing the North Vietnamese. This is understandable, of course, because Hanoi had already made some real progress in getting the United States negotiators to agree with their viewpoint. Furthermore, North Vietnam did not want to have to reveal officially the inescapable fact that they had many regular troops operating against us.

Politically, Kissinger gradually made greater concessions to the North Vietnamese delegates in these secret negotiations, equally as damaging to South Vietnam as the military concessions had been. The proposed mutual withdrawal of troops was initially tied to a move to pressure Saigon to accept a political compromise. Agreeing finally to the total withdrawal of American forces, the United States then in a reversal of policy agreed that President Thieu would resign one month before general elections in South Vietnam and that the United States would observe absolute neutrality in them. Little by little, concession by concession, Le Duc Tho induced Kissinger to accept his mounting political demands, so compromising to South Vietnam's future.

These long and arduous negotiations finally resulted in the Paris Accords of January 27, 1973, the document so keenly hoped for by the Nixon Administration. The timing of the drafting and signing of the cease-fire agreement, anticipated as far back as October 1972, contributed greatly to ensuring Nixon's landslide vote in the presidential election of November 3, although Kissinger denied there was any connection.

In arriving at that pact, Kissinger and Le Duc Tho, its foremost artisans, had to go through several series of meetings, broken off and resumed according to the cycle of combat and truce on the battlefield. The Communists were still hoping to achieve an easy victory over the Army of Vietnam, which, since Vietnamization began, was receiving nothing more from the Americans than logistical support. The withdrawals of U.S. combat troops were expected to weaken the capabilities of Saigon's Army enormously, so, on March 31, 1972, North Vietnam launched a large-scale operation, similar to the 1968 Tet offensive, hitting on several fronts, especially at Quang Tri, Hue, Kontum, and An Loc. This provoked a vigorous response from Nixon. On April 15 he ordered a massive B-52 bombardment of the cities of Hanoi and Haiphong and of diverse military targets above the 17th parallel.

The fall of Quang Tri, a province bordering on the DMZ, on May 1, 1972, redoubled the Communists' desire to seek a settlement by force and hardened their intractability at the conferences, both official and secret. Meeting with Kissinger the day after the Communist entry into Quang Tri, Le Duc Tho proved less inclined than ever to cooperate. He demanded the immediate resignation of Nguyen Van Thieu and his whole team and the establishment in its place of a coalition government. On May 8, Nixon answered by mining the North's harbors and coastline and bombing enemy roads, railways, and river navigation routes.

Quang Tri Province was retaken by our government troops in a well-coordinated joint operation of airborne, marine, and ranger units which took some seven weeks to complete. We were aided by American air cover, but the ground operation was entirely Vietnamese. The North Vietnamese fired their largest caliber artillery against our troops from above the 17th parallel, but this did not prevent our successful completion of our mission.

Our counteroffensive showed the world and especially our adversaries that we were capable of effective combat action and could not be overcome summarily. Signs to resume negotiations from the enemy side began to appear and on the advice of the USSR, following the Nixon-Brezhnev summit conference of May 22 to 26, Hanoi returned to the conference table on August 1. The talks continued at an accelerated pace, winding up on October 10, 1972, with a draft of an agreement provisionally endorsed by Kissinger and Le Duc Tho. It remained to be submitted for the approval of the American and North Vietnamese governments and accepted by Saigon.

A tentative timetable of implementation was set up:

October 21: End of mining of ports and American bombing in North.

October 22: Signing of the draft agreement in Hanoi by

197

	Tho and Kissinger, after the latter had obtained Thieu's assent on its contents.
October 30:	Signing of the pact in Paris by the North Vietnamese Foreign Minister and the American Secretary of State.
October 30:	Immediate cease-fire in place throughout the territory of South Vietnam.

Saigon building constructed as conference site for Colombo Plan Conference, used as Senate of Vietnam from 1967 to 1975.

CHAPTER TWELVE

Too Much
Taken for Granted

On October 18, 1972, Kissinger went to Saigon to present the draft peace plan to Thieu. With him he took several civilian and military officials whose degree of prestige was supposed to impress the South Vietnamese leaders. These included General Creighton Abrams, Chief of Staff of the Army and former U.S. Commander in Vietnam, Philip Habib, Ambassador to South Korea and former political advisor to the U.S. delegation at the Paris peace conference, and the commander in chief of the American forces in the Pacific, Admiral Noel Gaylor.

The first meeting was held from 11 A.M. to 12:45 P.M. on October 19 in the military operations room adjoining Thieu's presidential office in Independence Palace. In that room bursting with maps, statistics, and telephones linking him directly to the corps and division commanders, Nguyen Van Thieu himself conducted the debate for the Vietnamese side. Kissinger's retinue was joined by Ambassador Bunker and General Frederick Weyand, Abrams's successor as American commander in Vietnam. Beside Thieu sat Vice President Tran Van Huong, Prime Minister Tran Thien Khiem, Foreign Affairs Minister Tran Van Lam, Deputy Foreign Minister Nguyen Phu Duc, South Vietnamese Ambassador to Washington Tran Kim Phuong, Ambassador Pham Dang Lam (chief of the South Vietnamese delegation in Paris), Chief of General Staff Cao Van Vien, and Hoang Duc Nha, special advisor to the president.

Kissinger made a five-point presentation of the proposed accord and concluded that in adhering to the accord, Saigon ran no risks. He emphasized that Thieu would retain power and affirmed that American military and economic assistance would continue. He gave Thieu the English text of the draft but withheld from him the timetable he and Tho worked out for the signing.

Thieu undoubtedly was offended at being the last man consulted and then having no real voice because the matter was already decided. Nevertheless, he did not openly display his resentment. He remained impassive, wearing his courteous smile, and promised only a careful study of the draft before giving his opinion.

Kissinger did not, however, get what he had bargained for, largely because he failed to accurately appreciate the psychology of the Asiatic. Characteristically, the Asian prefers to avoid direct confrontation, especially upon first contact with a stranger. The refinement and courtesy of his welcome are no key to his interior reflections, which take time to express themselves. Kissinger, accustomed to conversing privately with Le Duc Tho and Xuan Thuy, had known only their "Communist" reactions, and not authentic "Vietnamese" responses. Moreover, during the long months they had been meeting, the ambiance of fraternity that usually permeates relationships between partners in any secret understanding had sprung up among them. He was totally unaware that even those in the capital of the South who seemed at first to accede to anything in order to save their official positions could, when the time was at hand, utter an obstinate "No" to his injunctions.

Thieu gave Hoang Duc Nha the English version and instructed him to analyze it and give a full report on it that same afternoon before the National Security Council. Nha spent three hours dissecting the text and collecting such information as might be relayed to him by teletype from Paris and Washington concerning the secret meetings between Kissinger and Le Duc Tho.

The Council met at 5 P.M. The Vietnamese side delineated 26 separate points in the English version which required clarification. Thieu was especially concerned with the National Council of Reconciliation and Concord referred to in several clauses as an "administrative structure." The Vietnamese translation of that phrase *(co cau hanh chanh)* could be very easily confused with the related expression "governmental structure" *(co cau chanh quyen)* which would mean a sort of coalition government in disguise. Thieu suspended the session, deciding that he had better ask for explanations from Dr. Kissinger and at the same time request the Viet-

202

namese translation of the document. Special Presidential Counselor Nha contacted Ambassador Bunker who promised him a satisfactory answer by the next day.

At 7 P.M., Kissinger returned to the palace with Bunker. Although Thieu spoke fluent English, he asked Kissinger several questions in Vietnamese, probably to make the meetings more formal, which Nha translated as he went along. The questions centered on three points of principle, as follows:

The draft mentioned the "three nations of Indochina" and three Vietnams. However, since 1954, four countries had existed on the Indochinese peninsula, not just *de facto* but *de jure*, as sanctioned by the Geneva Convention and through diplomatic recognition by many nations on every continent. These four nations were North Vietnam, South Vietnam, Laos, and Cambodia. Conversely, there could in no way be discussion of "Three Vietnams" since the National Liberation Front as a puppet of Hanoi could not pretend to represent a second state south of the 17th parallel.

What significance was to be attributed to the expression "administrative structure" used to designate the National Council of Reconciliation and Concord?

What would happen to the North Vietnamese soldiers stationed in the South when the document went into effect?

Kissinger answered the first point by saying it was a typographical error. As for the Council, it could not be anything more than an administrative body, and should not be mistaken for a camouflaged form of coalition government. He added that in any case Thieu would retain veto power over all deliberations of that body. Finally, he said, South Vietnam with a standing army 1,100,000 strong would have nothing to fear from the presence of 140,000 members of North Vietnamese units stationed on its territory.

Thieu thought it necessary to have these essential and potentially controversial points cleared up by a committee comprised of both Vietnamese and Americans, before moving on to the details of other clauses of the draft. Kissinger then suggested that the meetings be limited to four participants, Thieu and Nha for the Vietnamese side and Bunker and himself for the Americans.

The Thieu-Kissinger talks had scarcely begun when the Communists

203

made their presence felt. On October 20, they attacked on a wide front. This act of deliberate aggression entered into Hanoi's strategy in direct consequence of the secret calendar concluded between Kissinger and Tho. The attacks were timed to coincide with the assignment of 10,000 Communist cadres at various echelons to take charge of the South Vietnamese government as soon as the cease-fire agreement went into effect and the Thieu government fell in accord with the Kissinger-Tho secret protocols.

The hesitation and protests of Thieu upset Hanoi's premature arrangements. As a consequence, many of the 10,000 advance cadres were arrested.

Despite the furious battles going on, the committee established at Thieu's behest met the same day, October 20, at the official residence of the Minister of Foreign Affairs, Tran Van Lam, a Catholic, who proposed an opening prayer: "May God bless this meeting between the representatives of the Republic of South Vietnam and Dr. Kissinger!"

Nha set forth in order the 26 points requiring elucidation, emphasizing the existence of four, and not three, sovereign states in Indochina, the proposed National Council of Reconciliation, the reestablishment of the DMZ, and the withdrawal of Hanoi's troops from South Vietnam, Laos, and Cambodia. North Vietnam had used both Laos and Cambodia as an avenue for men, weapons, and ammunition, and as a practically inviolable sanctuary and weapons storehouse.

Kissinger countered, as usual, with evasive and unconvincing explanations. In speaking of the presence of Hanoi's Communist troops, he reminded the Vietnamese delegation of the advisability of looking at things from a more realistic instead of theoretical point of view.

The Vietnamese side responded that the document presented by Dr. Kissinger was marred by faults and weaknesses in its substance and full of confusion and errors in its form. The mistake Kissinger called typographical, recurring twice in the same text, the Vietnamese insisted, could not have been involuntary, but had to have been consciously committed to paper. Nha exploded in anger and charged that in its current composition, the Kissinger plan had to be unacceptable to the Nguyen Van Thieu government. Tension was mounting visibly, so Foreign Minister Lam suggested that the meeting be adjourned, and Kissinger returned to the American Embassy.

In the afternoon of October 20, Dr. Kissinger received a telephone call

204

from the United States Ambassador to Laos and Arnaud de Borchgrave, a *Newsweek* senior correspondent who had just returned from interviewing Prime Minister Pham Van Dong in Hanoi. According to the North Vietnamese leader, an accord between Hanoi and Washington had already been reached, the American POWs would be freed before the complete withdrawal of United States forces, and a coalition government would be constituted—without the participation of Thieu, considered to be already out of the picture. Borchgrave informed Kissinger that the interview would be published in the next issue of the weekly magazine.

Meanwhile, President Thieu learned from his intelligence aides that a timetable for the signing of the draft agreement had effectively been drawn up by Kissinger and Tho in Paris.

To delay Kissinger and Tho's secret maneuver, Thieu decided to avoid a new encounter with Kissinger. An emergency meeting was called at the presidential palace of all the generals in command of army corps and divisions and the colonels in charge of the provinces to study the measures to be taken in view of the gravity of the military situation. When Ambassador Bunker phoned trying to obtain a personal interview for Kissinger with Thieu for that evening, Special Counselor Nha replied that it was impossible, the president was tied up in conference with his commanders.

Kissinger, anxious to forewarn Thieu of *Newsweek's* coming revelations and to dispel any misunderstandings resulting from them, insisted on being received without delay. Nha repeated to him the recent conversation with Bunker. Kissinger said, "I am the envoy of the President of the United States, not an errand boy. I insist on seeing President Thieu tonight."

Nha replied calmly but firmly, "Don't take offense, I never considered you an errand boy. The president cannot see you and it truly is because of the meeting with the military chiefs. It will last for hours."

In an attempt to keep his promises to Le Duc Tho, Kissinger had to cable Hanoi proposing an adjustment to the previously arranged schedule. Now the bombing and mining would end on October 23, the preliminary signature of the agreement in Hanoi would take place on October 24, and the final signing in Paris on October 31. Hanoi sent a telegram of agreement, but they warned Kissinger against any further changes.

Borchgrave arrived in Saigon and sought an interview with Thieu in order to make *Newsweek's* publishing deadline, but Nha opposed the

205

request. Discovering that frequently difficult missions abroad had been entrusted to me by the president, Borchgrave came to see me and ask my help so that the two interviews with Dong and Thieu could be published in the same issue. In our conversation he spoke of the Hanoi leaders' inflexible attitude toward the negotiations. Dong had told Borchgrave that it was up to the Americans to make concessions if they wanted to recover their prisoners. I tried to arrange a meeting between Borchgrave and Thieu but the latter refused, so the *Newsweek* article never appeared.

Borchgrave had witnessed an incident which pointedly depicted the harshness of the North Vietnamese regime. One day the Russian director of the Tass News Agency came to the Agence France Presse bureau in Hanoi. Some officials had done something to upset him and he was in a blind rage, waving his arms and shouting in French, "This country is still at the Stalinist stage. Worse than that—they're trying to out-Stalin Stalin!"

In Borchgrave's opinion, "It would be astonishing if Thieu agreed to sign the agreement that Pham Van Dong disclosed to me as it stood when I interviewed him on October 18."

Meeting with Nha, Thieu asked his special assistant not to vent his feelings as he had done in the previous meeting. "I don't think," he reportedly said, "that Kissinger was trying to dupe us with the plan he brought to Saigon. He must have been tricked by Tho."

Hoping to finish up the talks in Saigon quickly, Kissinger suggested another meeting with Thieu at 10 A.M. on October 21.

The climate of suspicion and resentment which had hung over the deliberations of the day before persisted. However, Thieu and Kissinger did their best to control themselves and be polite throughout the debates.

Thieu began with the same three basic questions:

Was the National Council for Reconciliation and Concord actually a cover for a coalition government?

What did the phrase "three Vietnams" signify?

Why was no mention made of North Vietnamese troop withdrawals?

Kissinger answered that the misunderstanding about the Council would be cleared up in a future session with North Vietnam's Tho. As for Hanoi's 140,000 men, they could not pose a serious threat to South Vietnam's army of 1,100,000 backed by the Americans. Kissinger offered to make an effort to get Hanoi to pull out several of its divisions in the South if that was what Thieu wanted. Thieu declined to settle for a vague verbal promise, declaring that it would have to be put in writing in the document.

Thieu also said he wished to defer his response until after consultation with the National Security Council. Dr. Kissinger proposed a new meeting at the palace at 8:00 the next morning, October 22.

As soon as the meeting started, Thieu stated he could not approve the peace plan because of the 26 ambiguous points insufficiently clarified by Dr. Kissinger. He insisted that the ratification of this agreement would be an intolerable negation of the sacrifices of thousands of Vietnamese and Americans in their common defense of liberty.

Rather than burning his bridges behind him, however, Thieu pledged to develop some other peace proposals after serious open discussions with the enemy, instead of working through secret negotiations or articles in the press. Without consulting his military commanders, he even let it be understood that he would, if absolutely necessary, consent to a standstill cease-fire. He asked Kissinger to visit him at 5:00 that evening after his return to South Vietnam from Phnom Penh.

Thieu was offering a very grave concession, one that had originally been suggested to President Nixon by Henry Kissinger, probably because of something Le Duc Tho had said. At that time Thieu did not quite realize the deadly risks to South Vietnam if a cease-fire in place were allowed. If the enemy forces were not regrouped into strictly defined zones, how could we be sure that the mutual commitments of the armistice agreement would be honestly observed all across the country?

After the Thieu-Kissinger talks, Prime Minister Tran Thien Khiem and Foreign Minister Tran Van Lam were contacted by Deputy Ambassador Charles Whitehouse and Deputy Assistant Secretary of State for East Asian Affairs William H. Sullivan. They suggested that it would be best not to defy the Americans nor to totally reject their proposals.

Whitehouse was exceedingly active in efforts to persuade not only Khiem and Lam, but other government officials including senators, deputies, and members of religious and political groups. He said to me, "This agreement has its good side. It must be signed. It is only a piece of paper and will change nothing. You'll see!"

In spite of all the persuasion, Thieu persisted. A less firm position would have led to Thieu's downfall, and his replacement by a coalition government. Thus, Thieu's foes reasoned, Thieu's firmness was dictated not only by the fear of losing his fatherland but also by the fear of being deprived of his official position.

While Kissinger was in Phnom Penh, Thieu assured his associates and the large number of members of parliament he had assembled at the palace that he would never permit the formation of a disguised coalition government.

Other high-ranking officials, including Foreign Minister Tran Van Lam and General Cao Van Vien, discreetly said that South Vietnam was being abandoned by the Americans. Special Advisor Hoang Duc Nha was the only one who applauded Thieu's decision to reject the American peace plan.

At 5 P.M. on Sunday, October 22, Kissinger and Thieu met at the palace. Bunker and Nha were also in attendance. Thieu announced his refusal to sign the accord as it was currently written. It would require substantial revision before it would be acceptable. While Thieu had his back turned looking at some maps on the wall, Kissinger said to Nha: "The President has chosen to act the martyr, but he hasn't got what it takes! If we have to, the United States can sign a separate peace treaty with Hanoi. As for me, I'll never set foot in Saigon again. Not after this. This is the worst failure of my diplomatic career!"

"We are so sorry," answered Nha, "but you must remember that we have our country to defend!"

Thieu, turning around, asked Kissinger to communicate his fears to Nixon. He pointed at the maps and said, "What does it matter to the United States to lose a small country like South Vietnam? We're scarcely more than a dot on the map of the world to you. If you want to give up the struggle, we will fight on alone until our resources are gone, and then we will die. The United States' world policy dictates that you dance lightly with Moscow and Peking, that you make different choices to follow your new strategies. But for us, the choice is between life and death. For us to put our signature to an accord which is tantamount to surrender would be accepting a death sentence, because life without liberty is death. No, it's worse than death!"

Kissinger proposed a final audience, to last about 45 minutes, on Monday before he was to leave for Washington. He emphasized the advisability of revealing nothing to the press in order to prevent the spread of alarming and distorted rumors. So at 8 A.M. on October 23, Kissinger returned to the palace. He was counting on the intense pressure put on Thieu's people by the American Embassy to effect an abrupt about-face from the Saigon leader.

Changing his tactics, Kissinger reassuringly told Thieu that there was no need for him to worry because President Nixon was certain to be reelected.

"Please sign the accord. If they violate it, we will launch an operation into North Vietnam."

"But where?" Thieu queried. "A landing or an invasion through the 17th parallel?"

Kissinger replied: "In the region just north of the DMZ."

Thieu disagreed with Dr. Kissinger, saying, "To be effective, the landing should be in the vicinity of Vinh."*

To this statement, Kissinger made no further comment and the conversation ended with no real agreement between the two men.

In a subsequent meeting with his generals, President Thieu casually referred to Dr. Kissinger's commitment.

Lon Nol was the other Chief of State in Indochina Kissinger had to convince of the advisability of signing the Paris agreement.

A high-ranking Cambodian personality later told me that during his meeting with President Lon Nol, Kissinger behaved as if President Thieu had fully endorsed the accords. A smiling Lon Nol ordered champagne to be served. "Peace is at last coming. We are going to drink to it and to compliment Dr. Kissinger on his mission," Lon Nol said.

In an effort to square his "inflexible" policy with Dr. Kissinger's visit to Saigon, President Thieu addressed the nation on television on Tuesday, October 24. Thieu denounced the secret United States-Hanoi negotiations and the unacceptable clauses of the peace plan presented for his approval. He reaffirmed his opposition to the establishment of a coalition government in any guise and to the continued presence of Communist troops in the South.

His speech was received with mixed feelings within and outside South

---

*Vinh is a locality about 200 miles north of the 17th parallel and 180 miles south of Hanoi.

Vietnam. On October 25 at the palace, elected officials from the national to the provincial level turned out in full force to join a demonstration of support for the president.

For his part, North Vietnam's Premier Pham Van Dong on October 26 released the text of the draft agreement reached with Kissinger and the timetable for its preliminary and official signings. He tongue-lashed the Nixon administration for failing to keep its bargain and accused it of using the talks solely for electoral gain.

The revelations from Saigon and Hanoi forced Kissinger to hold an impromptu press conference the same day in Washington. He confirmed the existence of the document and the timetable he had concluded with Le Duc Tho. "Although peace is at hand," he said, "the October 31 date prearranged for the signature of the document may be changed, permitting modification of certain details."

Six hours later Le Duc Tho sent a cable to Kissinger from Hanoi with a proposal to take up the study of the plan again at a future date he did not name.

In order to keep closely posted on what might happen in Paris, Thieu asked me to go there. I left on Friday, October 27. In the French capital I found opinion split within Vietnamese, French, and foreign circles. Hope, disappointment, and anticipation were the diverse feelings I noted from reactions to statements issued from Hanoi, Saigon, and Washington. The majority of Vietnamese believed the accord would be signed October 31 despite Thieu's misgivings.

I contacted Jean Sainteny, still regarded at the Elysée as the expert in Vietnamese affairs, Froment-Morice, in charge of Asian affairs at the Quai d'Orsay (the French Foreign Office), and Foreign Minister Maurice Schuman. I wanted to hear their opinions and to learn from them anything that might be of interest to us. I had to explain to each why President Thieu could not approve the peace plan in its current form.

The Vietnamese in Paris for the most part favored the institution of a National Council for Reconciliation and Concord, in other words an understanding between the Saigon regime and the National Liberation Front. They conceded that Thieu was far from being the American stooge the Communists had until now painted him. In those last days of October 1972, he acquired a new stature, but unfortunately it soon faded.

Aircraft of South Vietnamese Air Force in a fly-by over Saigon.

CHAPTER THIRTEEN

Still Talking:

An Ironic Peace

On November 8, 1972, Thieu convened the National Assembly to hear Nha's detailed report on the Tho-Kissinger negotiations and the Kissinger mission in Saigon (October 18–23).

To reassure Thieu that American aid would continue to provide him plenty of resources even in the event of a standstill cease-fire agreement, Nixon flooded South Vietnam with war machinery and munitions, largely resupplying us for what had been expended in the Quang Tri operation. He also sent Thieu a personal letter* developing some new peace proposals. His messenger this time was General Alexander Haig. Accompanied by Ambassador Bunker, Haig had two conversations with Thieu. Besides the assurances of American espousal of South Vietnam's cause, Haig imparted an implicit warning from the newly reelected Nixon that a separate peace between Hanoi and Washington could be expected if Thieu maintained too rigid and recalcitrant a stand. Kissinger, too, alluded to such an alternative in a November 14 newspaper interview.

Le Duc Tho met with Kissinger again in Paris between November 20 and 25, and again between December 6 and 13 to preview the entire draft agreement.

I was still in Paris at that time so I was able to follow the evolution of the talks. The Saigon regime had succeeded in getting the head of its delegation, Pham Dang Lam, to the Paris conference where he was briefed by either Kissinger or his aide Sullivan on the topics of the day's discussions. Of course, not everything was disclosed but he learned the essentials. Thus

*A copy of this letter is an appendix to this book.

we found out that Tho had consented to rectify the linguistic errors or ambiguities; to specify to some degree the characteristics of the National Council for Reconciliation and Concord and to eliminate the term "administrative structure" formerly used to designate it; to withdraw five thousand North Vietnamese soldiers stationed in the South as a sign of Hanoi's good faith; and to stop insisting on the resignation of Thieu and his cabinet as a *sine qua non* for a cease-fire. However, the deliberations on the establishment of protocols and agencies for enforcement ended in a standoff.

In the meantime, a government-inspired press campaign was launched against Kissinger in Saigon. He was accused of imposing upon Thieu a kind of capitulation to Hanoi's inordinate demands so that he could win the Nobel Peace Prize or share it with Le Duc Tho. This accusation exasperated Kissinger, and he had Ambassador Bunker express to Special Advisor Nha his vehement protest against these vicious attacks. But Nha replied that there was nothing he could do, South Vietnam being a democratic country where freedom of speech was respected.

Thieu proposed a meeting with Nixon in Honolulu. Nixon said that because of his heavy duties at the beginning of his second term as president, he could not come right away. He preferred to postpone the session until after the signing of the agreement, and at San Clemente rather than at Honolulu.

Thieu then asked Nixon to receive an emissary from Saigon to explain GVN's position. Thieu then asked Nixon to receive an emissary from Saigon to explain GVN's position. Nixon agreed and Thieu then sent his foreign affairs assistant, Nguyen Phu Duc, to Washington—not foreign minister Tran Van Lam. His intention was to underline his resentment at not being able to meet the U.S. president immediately and to show the American and Vietnamese peoples that Washington consulted Saigon on nothing but very ordinary issues, while Kissinger and Le Duc Tho carried on deliberations of an entirely more vital character in Paris.

Nguyen Phu Duc* was a rather low-level functionary who had risen to the rank of ambassador purely through administrative routine. Thieu chose him deliberately, although he did not trust him to show any initiative or make any decisions. Nixon and Kissinger knew this about Thieu's envoy,

---

*Duc later was appointed ambassador to Belgium.

but Kissinger insisted on being on hand for the Nixon-Duc interview.

Duc arrived in Paris on November 25, still not having received exact instructions from Thieu. Thieu wanted to hold off on giving them until he knew the date of the audience with Nixon. In addition, Thieu was stalling for time, hoping to provoke new air raids over North Vietnam, which had become more vulnerable because of a shortage of SAM munitions. According to intelligence reports, Hanoi had perhaps no more than one thousand tactical missiles in stock.

Nixon ordered Kissinger to suspend his sessions with Tho until December 4 and to return to Washington to be present when he met with Duc.

In order to draw up Duc's letter of accreditation to the White House, Nha flew to Paris on November 26 with a blank paper signed by President Thieu. In Paris he gathered the most up-to-date information and wrote the fourteen-page letter which Duc would be given when he left for Washington on November 28.

This message recapped the political line followed by the Republic of South Vietnam in accordance with its 1967 Constitution and the American commitment to provide assistance in the struggle. It also repeated Thieu's vow to subscribe to no peace agreement with the North that did not meet the four basic conditions of:

> No coalition government.
> Retreat of North Vietnamese troops from the South.
> Respect of the neutrality of the DMZ.
> Settlement of political differences to be left to the
>   two Vietnams without foreign meddling.

The letter ended with the reiteration of Thieu's wish to speak personally with Nixon before the conclusion and signing of any cease-fire convention.

Duc received discreet directions to remain as ambiguous as possible to gain time while awaiting developments in the military situation. He was also instructed by Thieu to make Nixon understand Kissinger had overstepped his bounds in the talks with Le Duc Tho. To show his endorsement of Kissinger, Nixon refused to see Duc alone. At two successive meetings arranged for Thieu's special envoy, Secretary Kissinger and General Haig were present from start to finish. Nixon also rejected the proposed summit

215

conference with Thieu. The signing of the accord would evidently be soon, before December 15, General Haig had said when he was in Saigon in mid-November.

When Duc returned, Nha leaked a story to a local newspaper he sponsored, saying that Nixon had given Saigon an ultimatum. His aim was to awaken the conscience of Americans, especially conservatives, to the tragic fate that South Vietnam could expect if her ally concluded a peace agreement clearly damaging to her cause.

The same progovernment newspaper recommended direct negotiations between Saigon and Hanoi as the only way to achieve a fair and final settlement of the remaining political and military problems.

I had had the feeling that the Nixon administration, and particularly Secretary Kissinger, was determined to limit the Paris peace talks to a strict dialogue between Hanoi and Washington.

During each of my visits to Paris during the talks, I was under continual close surveillance by CIA agents. Apparently, they had reason to fear any direct contact between me and the "other side."

Thieu's hope for discord between Nixon and Dr. Kissinger over the matter of the negotiations was dampened when the president officially reaffirmed Kissinger in his White House post. Encouraged by Nixon's publicly expressed confidence, Kissinger pursued the policy he had designed, and showed more esteem for Le Duc Tho than for Thieu. A close associate of former Defense Secretary Melvin Laird told me recently that he thought Kissinger amoral since he had been sure since 1965 that South Vietnam would not survive.

Could this gloomy conviction have been at the root of some secret pact between him and Tho for the swift annihilation of the United States's bothersome ally, South Vietnam? Did it, directly or indirectly, inspire Nixon's declaration in February 1973 that "peace will be reestablished little by little in Indochina and Vietnam will be united?" This statement was made by Nixon shortly after a Kissinger trip to Hanoi which received absolutely no publicity. Few people paid attention to that prophetic opinion of yesterday which is today's raw reality.

After a break of about ten days, Kissinger and Tho resumed their talks in Paris on December 6, but they broke up shortly thereafter because Tho quickly perceived that the goal Kissinger was driving at was the liberation of

216

the American prisoners of war as early as could be arranged. He found that knowledge a useful pawn in his bargaining to avoid having to compromise on the neutrality of the demilitarized zone, the presence of North Vietnamese soldiers in South Vietnam, Laos, and Cambodia, and the establishment of international supervisory agencies authoritative enough to prevent any violations of the cease-fire convention.

In the meantime Thieu stubbornly resisted any agreement. Nixon, at the end of his patience, dashed off a warning simultaneously to Hanoi and Saigon wherein he let it be known that he would tolerate no blackmail from either side. He cabled the North Vietnamese government calling upon them to return to the conference table within 72 hours or he would begin the bombing once again.

December 17 came and went without a response from Hanoi, so he gave the green light to recommence air strikes on the cities of Hanoi and Haiphong, industrial complexes, and various military targets above the 17th parallel.

It is probable that this dynamic course of action was counseled by General Haig, who had reported to Nixon Kissinger's lack of firmness in conversation with Le Duc Tho. Announcing the new bombings, Haig declared that the B-52 bombers would show North Vietnam that Nixon was not just bluffing.

While he was escalating the violence against the North, Nixon assigned General Haig the tricky task of making President Thieu and the Saigon government understand that the United States would not hesitate, if the situation demanded it, to sign its own peace treaty with Hanoi. In that eventuality, all military and economic aid to South Vietnam would be immediately and totally cut off. This came in a letter from Nixon carried by Haig on his visit of January 16, 1973.

Thieu gave in, realizing that to continue the fight without American support would result in a grand disaster, as long as the enemy was still backed by its powerful allies. So he resigned himself to accepting the presence of North Vietnamese troops in the South, the entity called "the Provisional Revolutionary Government of South Vietnam," and Henry Kissinger's word on the nongovernmental nature of the National Council for Reconciliation and Concord and the reduction of Chinese and Russian military assistance to the Communists.

217

The B-52s however continued to pound important targets in North Vietnam, raining terror and destruction from the skies for twelve days in a row. On January 3, 1973, a battered Hanoi had to send a message to Washington proposing an end to the bombardment and the reopening of bipartite negotiations.

Fifteen B-52s and several dozen other planes were lost with their pilots, but reliable information reported that if the hammering of North Vietnam by the big bombers had gone on for one week longer, the Communists might well have been beaten.

On January 5, Nixon sent a letter* to Thieu which said in part:

> Should you decide, as I trust you will, to go with us, you have my assurance of continued assistance in the post-settlement period and that we will respond with full force should the settlement be violated by North Vietnam. So, once more, I conclude with an appeal to you to close ranks with us.

Unfortunately these terms were not remembered when the Communists committed their ruthless violations of the truce agreement by opening unlimited warfare against us.

On January 15, Nixon ordered a full halt to military operations against North Vietnam. General Haig arrived in Saigon on January 16, bearing a letter from the American president urging Thieu to sign the accord.

Keeping up the pressure on Thieu, a couple of days later, American Vice President Spiro Agnew also visited our capital to tell the government that the United States would recognize the Thieu government as the only legitimate one in South Vietnam. Further, Agnew pledged that the United States would deny the right of any foreign troops to remain on the soil of South Vietnam and that the Americans would react vigorously against violations of the cease-fire, once imposed. He also relayed an invitation from Nixon to Thieu to visit him in San Clemente, California, three or four weeks later, "to demonstrate the trust and cooperation between the two countries in peace as well as in war."

Ambassador Bunker, speaking for Nixon, notified Thieu that January 27 had been designated for the signature of the agreement. It was to take

*Reproduced in full as an appendix to this book.

218

place in Paris, not in Hanoi as Kissinger and Le Duc Tho had earlier planned.

The National Security Council was called together by Thieu at the presidential palace with the task of determining the best ways to thwart the enemy's efforts to make its presence felt everywhere in order to profit from the cease-fire. In fairness it must be said that the ARVN also was preoccupied with extending its presence and had located forward posts in areas frequently claimed by the Communists. Because the opposing armies had not first been regrouped into strictly delimited zones, it became a hopelessly entangled and tricky job to administer the standstill cease-fire.

The South Vietnamese Army was still capable of putting up a good fight, as was demonstrated during our seven-week operation to regain Quang Tri province. The Vietnamese Air Force, on the other hand, did not have sufficient capability to provide the close support so needed by our ground forces in a combined exercise.

The argument could be made, I suppose, that our adversaries did not have much strength in the air, either. This is true, but one must remember that our tactics, learned from the Americans, involved heavy use of air power: fighter-type planes to provide close support and helicopters for fire support and airlift.

Had our army been able to devote itself alone to combating enemy soldiers we would have been able to continue the fight for a long time. But the army also had to perform a territorial mission that should have been accomplished by regional or popular forces, which proved time and time again to be incapable. The fighting strength of the army was frittered away in trying to secure the countryside, and thus it became too weak to engage successfully with regular enemy troop formations.

President Thieu called a meeting of the National Security Council on January 21, 1973. He invited me to attend to give me an assignment to study how to regain as much of our territory as possible during the cease-fire period. The text of the peace agreement did not mention any regroupment of either force and the International Control Commission personnel had not yet had a chance to get into position to supervise the truce.

As part of my mission, Thieu asked me to return to Paris on January 22 to help keep him abreast of events as they happened there. He then named a military team led by General Vinh Loc to attend the signature ceremony.

219

The definitive text of the agreement had been drawn up with partial consideration taken of the corrections and clarifications requested by President Thieu.

The Paris peace agreement was signed on January 27, 1973, in the presence of the Secretary General of the United Nations, representatives of the nations acting as guarantors of the pact, and officials from the United States, North Vietnam, South Vietnam, and the Provisional Revolutionary Government.

Kissinger, Le Duc Tho, Nguyen Duy Trinh, and Nguyen Thi Binh were plainly jubilant, their faces lit by large smiles for the hordes of photographers and television cameramen who surrounded them. In contrast, the blank, leaden looks of our delegates, Tran Van Lam and Pham Dang Lam, were pitiful to behold.

Everyone else had something to gain from the conclusion of this fateful agreement.

North Vietnam was on the verge of realizing its dream of conquest of the South by force, and the self-styled National Liberation Front was now recognized as being a legal entity.

The United States could bring home its soldiers and POWs with its honor intact.

The Soviet Union's influence in Southeast Asia and in the other continents would continue to grow, profiting from the success of its protegé, North Vietnam, both on the battlefield and at the conference table.

China's absence of several decades from the world scene had happily come to an end.

Richard Nixon won his second presidential term handily.

Henry Kissinger's growing reputation opened the way for his appointment to the more important post of Secretary of State.

Kissinger and Le Duc Tho were jointly awarded the Nobel Peace Prize for their roles in "ending the Vietnam conflict."

The only losers were the people, the sad people, of South Vietnam. Their future and interests and right of self-determination were ignored or waived away by everyone—Northern leaders, Southern leaders, allies and neutral nations, by a frightened world divided into irreconcilable and implacable blocs. Within South Vietnam, perhaps the group which lost the most was the NLF itself. It was dissolved in early 1977, after fighting the

220

war for fifteen years (1960-75) and having been used as the front for the northern conquest. The NLF was merged into a loose organization called "Vietnam Fatherland Front." According to some reports, several of its leaders have been arrested and executed.

After the signing of the agreement, I unexpectedly encountered Dr. Kissinger in Paris on January 24, the day after the initialling of the peace pact by Le Duc Tho and himself. So remarkable was his memory that as he shook my hand he reminded me, "I tried to see you in Saigon in 1965, but you were in Dalat." I felt more certain than ever that he had changed neither his feelings nor his pessimistic vision of South Vietnam's fate since his first visits to Saigon in 1965 and 1966.

After observing the wind up of negotiations in Paris and the signing of the document, I flew back to Saigon on January 29. I traveled incognito, as I had done so often before. I discovered that by a curious coincidence the other passengers on the plane included the Polish representative on the new International Commission of Control and Supervision and the ten members of the Provisional Revolutionary Government delegation to the Four-Party Joint Military Commission in charge of enforcing the terms of the cease-fire pact. The NLF colonel in command of the delegation introduced himself to the Polish official and they began to converse loudly in French. The colonel was between fifty-five and sixty years of age, and was modestly dressed, but his colleagues, in their new tailored suits of a peculiar style, seemed to have just stepped out of the jungle.

A reception had been organized for them in the VIP lounge at the airport in Bangkok by representatives of the Thai government. Afterwards they boarded a South Vietnamese Air Force C-47 to continue their voyage to Saigon. I flew on to Saigon on an Air Vietnam plane and arrived at Tan Son Nhut at 4 P.M. I was surprised to see security guards waiting for these delegates, who arrived one hour later. However, they were not permitted to disembark because their passports were issued by Hanoi and they refused to have them stamped by the South Vietnamese authorities.

They were forced to spend the night on the airplane. Even the Americans, who had taken the responsibility of transporting them to Tan Son Nhut, could not go near them. After some bargaining between the Americans and the police, they were given some milk for nourishment, just enough to ease their hunger. But they drank so much that they all got diarrhea, which made the atmosphere in the airplane somewhat less than pleasant. The next morning the Americans persuaded Prime Minister Khiem to authorize the PRG delegation to disembark.

The same delay beset the members of the North Vietnamese delegation when they were brought into Saigon in large American C-130 aircraft. Because they would not comply with police formalities at the airport they could not leave for their lodgings until after other hurried American arrangements with the prime minister. It was not an auspicious omen for the implementation of the Paris peace agreement.

Because it was written by the representatives of the United States and North Vietnam only, the Paris Accords of January 27, 1973, should not have been anything more than a simple cease-fire agreement. Clauses dealing with political issues should have been excluded.

At the time of the negotiations and the signing of the agreement, North Vietnam and South Vietnam were two separate, independent states divided at the 17th parallel, recognized as such by dozens of nations. Their status was similar to that of the two Germanies, the two Koreas, or the two Chinas since the end of World War II. They existed under entirely different politico-social regimes and with different institutions. The problems of their unification, of general elections, of new governmental structures, and alliances could not be settled except by the two countries themselves.

The United States came into South Vietnam to help us defend our freedom. As a foreign government, the United States was not entitled to substitute for us in negotiations with the enemy, especially on questions of an essentially political nature. Had we not already recorded our protests against this kind of usurpation of sovereign rights in 1954? South Vietnam's representatives questioned the legality of the Geneva Convention and refused to sign it because they opposed partitioning the country and the arbitrary fixing of the date for general elections written into that document. The repetition of the same mistake in the Paris armistice agreement was still more inexcusable in that the United States and Vietnam did not even have the same relationship as the one existing between France and her former colony during the transition period when sovereignty was being transferred.

Every government in South Vietnam from those of Bao Dai to Ngo Dinh Diem to Nguyen Van Thieu denied the legitimacy of the regime in the

North. Their contentions were neither false nor self-deluding, because they were built on indisputable arguments grounded in the principles of international law.

In fact, with the Elysée Accord of March 8, 1949, signed by the Emperor Bao Dai (Head of State again at that time) and French President Vincent Auriol, France replaced sovereignty over all of Vietnam in the hands of Bao Dai, the last heir to the Nguyen Dynasty, which had reigned in the second half of the nineteenth century when France completed her conquest. Since that time, France had recognized Vietnam as a sovereign state with Bao Dai at its head.

One week after the end of the 1954 Geneva Conference, the government of French Premier Mendès-France unilaterally recognized Ngo Dinh Diem's government as the only constituted authority over Vietnam. Further, the French agreed that Diem had complete control over all civil and military affairs of the nation. The French did not recognize the government in Hanoi until 1973, when ambassadors were finally exchanged.

At this same time in 1954, General Paul Ely, the French High Commissioner in Indochina, proclaimed that South Vietnam was the true state of the Vietnamese people and that Ngo Dinh Diem's government represented them.

Therefore, certain clauses of the 1973 cease-fire agreement should have been eliminated because they were internal political affairs of North and South Vietnam and not any business of the United States:

> a. The section of the preamble referring to the fundamental rights of the Vietnamese people and the right of the South Vietnamese people to self-determination.
>
> b. Article 9, calling upon the United States and North Vietnam to respect the exercise by the people of South Vietnam of their right to decide their own political future in free and democratic elections under international supervision, and enjoining foreign countries to refrain from foisting political tendencies or personalities on the South Vietnamese people.

      c. Article 11 which recommended national reconciliation and concord and respect for democratic liberties.

      d. Article 12 concerning the formation of a National Council of Reconciliation and Concord, and establishing its duties, notably the organization of general elections.

      e. Article 13 relating to the reduction of strength and demobilization of troops of the two South Vietnamese parties.

      f. Article 14 which referred to the foreign policy which South Vietnam would adopt.

      g. Article 15 defining the ways and means of reunifying the North and South and reestablishing normal relations between the two in various fields.

While every one of the above cited clauses lacks any validity in international law, one in particular is of great interest in the light of recent events. I speak of Article 11, which reads:

> Immediately after the cease-fire, the two South Vietnamese parties will:
>
> —Achieve national reconciliation and concord, end hatred and enmity, prohibit all acts of reprisal and discrimination against individuals or organizations that have collaborated with one side or the other;
>
> —Ensure the democratic liberties of the people: personal freedom, freedom of speech, freedom of the press, freedom of meeting, freedom of organization, freedom of political activities, freedom of belief, freedom of movement, freedom of residence, freedom of work, right to property ownership, and the right of free enterprise.

Have these provisions so glowingly inscribed in the Paris Accords been sincerely administered by their authors? Will they be in the future? I leave these questions to the present leaders of Vietnam and to the world's impartial observers. May all reflect wisely upon them.

The secret talks between Kissinger and Tho, carried on without the Saigon regime's knowledge, stripped the official conference in Paris of its usefulness. The South Vietnamese delegates wasted their time and their prestige there.

The desperate desire of the families of American prisoners of war to have their men home again as quickly as possible and the defeatist influence of leftist, antiwar groups were legitimate political concerns. They should not, however, have monopolized the judgment of President Nixon and Dr. Kissinger to the point where they ignored the fate of an entire people. To desert an ally in the midst of a deadly battle, to cut off his military and monetary resources without any transition period was, in Kissinger's own words, "throwing him to the wolves."

But, there was a viable alternative available to the United States, completely unexplored by these gentlemen or their predecessors. Given the political necessity for the United States to pull out, consultation with the real nationalists who were not mere sheep would have provided a means of effecting a gradual change in South Vietnam's interior and exterior policies. Over the years, these nationalists appeared to be ignored or dismissed by the Americans. Meaningful talks between Hanoi and Saigon could well have occurred if directed and initiated by those nationalist leaders. Instead, American influence was responsible for holding down nationalist politicians and military leaders who could have made a real difference, such as the American-provoked dismissal of Nguyen Van Thoai, fine patriot and minister of planning under Ngo Dinh Diem, for having supported, in the name of South Vietnam, the proclamation of the nonaligned countries which came out of the important Bandung Conference organized in 1955 by Sukarno, Nehru, Nasser, and Tito.

The Americans abetted the countercoup of January 30, 1964, perpetrated by Nguyen Khanh who accused my associates and me of being "pro-French neutralists," and then removed us from office while we were just getting our political program underway.

South Vietnamese political leaders who were anti-Communist but not servilely pro-American should have been heard. These were men who advocated a policy of nonalignment and a reasonable reconciliation with the nationalist elements of the NLF which were in overt opposition to the hardline policies of Hanoi.

The most frequently heard argument in defense of American withdrawal was that in spite of abundant foreign aid, South Vietnam could not manage to defeat the enemy and was beginning to be the despair of her most loyal allies. Condemnation for becoming embroiled in all kinds of corruption and intrigue was also laid at her door.

I won't deny the soundness of some of these criticisms, but I do not believe that they were all true. Nor was the situation that simple. I hope through my account to have shown that American policy had its blind spots, its devotion to self-interest and lack of candor, and that there were alternative courses which, if followed, might have led to a very different life for my people. The present regime has destroyed much of the regular life of the people. Recent reports attest to the fact that tens of thousands have lost their homes in the cities and towns in southern Vietnam and been sent into rural and mountain areas to build new economic zones.

We had to endure a long, long war and the multiple problems war inevitably creates. Furthermore, the North Vietnamese received heavy support from Soviet Russia and Communist China. They spent many years inching toward their hard-won victory, and it was only the unflagging assistance of their powerful allies and their extremely artful propaganda network (especially effective in the United States) that finally earned them their prize.

Former Ambassador Graham Martin in testimony before the Foreign Relations Committee of the U.S. Senate entirely verified these, my own, allegations. I hope that the people of the United States as well as the rest of the Free World, particularly the emerging countries, profit from this sad experience of my country.

The ultimate victor, Ho Chi Minh.

CHAPTER FOURTEEN

The Agony Begins

As I described in the last chapter, no patriotic Vietnamese could in any way approve of the United States-North Vietnam cease-fire agreement, covering, as it did, matters that were properly the business of the two Vietnamese entities. Strangely enough, however, our military situation at that time was probably the best it had ever been, including the time of maximum buildup of U.S. forces in our country.

Directly after the signing of the agreement, the two opposing sides began a jockeying of positions to try to occupy as much of the most advantageous land as possible. As an example, in my legislative district of Quang Ngai province, the Communists tried to cut National Highway 1 by occupying two strategic villages. This was a small, but highly critical section, vital to both sides. If the enemy occupied it, they would practically divide the country in two. Our troops immediately began a military operation that retook the contested zone and reestablished our control over the highway. In fact, at that time, we had the best control over our highways, roads, and other lines of communications that I can remember since the relatively safe days right after the 1954 Geneva Accords.

The situation was so secure that Senator Ton That Dinh and I, accompanied by a group of ten staff assistants, in May 1973 drove from Saigon to Hue (about 750 miles) and back to assess the overall military situation, which proved quite good. We spent about ten days on the road, traveling openly with no armed escort whatsoever and had not the slightest difficulty. The countryside was as peaceful as it had been in 1954. The two opposing sides tried their best to influence peacefully as much of the population as they could. In general, we were able to control all province and district cities, but Communists had many of the small villages and hamlets which contained the bulk of the people.

On the international political scene, Hanoi tried at various conferences to get agreements for admitting its NLF representatives to such organizations as the International Parliamentary Union, Asian Parliamentary Union, and UNESCO. As a leading member of our House of Representatives, I was asked by President Thieu to attend and monitor many of these conferences. Generally, our views prevailed and the NLF was not seated.

But, in 1974, the Communists began their generalized attacks against governmental outposts, small villages, and province towns in order to test American promises to help us when faced with danger from the North. They reorganized their forces and changed their tactics, reinforced with supplies and new equipment from the North as well as with regular North Vietnamese army units. They began their offensive gradually, attacking to inflict the greatest number of casualties where they were certain of success. As the year went on, they increased the tempo of their attacks, moving from one success to another.

On our side, we did not adopt correct military strategy to deal with the inexorable Communist steamroller. We spread our forces too thin, trying to maintain a presence in and defend each province town, an ambition clearly beyond our capability. Although by this time we had an armed force of over one million men, such a method of defense did not have a chance for success. We also had become used to American military methods which are fine when you have all the supplies and equipment needed to fight an American-style war. On this, too, we failed to reckon with the facts of life in 1974.

This was, of course, one of the worst periods in American political history. Watergate with its fantastic exposure of corruption at highest levels in the American government dominated the political scene and preoccupied the American public. Before the end of the year Vice President Agnew and President Nixon had resigned, a situation unprecedented in the political life of the United States. It is understandable that conditions in poor little Vietnam, America's troublesome ward, could be ignored by an otherwise sympathetic people. Watergate also gave Nixon's many enemies a chance to repudiate promises made by his administration, such as guarantees to Vietnam of prompt and effective aid should the Communists not keep their part of the bargain. Finally, the deceptively peaceful conditions in the country could logically lead the unwary to believe that aid funds could be reduced safely, as was actually done by the U.S. Congress.

230

In any event, aid to our country began perceptibly to decrease in all areas. Tied as we were to American concepts of mobility and firepower, we sorely missed the fuel for our vehicles and ammunition for our artillery that failed to arrive. Both our mobility and firepower were reduced at a time when we needed more of both. This slowup in aid, tied to congressional monetary reductions, caused us to fall behind our Communist adversary in strength since he was receiving ample supplies from his friends. Our units became less and less capable and more susceptible to defeat by the enemy; and the defeats multiplied.

I visited an infantry unit in the Delta in 1974. The company commander was quite discouraged because he was getting a lot of harassment from the enemy at night and could not get any really effective artillery support. For example, the neighboring battery would fire one round at the enemy when perhaps twenty were needed. This was not the artillery commander's fault. He simply did not have sufficient ammunition available to provide the fire needed.

Another trouble besetting our units was the presence of wives, children, and other family members living in and around the tactical positions of the troops. Suppose, for instance, the Communists attacked a government position with enough strength to cause the local commander to order a logical withdrawal to a more defensible position, a movement practiced by all armies throughout history. Normally, such a tactical move would be achieved without difficulty and with few losses, resulting in a better military situation than before. In our case, the order would be given, but before that the dependents of our soldiers would have started their movement first, simply trying to get out of the zone of enemy attack. Our soldiers were naturally motivated to protect their families and individual possessions, so they might very well have left their posts to see to them. This would, of course, weaken the defensive position, the enemy would exploit the situation further, and eventually what had started as an orderly retreat for good purposes would turn into an utter rout. This happened both with small formations such as platoons and companies and large organizations such as regiments and divisions. At Da Nang and Hue, for example, strong defensive positions were abandoned disgracefully, with supplies, weapons, artillery, armor, and other equipment left on the battlefield to be picked up at will by the advancing North Vietnamese troops.

231

In February 1974, President Thieu, in order to show a new face to the world, reshuffled his government again and appointed me vice premier under Khiem who retained his dual role of premier and minister of defense.

Until then, I was the parliamentary opposition leader and accepted Thieu's offer only after an agonizing debate within our political group. We concluded that the best way of talking Thieu and the United States into reaching a negotiated settlement with the other side was to work with the Saigon government.

My duties were to inspect governmental programs of national development that included projects to stimulate the overall economy and to act as liaison with the Congress, since I was still an elected representative. One day I casually asked Khiem why I was given this position without any specific department to supervise. Unaware of my real intention, he responded that Thieu wanted my name in the government as a show of national concord.

With a team of young, but dedicated, technicians I determined that the greatest problem with the administration of the aid we did get from the United States was not with the individuals working at the grass roots, but with the organized system of corruption at all levels of our administration. I have described this in relation to the Diem regime but the situation was no better under his successors. I naturally took my findings to Thieu and Khiem, but they did nothing to reform the situation.

Thieu one day complained to me that his two key assistants, Khiem as premier and defense minister and Vien as army chief, were not getting enough work done. He also said that Khiem had given many key jobs to his brothers and cousins. One cousin, for example, was the director of the port of Saigon and a brother-in-law was ambassador to Switzerland. A system of illegal traffic had been set up which yielded great riches to them. I suggested to Thieu that he fire both Khiem and Vien, but he told me that pressure from the American Embassy prevented this.

As I have recounted, because of my congressional and ministerial status, I was sent on many special diplomatic missions for President Thieu during 1973, 1974, and 1975. During these years I headed Vietnamese delegations trying to get financial and economic aid from Japan and France. Prior to that I had, of course, headed a political group opposed to Thieu's policies and openly advocating a policy of reconciliation with non-Communist nationalistic members of the NLF. During these trips abroad to Africa, France, England, Hong Kong, and many other countries, my discussions with leading officials, such as Vice President Ford of the U.S., Premier Miki of Japan, and Finance Minister Giscard D'Estaing of France, even more strongly convinced me that reform was vital to our survival.

Accordingly, after my return from Paris on February 7, 1973, I had a meeting with Thieu to propose formally to him that he establish a "Peace Government" to cope with the new political situation developing from the cease-fire. This was the best possible time to do this because our military situation was still strong, and the eyes of the world were then on us. I described to him a study I had made with my political friends, Professor Bui Anh Tuan and Dr. Tran Van Du on the establishment of such a government and the different phases of application of the cease-fire agreement.

I handed him a draft of our project, which included the provision that he remain president of the Republic, but delegate all power to negotiate to myself as the new prime minister. After discussing several details he gave me his agreement in principle. I asked him if I might bring it up right away with Premier Khiem. He thought a few seconds, then said, "Let me mention it to him. It would be more correct coming from me than from his replacement." But there was no follow-up to his tentative acceptance of the plan.

Tuan and Du were leading members of a tightly knit political group that had been secretly but closely associated with me since the late 1960s. The group represented a miniature version of a coalition government.

Tuan was imprisoned by both the Viet Minh in Hanoi and the Nguyen Khanh regime in Saigon. He was known not only for his pro-U.S. stance, but also for his deep commitment to nonalignment and extensive social reforms for South Vietnam.

A seasoned Marxist intellectual, Du belonged to the French Communist Party in the early 1940s when he went to Paris to pursue graduate veterinary studies. Du was arrested in 1954 in Saigon by the Diem government for organizing a pro-Communist peace movement. His pro-Communist views did not prevent him working for a balanced peace settlement with non-Communist and formerly anti-Communist elements.

Another member, Harvard-trained Professor Nguyen Xuan Oanh, formerly deputy prime minister in 1964, was usually referred to as a pro-

American politician, but in fact he had been blacklisted by the Central Intelligence Agency. Oanh was accused by the Americans of supporting Japan during World War II while he was in Tokyo as a student.

Our group included two less important members. One was Professor Pham Van Dieu, a nephew of North Vietnam's Premier Pham Van Dong, and an anti-American politician. He kept himself ready to go to Hanoi to meet with his uncle whenever the government desired. The other, Professor N,* was our contact with the NLF.

After the April 1975 collapse, all members of our group except Professor Tuan and I chose to remain in Saigon.

Despite differences in political backgrounds and affinities, we were able to come to a consensus: Vietnam should become a nonaligned country; and a fratricidal war could be avoided only by forming a national coalition government, and carrying out genuine political, social, and cultural reforms.

The group decided to keep the Americans informed of our discussions and proposals. We reasoned that Thieu, the main obstacle to peace, could easily be removed from office by the Americans.

In early 1971, as the presidential elections drew near, the group suggested that I arrange a meeting between General Big Minh and two members, Professor Tuan and Dr. Du.

A secret meeting was held at my house in the Chinese city of Cholon. During the conversation we suggested that Big Minh, who was willing to run for president against President Thieu and General Ky, offer the vice presidential slot to Dr. Du. Big Minh replied he had to consult with his advisors. A week later, he came up with a flat "no."

"I can't accept Dr. Du," he mumbled embarrassingly. "The reason is simple but clear. Dr. Du is a Communist."

"If you don't like Dr. Du, how can you form a coalition government with the Communists?" I retorted.

Information about our group's activities was relayed to Washington, I believed, by two American officials, Landreth and Wittinghill. I once asked Ambassador Martin about the American reaction. He didn't think that my group had "real" contacts with Communist leaders in Hanoi and in the jungle. At least a dozen times I told the Americans that "it's not difficult to

*True name withheld to protect the professor.

234

verify our credibility with the other side." "Give us a chance," I would insist, "within 24 hours, we'll send one man to Hanoi, and another man into the jungle. Why go to Paris? We can make peace here, between Hanoi and Saigon, provided that we are allowed to negotiate with the other side."

Again and again our peace proposals fell on unreceptive ears. According to our information, I believed that even in mid-April 1975, about one week before Thieu resigned, setting the stage for a free-for-all exodus, we still had a chance of coming to some kind of peaceful settlement with Hanoi. But, this chance soon vanished.

So, after the signing of the Paris Peace Agreements, President Thieu continued to preserve the political status quo with a tired and incapable cabinet, unable or unwilling to make the changes necessary to adjust to the new situation. Our military posture declined day by day, in face of the communist attacks and the rapid decline of assistance from the United States.

In April and September 1974, I traveled to Washington to plead our cause before such American military leaders as Secretary of Defense Schlesinger, Admiral Zumwalt, and General Abrams. They were entirely sympathetic, understanding my arguments completely, but explained that their hands were tied; that the funds came from Congress, and despite their protestations, the House and Senate continued to decrease aid to us.

To gauge the American reaction, the enemy made a defiant gesture in December 1974 by attempting to capture Phuoc Long province, 200 miles northeast of Saigon on the Cambodian border. The Communists had completed a petroleum pipeline to this point from the 17th parallel along the border. Using this they could easily resupply their vehicles later when they introduced fully conventional warfare.

In Saigon, the political situation quickly deteriorated with demonstrations by religious groups, politicians, legislators, and students, all against the Thieu government. A list of ten accusations* was published by a group whose spokesman was Father Thanh, a Catholic priest.

Nguyen Van Ngan, one of President Thieu's closest aides, was discharged for his alleged involvement in a campaign against cronyism and

---

*Three of these accusations involved the immediate family of the President. The first of trafficking illegally in fertilizer was described in Chapter 10. The other two, which implicated Thieu's wife, come later in this chapter.

235

corruption; he was later arrested for being under suspicion as a coup plotter. Ngan played a major role if not the most important, in organizing Thieu's Democratic ruling party, the members of which held leading posts in the government as well as the armed forces. In 1974, Ngan talked influential Democratic members in South Vietnam's Congress into alerting Thieu to corrupt officials from the central down to the district levels.

The figures were unusually grim. Of sixty generals and two hundred full colonels, fewer than one-third were "clean." A two star general in the First Corps, Vietnam's most exposed area, was involved in a massive "rice scandal." Official investigation showed that he illegally sold rice to the Communists.

Corruption was rampant in the Highlands military region under General Nguyen Van Phu. All positions of command from district to provincial levels—even that of regimental commanders—were "purchasable." This was later confirmed to me by Colonel Le Khac Ly, now a refugee in the United States. The pattern of "selling" and "buying" official jobs, in the military as well as in the administration, was tolerated by the administration. Its ramifications reached deeply into every corner of the country. In the midst of Saigon, only a few miles from the presidential palace, a governmental minister owned an illegal gambling center.

Another high official controlled a wide range of illicit enterprises, from drugs and smuggling to a passport racket. Despite mounting evidence, President Thieu continued to retain him as an influential advisor.

Nguyen Van Ngan and his friends committed a fatal mistake in trying to expose the mesh of corruption that involved some members of the President's and the Prime Minister's immediate families. Thieu's brother accused him of "pro-Communist connections," so the President dismissed Ngan from his position. Ngan told me that until 1973 President Thieu was relatively honest, but he changed after the signing of the Paris Peace Agreements.

In October 1972, Thieu, who then placed complete confidence in his assistant, confided to Ngan that "we are going to be sold down the river."

"What are you going to do?" Ngan asked.

"We'll use dilatory tactics. We'll do everything to delay the signing," President Thieu replied. As it turned out, he was so right in believing that the Paris Agreement was a death warrant for South Vietnam.

236

In March 1973, after his return from the United States, Nguyen Van Ngan added, President Thieu became very pessimistic about the future of Vietnam. At the same time he shut his eyes to what his family was doing and continued to keep some of the well-known corrupt officials in power.

Thieu once told an aide, "The best way of avoiding coups d'etat is to have these loyal subordinates." On another occasion, when asked why he did not prosecute the most obvious cases of corruption, Thieu gave this explanation, "I can't. These trials would impair our relationships with the Americans." Thieu's statement is a hint that the mesh of corruption possibly also involved American officials.

One thing that deserves close scrutiny by historians who want to seek out the roots of South Vietnam's social and political problems: the incredible "clout" exerted on our powerful leaders by their wives. There were a thousand ways, both legal and illegal, of making money in war-torn Vietnam. And the wives of our leaders mastered all of them. A survey conducted by an opposition group in Saigon weeks before the 1975 collapse estimated that between 1954 and 1975 these mighty wives pocketed an equivalent of $500 million. There is an old saying in our country calling the wives "the generals of the internal affairs" (Nôi Túong).

There was one accusation, which shocked all of Saigon, including myself. President Thieu's wife was instrumental in supporting the Vi Dan Hospital, a nonprofit charity which existed on grants from various foreign agencies and which was staffed largely by volunteer labor. It was alleged that she took advantage of her situation by having the hospital import many items of trade which she then resold at a profit. Because of the favored situation of the hospital, no customs duty was paid on these items, so this illegal traffic helped add to her wealth.

Considering the fact that Thieu and his family were far from rich before his entry into politics we all knew that any major real estate transaction made by his wife could not have come from his salary. She purchased, for 92 million piasters, an opulent villa in 1972 on Cong Ly Street, which had previously belonged to the proprietors of a rubber plantation. At the black market exchange rate at the time, this was the equivalent of more than $400,000.

Mrs. Thieu was not the only "poor" wife who managed to leave Vietnam in a quite wealthy condition. Another was the notorious wife of

237

Premier Khiem whose black market and other illegal activities were a continuous scandal in the country.

To be true, "clean" leaders and "clean" wives were many. But, often these honest military leaders such as generals Nguyen Duc Thang and Nguyen Van Hieu were removed from leading jobs or demoted to obscure positions.

Honesty is, indeed, a virtue; but, unfortunately, honesty alone can't help a general lead his troops and obtain success.

General Ngo Quang Truong, commander of Central Vietnam, usually known as the 1st Corps area, was a case in point. A "clean" commanding officer, he worked very hard but lived modestly. In 1973 and 1974, I told Truong that people were attempting to secure financial privileges through his wife. Truong immediately took drastic measures to neutralize these attempts.

At the time the Highlands were lost to Hanoi's invading army, General Truong still had under his command the best of our troops, but these elite troops disintegrated in a matter of days and the area under Truong's control was occupied by the Communists who were surprised not to have to face a major battle. When the moment of truth came, Truong was abandoned by his men, even his close bodyguards. He had to throw himself into the sea and swim alone and unaided to safety. He was honest, but also, unfortunately, incapable.

It is true that the debacle was caused partly by Thieu's strategic and tactical mistakes as Vietnam's commander-in-chief, and especially by Thieu's personal order to withdraw from the 1st Corps an airborne division, Vietnam's best army unit, allegedly to protect his palace in Saigon against an impending coup d'etat.

It is equally true that the unexpected stampede in the 1st Corps was traced back to General Truong's total dependence on the Americans. Until the last moment, he still hoped that the Americans were going to bail him out and so did not use his own troops effectively.

To a certain extent, General Ngo Quang Truong was comparable to President Nguyen Van Thieu. Both continued to believe in a miracle that failed to materialize.

My latest trip before the fall of South Vietnam was to the friendly non-aligned lands of Africa. By this time the disasters of Da Nang and Hue had

238

occurred with their huge problems of evacuees who were "voting with their feet," moving south ahead of the advancing Communist regular forces from North Vietnam. The invasion by major units feared so greatly by American advisors in 1954 had finally come to pass; but now we lacked the means to withstand them.

I arrived in Zaire on March 12 to be received by President Mobutu. I asked him to help us by mobilizing world opinion in our behalf toward some kind of political settlement leading to peace. He promised to help. On March 20, I traveled to Nigeria and on the 23rd to Upper Volta. There I received a cable from President Thieu asking me to cancel my proposed trips to Paris and Washington. After stops in Abidjean, Liberia, and Togo, I proceeded to London where I arrived April 1.

During my two-day stop in London, I learned some very important information, obtained by friends from M. Chirac, the Premier of France. "It's all over for South Vietnam," they reported. "The only thing to do now is to arrange the evacuation of those who don't want to live under a Communist regime. The three superpowers have agreed to the reunification of the two Vietnams under Hanoi's control." This information from a most reliable source was, of course, most distressing to receive.

I cabled Thieu, enroute from Hong Kong, asking that he see me on April 5 as soon as I could get back. I then met twice with the American Consul General in Hong Kong to discuss an evacuation plan for as many as one million people, a realistic figure considering the numbers who had escaped from North Vietnam in 1954 as well as those fleeing at this time before the advancing Communist armies. He took note of my recommendations and said that he would submit them to the State Department and to the Embassy in Saigon. He agreed that the plan should be kept secret. I was anguished, therefore, to see the news release stating that the United States had formulated a procedure for evacuating 250,000 people!

Destruction of the statue of a Vietnamese marine, last symbol in Saigon of the Armed Forces of South Vietnam.

CHAPTER FIFTEEN

The End

I returned to Saigon at 12:30 A.M., April 5, and proceeded directly to Independence Palace to brief President Thieu and his cabinet ministers. There I learned that a governmental reshuffle had occurred and that Premier Khiem had resigned under pressure from the president. Privately, I told Thieu of the information I had obtained from French sources concerning the joint decision of the superpowers to abandon South Vietnam. He professed not to believe me, but requested that I not spread this word around since it could be expected to destroy what morale was left in the country. He told me that he would check this with the American ambassador.

This was one other example of a lack of policy or advance planning by Thieu and his government. Instead of having a logical plan to meet such a contingency, Thieu had to turn to the Americans for advice. For years now, this deficiency had been apparent. At no time during his presidency did Thieu or his ministers try to think ahead to counter what was liable to happen in the future, both in the world political sphere and in the day-to-day conduct of our war against the Communists.

But, Thieu was really quite intelligent since he survived in power for about ten years by pleasing the Americans. At one time he told me that he had to fight more against our American friends than against the Communists, so I knew he was aware of the problem he and the country were in.

I then advanced some specific suggestions, pointing out that after less than a month's absence, I could see immediately how far the situation had deteriorated. I told him that to save the Saigon area and the Mekong Delta, we had to have a cabinet capable of holding out militarily, and of initiating negotiations with the NLF immediately. In effect, I was proposing an immediate coalition government, but Thieu professed to be so violently anti-Communist that he could not stand even to hear the word "coalition." On

241

the two previous occasions when I had proposed such a government to him, he had ignored my suggestions. By now, it was almost too late. Nevertheless, Thieu suggested that I discuss the matter with the new premier-designate, Nguyen Ba Can.

Can had been president of the House of Representatives since 1971; he belonged to an influential political party organized by Vietnam's prominent labor leaders and was from the South. Flexible and able, he was assured of attracting considerable support from all moderate factions. He was chosen for political reasons, to gain support for Thieu in the House since the Senate had already lodged a vote of "No Confidence" in the president. Choosing a civilian, however, was somewhat of a blow to the army so, when I spoke with him, Can asked me to join the cabinet as Deputy Premier and Minister of Defense. I accepted on April 7. Can took until April 14 to present his cabinet, so during the two weeks from the resignation of Tran Thien Khiem, Vietnam was without a government.

Khiem was no longer a prime minister, but was still powerful. He took special care to send his belongings to Taipei and Paris.

Days before Khiem officially resigned, the Vietnamese embassy in Paris received at one time dozens of crates totaling about nine tons of freight. These crates were sent from Saigon to Paris aboard an Air-France flight, bearing no indication who had sent it or the recipient. Ambassador Nguyen Duy Quang, a relative of Khiem by marriage, fired off an official query to Saigon. The explanation came later in a personal letter from the ex-premier to the ambassador.

During February and March 1975, copies of the cables exchanged between Ambassador Quang and Saigon were ordered by the ambassador to be removed from official files. This shipment alone cost the Vietnam government the amount of U.S. $80,000. The crates were later stored in a large mansion owned by Premier Khiem in Vincennes in the suburbs of Paris. It is also worth noting that long before the final collapse, large quantities of Khiem's belongings had been flown abroad by Air-Vietnam, whose director general was related by marriage to both President Thieu and Premier Khiem.

On April 15, during the first meeting of the Can cabinet, I called for a complete account of our military situation. On the same day I summoned the senior generals to General Staff Headquarters to instruct them to

242

continue to hold on to what we still commanded, and to seek to negotiate an honorable cease-fire to guarantee us control of the two tactical areas remaining (Saigon area and Mekong Delta). I made them understand that a political settlement would be impossible unless we held on in the battlefield.

Again on that same day, I flew to Phan Rang which was receiving enemy artillery fire. To give an idea of our abominable condition, a unit of rangers there had no communications equipment and thus had to abandon their positions; a battery of 105-mm howitzers could not shoot because they had no sights for the guns; and the aircraft had no bombs available to drop on readily identifiable targets. I promised to get them the things they needed and departed in great sorrow. Following up on these and other similar deficiencies, I had discussions with General Smith, the American Defense Attaché and our Air Force Commander, Tran Van Minh. Minh reported that the problem I had observed concerning munitions for the aircraft in Phan Rang was also a common problem for other bases.

I spent the next couple of days visiting military organizations in the entire area left to us, including some, like the 22nd Division, which had arrived almost intact from Qui Nhon in Central Vietnam. These personal contacts with our soldiers enabled me to reaffirm once again the reasons for our losing ground so rapidly against the invading Communists: poor logistics, lack of equipment, ammunition, fuel, and the abandonment of significant stocks of war material by commanders in the chaotic and poorly executed retreats from key positions. We could no longer implement American combat tactics and our soldiers were more involved with seeing to the welfare of their families than performing their military duties. Other mistakes, probably the most decisive ones, were made at the highest governmental levels where President Thieu centralized too much decision-making power in his own office and appointed inexperienced and incompetent officers to key positions.

There has been a consensus among foreign observers that our senseless withdrawal from the Highlands triggered the process of collapse, a view I share. However, I would like to insist that the truth of history was not fully reflected by Western reporters and columnists.

Two leaders were involved, President Thieu, as Vietnam's commander-in-chief, and General Pham Van Phu, commander of the Highlands area.

Phu died in Saigon of a dose of poison two days after the Communist troops took control of the city. He was a courageous captain in Dien Bien Phu in 1954. He could have been a famous colonel. But Thieu made him a general, and at Premier Khiem's personal recommendation gave him one of Vietnam's most difficult military jobs.

Ban Me Thout was not entirely occupied by the Communists on the day the foreign press said it fell. Two-thirds of the town was still in our hands, and our troops were well on their way to recapturing the city. Suddenly the local commander, personally chosen by General Phu, issued a withdrawal order. The bulk of our force was diverted to a nearby airfield. Our soldiers thought that fresh troops and ammunition were coming, but they were wrong. They were assigned to protect the airfield to ensure the safety of the families of their commanders leaving the combat area.

At a subsequent high-level meeting in Cam Ranh Bay, President Thieu ordered General Phu to retake Ban Me Thuot. "At any cost," he insisted.

Other generals in attendance, including Phu, agreed with Thieu that the loss of Ban Me Thuot could entail the most damaging psychological and political consequences. Thieu approved a request submitted by Phu regarding the formation of an ad hoc force to be sent to that city, under the command of a newly promoted general. As the overall commander of the area, Phu had to stay in his Pleiku headquarters, another strategic locality in the Central Highlands.

Hours after the high-level meeting, General Phu unilaterally ordered the withdrawal of his headquarters with all its supporting forces from Pleiku to Nha Trang, a safe area along the coast.

It is true that if no withdrawal had been made, General Phu might have been besieged by advancing Communist units, and even killed. But, at least the country would have avoided the chaotic exodus of thousands of panic-stricken highlanders which caused innumerable civilian casualties and prevented our relief columns from reaching Ban Me Thuot.

The withdrawal from Pleiku sealed the fate of the Highlands, and that of the whole nation. Mrs. Phu, who did not make that decision, was nevertheless held responsible for it by officers who succeeded in escaping from the ensuing inferno. She was very close to Mrs. Khiem, the powerful wife of our prime minister. Their relationship was not limited to purely nonprofit social and religious activities.

The fall of the Highlands was caused in great measure by our president's inaction and lack of leadership. Thieu's office in the Independence Palace in Saigon was equipped with the most sophisticated telecommunications devices with which he could contact any army unit across the nation at any time. General Phu's withdrawal move was instantaneously reported to Thieu, but Thieu did not countermand it when this is exactly what he should have done.

A Thieu close aide told me that at that moment the president knew that a Communist victory was only a matter of days away and Thieu needed a scapegoat. Later Phu was placed under house arrest in Saigon, where humiliated and abandoned, he took his own life. Mrs. Phu stayed in Communist-controlled Saigon.

The last days of Saigon were particularly rich in *coups de théâtre*.

Within the ranks of younger officers, there were many who harbored considerable resentment at the United States for failing to live up to promises made at the time of the signing of the cease-fire agreement. Some planned to seize as hostages about one thousand Americans, including the ambassador, his staff, and the military attaché. This was, of course, a ridiculous plan which I fortunately was able to defuse. Forgetting the barbarous nature of the scheme, it never could have worked in practice, as such coercion would not have intimidated the Americans. It would have been a grim last chapter to our relations with America to have seen United States Marines landing in Saigon to battle their former allies.

On the morning of April 19, after a meeting with the generals and admirals at General Staff Headquarters, I received a call from Air Force General and former Premier Nguyen Cao Ky asking me to meet him at his residence at Tan Son Nhut. At the meeting, he told me that he and his followers were ready for a type of coalition government with the NLF, that this had American Ambassador Martin's approval, and that the only obstacle was President Thieu. I told him to try to be patient, as I was working on this very thing. I was trying at the moment to introduce as Deputy Defense Minister General Nguyen Duc Thang, one of Ky's friends and partisans, well respected in the army for his competence, energy, and integrity.

I had also been approached by diverse political leaders in the past few days with the same suggestion to set up a coalition government but with me as premier, so that meaningful negotiations with the other side could commence speedily. I let them know that this might still be feasible if the military position permitted it.

In the relatively calm days following the installation of the Can Cabinet, I still felt that a political settlement was possible within our Constitutional framework. The brilliant resistance by the 18th Division under General Le Minh Dao, the Second Armored Brigade of General Khoi, and the 25th Division, commanded by General Ba, backed up by the still potent air force, had victoriously halted the Communist advance at Xuan Loc, about 40 miles from Saigon, causing some optimism to be reborn.

At 10 A.M. Sunday, April 20, Ambassador Martin met with Thieu in the Independence Palace. He tersely advised Thieu that in view of the disintegrating military situation, the only way to stop the Communist advance was to find with the utmost urgency a political settlement through negotiations with Hanoi.

Martin told Thieu that his contacts indicated that the only public figure acceptable to Hanoi was Big Minh and that the armed forces were willing to accept this solution, as evidenced by my meetings with my generals and with General Ky the day before. It has been reported that Martin demanded that Thieu resign from the presidency. This is not true. Martin's only request was that Big Minh be appointed premier with full power to negotiate with Hanoi. In their talk, however, Martin told Thieu that unless Big Minh was appointed, American aid would cease. If Thieu acceded to the request, aid might be continued. So, I think Thieu saw a good reason for resigning as he did later.

On the same day, I met with Martin. He told me that a new premier was required with as much power as Ngo Dinh Diem had been given in 1954. He also insisted that the new appointee would probably have to be Big Minh. However, "I prefer you," Martin added.

The next day, April 21, I again had an appointment with the American ambassador. This was a fateful day, because it was at this point that President Thieu decided to resign from office.

This was the worst possible time for Thieu's resignation—he should have done it much earlier or not at all. Under our constitution, someone like Big Minh could not succeed him, but Minh could have become premier and thus had power to commence negotiations with the Communists. The entire political situation had become worse with the fall of Phnom Penh the preceding week, and a cloud of gloom prevailed.

This same day, Thieu convened his National Security Council, but without me, the Defense Minister, and announced his resignation from office. The formal transfer of power to Vice President Huong occurred at 8:00 P.M. after a fifty-minute extemporaneous speech from Independence Palace during which Thieu exhorted both the armed forces and the people to continue the fight against the enemy. Huong had little to say, ending his statement mournfully, "I will share the fate of the soldiers on the battlefields."

On April 22, reports were flying around that I would take over as premier and commence negotiations. French diplomat Brochand saw me to advise me to scrap the idea. He asserted that the Communists would only negotiate with Big Minh.

I saw Minh later that day and asked him if he would be able to negotiate. He answered in the affirmative, but he insisted, "We have to act quickly." He assured me that Hanoi was only waiting for him to come to power before negotiations would commence.

Minh told me that getting 71-year old Huong to give up his power might be a problem. "He will listen only to the Americans," Big Minh added. "So, please ask Ambassador Martin to exert pressure on Huong."

I left Big Minh around midnight and went straight to Ambassador Martin's residence, delivering to him Minh's message. Martin agreed with the request.

On April 23, I had conversations with some senior generals about the necessity to replace General Cao Van Vien as Chief of the General Staff. Their first recommendations was General Nguyen Duc Thang, Ky's friend, who even at that late date could have restored a semblance of order to the battlefield. Plans were in existence for a last-ditch effort to save Saigon and the Mekong Delta, including help from a contingent of Americans remaining in Saigon who wanted to enlist in the Vietnamese Army. Openly disapproving American policies, they wanted to fight with us to reawaken the conscience of the United States and to force Washington out of its indifference to our fate. Events moved too quickly, however, preventing the participation of these concerned Americans in our last battle.

For the next couple of days, I ran around Saigon trying to mediate differences between various parties, principally between President Huong and Big Minh. Both of them were behaving unrealistically, seemingly unaware of the impending disaster apparent to everyone else. Huong desired to keep the power of the presidency, despite the obvious fact it could not last much longer. Big Minh, on his part, refused to take the position of premier, since he wanted to be head of state, thus losing several precious days when he might have accomplished something useful. I really could not believe what I was observing: responsible people were arguing over fine points of the Constitution while disaster was about to overcome us. Hanoi was said to be willing to talk only to Big Minh, Huong was standing pat on his prerogatives, and Minh refused to be anything but top dog. I saw Brochand again who told me that Hanoi was waiting until the 27th before it unleashed a final strong assault on Saigon.

In a desperate effort to save Saigon from destruction, I tried again to persuade Huong to step down in favor of Big Minh. To give more weight to my report that the military situation was no longer hopeful, I asked General Cao Van Vien, Chief of the General Staff, to accompany me. Again, Huong refused to budge.

On April 26, Huong addressed a special session of parliament outlining his meeting with Big Minh and his refusal to resign in his favor. He then put the question to the delegates to decide if he should hand power over to Minh or appoint a premier to bargain with the Communists. Debate then followed.

After his address, Huong called me to announce that he intended to appoint me as premier of a negotiating government. I thanked him for his choice, but politely declined, saying that intelligence reports made available by both France and the United States were overwhelmingly favorable to Big Minh. The president replied that my appointment was prompted by two factors: the National Assembly did not think that Big Minh was able to restore peace, and that he had just received solid reports that my name was acceptable to the NLF.

Encouraged by Huong's revelations, I began to line up support in case this nomination came through. I first called General Ky who was enthusiastic about the idea, recommending General Thang as Defense Minister. My appointment would only make sense if it were, directly or indirectly, accepted by the NLF, as President Huong had said.

248

I convened an emergency meeting at my residence, where we made a careful survey of the military situation. Our defenders could stall the enemy forces around Saigon for only a short time, about five to seven days.

This deadline would be more than enough for me to carry out the plan drawn up months ago by our group. At 8:00 that evening I asked our usual contact with the NLF if they would accept me as premier.

The contact replied that 16 hours would be needed for the NLF to acknowledge my message and reply to it. According to our plan, my "cabinet" would include a NLF vice premier. The NLF would control the ministries of information and economy. General Thang would be Chief of the General Staff. Members of our political group, half pro-U.S., half pro-NLF, would hold the sensitive posts of security, intelligence, and negotiations. Pro-Thieu people would be allowed to leave Saigon. There would be no massive evacuation; however, those who wanted to leave would be permitted to do so.

In the meantime, unbearable pressures were exerted on me supporting Big Minh's candidacy. French Ambassador Merillon insisted that I reject President Huong's offer, saying that if Minh were not chosen, the Communists would attack Saigon tonight. I visited Ambassador Martin to confirm. The American ambassador unequivocally confirmed Merillon's information which, he said, came from Hanoi. I saw Huong again to impress on him that time was running out. He finally agreed to transfer power to Big Minh. I then notified Minh and Ambassadors Martin and Merillon.

On April 27, Huong convened a meeting of notables, publicly announcing his decision to step down in favor of Big Minh.

At 9:00 A.M. my NLF contact told me that I was acceptable to them as premier. By then it was too late since Minh was already set up as Huong's replacement.

At 3:00 P.M., Ambassador Merillon called to say that the Communist bombardment of the city would begin at 6:00 P.M. unless word was received that Minh was named as president. I immediately sent my staff to round up our National Assembly representatives and personally contacted the Senate president to urge him to act speedily. A quorum was attained at about 7:30 P.M. I appeared before the delegates with several well-informed generals to review the military situation with them. I told them that sixteen enemy

249

divisions equipped with armor and heavy artillery were tightening their ring around Saigon; that we were clinging to the Delta, but had no reserves at our disposal.

After a small amount of bickering and with American officials watching the entire process, the Assembly voted reluctantly to transfer power from President Huong to Big Minh. Huong asked me to tell Minh that he could take the power whenever he was ready, which I did after notifying Merillon and Martin. I recommended to Minh that he get sworn in that very night, but he decided to wait until the next day. Finally in a ceremony at 5:00 P.M. April 28, Minh took his oath in the same room as had Huong a week earlier. Minh appeared courageous and calm, announcing his determination to end the war by negotiating directly with Hanoi. A wisp of hope came as Minh talked of peace, national reconciliation, and harmony. It was, of course, only a fleeting hope, dissipated quickly.

That night, the Communists bombed Ton Son Nhut Airport and during the dark hours of the 28th and 29th they rained shells on Saigon. The echoes of Big Minh's call for peace and reconciliation were drowned in the noise of exploding artillery rounds. The defense perimeter around the city still held, however, due largely to the heroic efforts of the Saigon sector commander, General Nguyen Van Minh. A 24-hour curfew was proclaimed, with the people ordered to remain at home. This prevented the panic that had occurred previously in Da Nang. But, it also had a lamentable consequence. Many people who should have been evacuated missed getting to pickup points to be airlifted or boated to safety.

April 29, 1975, was one of the most painful days of my life. At 8:00 A.M. I went to General Staff Headquarters, although I was no longer officially in the government, to get the latest information. I heard that General Ky had been up in his helicopter observing the enemy's activities. He returned a little later, feeling that all was lost and took off with General Ngo Quang Truong to land on a carrier of the American Seventh Fleet.

I then went to my old office and telephoned Big Minh to tell him of the pressing necessity to name a new chief of staff. My call had interrupted his conversation with French Ambassador Merillon who had come to communicate Hanoi's latest demand: before cease-fire negotiations could begin, all American agencies must leave Vietnam.

I attended the swearing-in ceremony of the new cabinet of Premier Vu Van Mau at 11:30 A.M. where Mau explained to his new ministers that he had made a radio speech demanding that the American Defense Attaché Office (DAO) leave the country in twenty-four hours. Hearing this I called the American embassy and asked, "Is it true that the new premier has insisted that DAO clear out?"

"Not just DAO," he responded, "but every single American. We are in the process of leaving. If you want to go, yourself, be at the Embassy before 2:00 this afternoon."

I decided at that instant to join them. Others made their individual decisions, some staying, some going. Big Minh's wife decided to remain at his side despite his urging her to leave.

As soon as Minh had taken office he had begun urgent talks with the Communists. At about 4:30 P.M., Ambassador Merillon went to Minh to bring him the answer to his plea for cease-fire negotiations. The Communist answer was a resounding, "No." Merillon had tears in his eyes and Minh was completely crushed. There would be no truce. It would only be the spectacular victory the other side sought, won with the least trouble, aided by their shrewd diplomatic maneuvers and military pressure. All of us had been duped, Minh, Merillon, Martin, and myself. Our feverish activities went for naught; our disillusionment was complete.

Minh's last gesture, however, deserves to be retold.

With his wife and other political and military aides he decided to spend the night of the 29th in the presidential palace, waiting for the inexorable invaders. He would try to have the honor of a head of state capitulating at his post. This was a logical move. It was better this way than to be arrested at his private residence, in which event he could have been accused of cowardice or shirking his duty. The foreign newspeople who witnessed the entry of Communist tanks into the presidential palace at 8:30 on the morning of April 30 related what the whole world already knew.

The first Communists on the scene, all officers, were greeted by Minh. He stood, flanked by the members of his government, ready for a possible transfer of power. The conquerors replied with perfect scorn, "Loser! You have nothing to transfer. You can only surrender."

One must see the photographs taken by foreign reporters to realize the whole pitiless aspect of the treatment inflicted by the victors on Minh whose innocent trust unwittingly opened the floodgates for their triumphal and unhampered penetration into his own palace. The photos show us the poignant image of Minh and his advisors, heads lowered, being led away to imprisonment between two rows of heavily armed, scowling Communist soldiers.

In a sense Minh's accomplishment was laudable, despite this humiliation. He was responsible for saving Saigon from unnecessary destruction and by his actions, he indirectly permitted over 130,000 Vietnamese to leave their homeland and seek new lives away from Communist oppression. By sunrise on April 30, 1975, the evacuation had ended, and Saigon had not been shelled extensively.

I am convinced that without the personal sacrifice of Big Minh, Saigon, now renamed Ho Chi Minh City, would have been reduced to shambles by both the defending and attacking Vietnamese. As a seasoned military commander he could not be unaware of the improbability of talking the victor into making concessions to the vanquished. He betrayed this awareness by taking special care to send away his daughter and grand-children on April 24, and his son-in-law and nephew, just hours before the final collapse.

Big Minh's closest aides told me that shortly before taking over he had come to the conclusion that Hanoi had no intention of dealing with him. He became more optimistic, however, because of the rosy reports from the French ambassador coupled with repeated reassurances from American diplomats. Finally, doublecrossed and deserted, he resigned himself to his own sacrifice so that those of his countrymen who could not accept the Communist domination could emigrate in safety and to ensure that those who chose to remain did not suffer the horrors of total destruction.

Despite his mistakes, Big Minh deserves our respect.

My respect also goes to our non-Communist friends in the NLF. As promised, the NLF responded to my last query for national concord. Their favorable reply was transmitted to me at 9:00, April 27, four hours before the expected time.

Our NLF contact said that a government headed by the NLF, with the participation of other patriotic elements in Saigon, would be the only way to save South Vietnam. "Hanoi is going to seize Saigon militarily, at any costs. Of the troops surrounding Saigon, only 5 percent are NLF. A government led by you, or by Big Minh, could be called 'puppet' or 'reactionary' by Hanoi, but not an NLF government."

Recently, I have been able to confirm the information given us by the NLF through highly placed American and French intelligence sources. Since the time I left Saigon as a political refugee, I have travelled extensively in Europe and the United States, talking with a variety of informed people, writing investigative requests, and interviewing former intelligence officials in depth. The results of this probe are horrifying to me.

Contrary to published reports and official statements, the government of the United States, particularly President Ford, Secretary of State Kissinger, and the Central Intelligence Agency knew at least two weeks before Communist tanks entered Saigon that Hanoi had refused to settle for anything less than total surrender, military occupation of the South, and unconditional withdrawal of United States personnel.

In Saigon on April 15, 1975, while my political group was making exploratory contacts with the nonmilitary branch of the NLF, the head of the American CIA office in Saigon received a most disturbing report. Despite the highest security measures imposed by the Communists, the CIA had managed to infiltrate an agent into the highest echelon of the Central Office for South Vietnam (COSVN), Hanoi's control headquarters in the South. This agent informed the Saigon CIA that the North Vietnamese Politburo had unanimously decided against a negotiated settlement, regardless of any political changes in Saigon. This decision was received in COSVN from Hanoi in early April. Further instructions told COSVN that Saigon must be occupied militarily at the latest before May 19th, Ho Chi Minh's birthday, but that all Americans and some of their "friends" could be evacuated safely before that date. Hanoi, however, would not permit a large-scale evacuation of South Vietnamese. In exchange for this concession, the United States was to leave behind all military equipment present in the country.

The CIA transmitted this startling report to Washington as soon as they could have it encoded. The State Department did not believe the report was accurate, and so began a last-ditch diplomatic effort with Moscow to try to stave off the final defeat. After this negotiation failed, Kissinger decided in favor of the withdrawal and evacuation which started quietly on April 20 and culminated with the massive airlift on April 29.

The CIA divulged the contents of this report to President Thieu on April 17, only four days before his resignation. It came to him through General Nguyen Khac Binh, South Vietnam's chief of police and intelligence. Binh left Saigon on a CIA aircraft on April 28. This makes it perfectly clear that Thieu's resignation could never have been considered as an attempt to obtain a peaceful settlement, either in his mind or by the Americans!

I do not know whether Ambassador Martin knew of this report, but it seems logical to assume that he did. If so, he certainly played his part effectively because none of us guessed the truth. There was one other individual who surely knew the facts, Premier Tran Thien Khiem.

For many years, probably since 1962, Khiem had been suspected by many Vietnamese of being a special agent of the CIA. This would explain many of his peculiar actions over the years when he seemed to place the interests of the United States above those of his own country. Khiem made the arrangements with the Americans which resulted in his and Thieu's early evacuation to Taipei.

One can only make suppositions of what might have occurred if Thieu had taken Big Minh and others like Premier Can, General Ky, and myself into his confidence. President Huong would have been forced to accept a coalition government with the NLF, certainly a more acceptable solution than total capitulation to the North Vietnamese. Had the NLF been in control in Saigon, the harder line Communists from the North would have had a much more difficult time seizing power without focusing on themselves the enmity of the entire world including the Chinese and Soviets.

Big Minh's hope of being able to negotiate directly with Hanoi was based on information received from French Ambassador Merillon. Although Minh thought that Merillon was in direct contact with Hanoi, he only had secondhand information obtained from the Polish and Hungarian ambassadors.

Minh and the rest of us acted in good faith, trying up to the last minute to avert disaster and convince both France and the United States to come to our aid. As most of us have become expatriates in other lands far from our beloved Vietnam, our only satisfaction is that we did our best for our country.

Afterword/Epilogue

The foregoing book has depicted a thirty-five year war with only a single theme: the struggle for independence and unity of Vietnam. It was a ghastly war, especially so because it was fratricidal. After literally millions of casualties on both sides, the expenditure of untold treasure, and the disruption of a way of life, a type of unification occurred which was available from the very first. What prevented this? The answer is, *many things*. But, two major reasons predominate.

First was the desire of foreign powers, France, the United States, Soviet Russia, and China to use Vietnam, North and South, for their own national interests. These great countries did not and still do not really care what happens to the Vietnamese people. France wanted our country as a colony, the United States saw us as a pawn in the struggle against world Communism, while China and the Soviet Union used us to extend Communist hegemony over a land having no need of their ideology.

In August 1945, the French and especially General de Gaulle, believed they could and should reestablish their old colonial order after Japan's defeat. This shortsighted policy led France to many setbacks, culminating with the defeat at Dien Bien Phu. Instead of entrusting leadership to the many Vietnamese patriots available who had planned a clear path toward independence, the French followed a dead-end road, mired in a war they did not have the heart or ability to win.

The United States's intervention in the war, although laudable in principle at the start, also failed to accomplish its purpose. In the long run, the Americans found themselves in almost the same position as the French. As in 1954, "peace" talks occurred, spurred on by political discontent at home at a time when the enemy was still strong in the field. Settled in too much of a hurry, the cease-fire agreement finally spelled the end of South Vietnam as a nation.

257

Second, and equally important, was a lack of political vision coupled by ideological stubbornness of Vietnamese leaders on both sides. This inability of Vietnamese, ourselves, to get our own political house together, coupled with foreigners avidly willing to exploit us, promoted disunity and thwarted the real peace which was within our grasp from the start. Many chances for this real peace were lost because of our inability to talk with one another. Now, we have a type of unity, but is it a truly peaceful country we see today?

Despite my personal reservations about Communism, I sincerely hope for a peaceful life for my countrymen. Certainly after thirty-five years of conflict, they richly deserve it. The Communists deserve my admiration for their courage, tenacity, and unified adherence to their goal and to their faithful allies who back their goal. While I cannot share the political philosophy of the victors, I can and do appeal to them to adopt a policy of true national reconciliation for the benefit of all the Vietnamese people which they have long promised.

Before the victory of North Vietnam, serious questions were raised by thoughtful Vietnamese concerning the ability of a unified Vietnam to chart its own course in the stormy seas of international Communism. How well will new Vietnam be able to resist the pressures of alliances and misalliances of a world divided into three blocs, Capitalist, Communist, and Third World?

We have seen the pressure commencing with Soviet use of Cam Ranh by her fleet and China's occupation of the Paracel Islands. They and other countries will wish to compete for Vietnam's natural resources such as the newly found oil on the southern coast. How can the rulers of new Vietnam trust a Soviet Russia whose brutal subjugation of captive nations like Hungary and Czechoslovakia is so well known? How can the rulers of new Vietnam forget the thousand years of Chinese domination? They might well ponder the experience of the North Koreans who are tying themselves more closely to the USSR in fear of their colossal neighbor, China. And, as the United States prepares to withdraw her troops from South Korea, what will her attitude be in light of new Soviet or Chinese attempts to export revolution and extend their spheres of influence?

Certainly, Vietnam cannot afford another war. She has suffered enough. What she needs is a period of peaceful reconstruction leading to a way of life preferred by the overwhelming millions of Vietnamese people. The life of the village with its bamboo hedge is still the best kind of life for my

258

ancient country. It can, of course, modernize itself in a gradual way, but today it needs a regroupment of the old ways, where the common people will not feel oppressed by a domineering central government.

We should strive for a Vietnam aligned with none of the world's great powers, a Vietnam that can stand for the best it is capable of producing. The American diplomat Averell Harriman was quoted as saying that Hanoi's leaders "had their hearts in Moscow but their stomachs in Peking." I would prefer to see them have their hearts in Hue, Hanoi, Saigon, Lang Son, and Ca Mau and their stomachs in the deltas of the Red River and the Mekong and in the rich red earth of the High Plateau. Vietnamese hearts must beat first for the love of fellow Vietnamese, not for foreigners with an unneeded political ideology.

A strong policy of nonalignment need not mean chauvinism or xenophobia, nor the closing of our country's borders to the outside. Other small nations like Switzerland and Yugoslavia have managed to exist and prosper with opposite political ideologies without surrendering their national independence. A country whose policies are based on true nonalignment can be open to all friendly diplomatic, cultural, scientific, and economic intercourse. Being opposed to the dominance of foreign powers, it can protect equally the independence of the nation, its pride, and its individual character.

We must never forget that Vietnam has a four-thousand year history and culture. Our country must not further spoil our culture and customs by slavish imitation of foreign economic or political systems which are not suited to us. We are a peculiar people and should remain so. We are neither Russian nor Chinese, neither French nor American; we are Vietnamese. We can borrow the good from the rest of the world, but can never forget our own heritage. Vietnamese, like other people of the world, can live happy and productive lives without dogged adherence to either the Communist or capitalist model. I do not believe that poor people are any better off under either Communist or capitalist systems; they continue to be poor. Governments everywhere should be guided by a higher ideal, the betterment of all people, rich and poor, and of all nations, large and small.

The unification of North and South Vietnam must not have a purely geographical meaning. True unification will not result from a new set of politicians, an armed occupation, reeducation camps, or flamboyant

259

speeches. It must express itself in a change in human hearts, else the union will be a facade, insincere and deceptive. Vietnam must renounce the slogans and prejudices of outdated propaganda. How can the boundaries of proletariat and bourgeoisie be defined when the country remains predominantly agricultural. There never existed giant corporations exploiting salaried manpower. There never existed great landowners exploiting a vulnerable peasantry. There never existed hereditary titles or privileged nobility. Our country must assimilate the entire spectrum of political thought, maintaining freedom for the individual expressions of all the people. Our historic tolerance for differing religious beliefs must extend over into differing political ideas.

If the present government of Vietnam can achieve a true sense of unity based on compassion and brotherhood and based on love for one's neighbor, all will be well. But, if the opposite prevails and a police state resorts to harsh exploitation of its people in order to build the so-called "socialism," where sons inform on parents, and neighbors cannot live together harmoniously as in the past, then the last battle of our lengthy war has not yet been fought. Vietnamese will never tolerate an oppression of the spirit; we must have our own peculiar freedom and way of life.

A popular adage known to Vietnamese since ancient times says,

> Let us bathe in our own family pond. Whether its waters are clear or muddy, it is still the best because it is ours.

I might bring this ancestral wisdom up to date by changing it to read,

> Let us bathe in our own pond and keep its water pure and clear, so that it will be the best pond anywhere.

I pray that other emerging countries in the world, but principally those of Southeast Asia and Africa, will not repeat the costly mistakes of my country as I have described them in this book. Let them keep themselves nonaligned, supporting each other, and maintaining enough strength to preserve their precious freedoms.

The great countries must stop their manipulation of others. Never again should there be a confrontation of superpowers using a poor country like Vietnam as a battlefield. The big nations must hear the voices of the economic have-nots and help them, not to gain further ascendency in the world, but for the good of those who need help. There is never a need for struggle among people. We must learn to live together without war, rancor, or bitterness to the ultimate benefit of mankind. Only the most clear-sighted leaders can forge a beautiful future for humanity. May they do their work well.

Let them and all of us, therefore, turn toward the Almighty and All-Knowing Creator of mankind and the universe to beg merciful guidance on the steep path to light, truth, and justice.

Appendix

THE WHITE HOUSE

WASHINGTON

November 14, 1972

Dear Mr. President:

I was pleased to learn from General Haig that you held useful and constructive discussions with him in Saigon in preparation for Dr. Kissinger's forthcoming meeting with North Vietnam's negotiators in Paris.

After studying your letter of November 11 with great care I have concluded that we have made substantial progress towards reaching a common understanding on many of the important issues before us. You can be sure that we will pursue the proposed changes in the draft agreement that General Haig discussed with you with the utmost firmness and that, as these discussions proceed, we shall keep you fully informed through your Ambassador to the Paris Conference on Vietnam who will be briefed daily by Dr. Kissinger.

I understand from your letter and from General Haig's personal report that your principal remaining concern with respect to the draft agreement is the status of North Vietnamese forces now in South Vietnam. As General Haig explained to you, it is our intention to deal with this problem first by seeking to insert a reference to respect for the demilitarized zone in the proposed agreement and, second, by proposing

263

a clause which provides for the reduction and demobilization of forces on both sides in South-Vietnam on a one-to-one basis and to have demobilized personnel return to their homes.

Upon reviewing this proposed language, it is my conviction that such a provision can go a long way towards dealing with your concern with respect to North Vietnamese forces. General Haig tells me, however, that you are also seriously concerned about the timing and verification of such reductions. In light of this, I have asked Dr. Kissinger to convey to you, through Ambassador Bunker, some additional clauses we would propose adding to the agreement dealing with each of these points. In addition, I have asked that Dr. Kissinger send you the other technical and less important substantive changes which General Haig did not have the opportunity to discuss with you because they had not yet been fully developed in Washington. With these proposed modifications, I think you will agree that we have done everything we can to improve the existing draft while remaining within its general framework.

You also raise in your letter the question of participation by other Asian countries in the International Conference. As you know, the presently contemplated composition are the permanent members of the United Nations Security Council, the members of the ICCS, the parties to the Paris Conference on Vietnam and the Secretary General of the United Nations. We seriously considered Cambodian and Laotian participation but decided that these would be unnecessary complications with respect to representation. We do not, however, exclude the possibility of delegations from these countries participating in an observer status at the invitation of the conference. As for Japan, this question was raised earlier in our negotiations with Hanoi and set aside because of their strenuous objections to any Japanese role in guaranteeing the settlement and also because it inevitably raises the possibility of Indian participation. I have, however, asked that Dr. Kissinger raise this matter again in Paris and he will inform your representative what progress we make on this. What we must recognize as a practical matter is that participation of Japan is very likely to lead to the participation of India. We would appreciate hearing your preference on whether it is better to include both countries or neither of them.

Finally, in respect to the composition of the ICCS, I must say in all candor that I do not share your view that its contemplated membership is unbalanced. I am hopeful that it will prove to be a useful mechanism in detecting and reporting violations of the agreement. In any event, what we both must recognize is that the supervisory mechanism in itself is in no measure as important as our own firm determination to see to it that the agreement works and our vigilance with respect to the prospect of its violation.

I will not repeat here all that I said to you in my letter of November 8, but I do wish to reaffirm its essential content and stress again my determination to work towards an early agreement along the lines of the schedule which General Haig explained to you. I must explain in all frankness that while we will do our very best to secure the changes in the agreement which General Haig discussed with you and those additional ones which Ambassador Bunker will bring you, we cannot expect to secure them all. For example, it is unrealistic to assume that we will be able to secure the absolute assurances which you would hope to have on the troop issue.

But far more important than what we say in the agreement on this issue is what we do in the event the enemy renews its aggression. You have my absolute assurance that if Hanoi fails to abide by the terms of this agreement it is my intention to take swift and severe retaliatory action.

I believe the existing agreement to be an essentially sound one which should become even more so if we succeed in obtaining some of the changes we have discussed. Our best assurance of success is to move into this new situation with confidence and cooperation.

With this attitude and the inherent strength of your government and army on the ground in South Vietnam, I am confident this agreement will be a successful one.

265

If, on the other hand, we are unable to agree on the course that I have outlined, it is difficult for me to see how we will be able to continue our common effort towards securing a just and honorable peace. As General Haig told you I would with great reluctance be forced to consider other alternatives. For this reason, it is essential that we have your agreement as we proceed into our next meeting with Hanoi's negotiators. And I strongly urge you and your advisors to work promptly with Ambassador Bunker and our Mission in Saigon on the many practical problems which will face us in implementing the agreement. I cannot overemphasize the urgency of the task at hand nor my unalterable determination to proceed along the course which we have outlined.

Above all we must bear in mind what will really maintain the agreement. It is not any particular clause in the agreement but our joint willingness to maintain its clauses. I repeat my personal assurances to you that the United States will react very strongly and rapidly to any violation of the agreement. But in order to do this effectively it is essential that I have public support and that your Government does not emerge as the obstacle to a peace which American public opinion now universally desires. It is for this reason that I am pressing for the acceptance of an agreement which I am convinced is honorable and fair and which can be made essentially secure by our joint determination.

Mrs. Nixon joins me in extending our warmest personal regards to Madame Thieu and to you. We look forward to seeing you again at our home in California once the just peace we have both fought for so long is finally achieved.

Sincerely,

Richard Nixon

His Excellency
Nguyen Van Thieu
President of the Republic of Vietnam
Saigon

THE WHITE HOUSE

WASHINGTON

January 5, 1973

Dear Mr. President:

This will acknowledge your letter of December 20, 1972.

There is nothing substantial that I can add to my many previous messages, including my December 17 letter, which clearly stated my opinions and intentions. With respect to the question of North Vietnamese troops, we will again present your views to the Communists as we have done vigorously at every other opportunity in the negotiations. The result is certain to be once more the rejection of our position. We have explained to you repeatedly why we believe the problem of North Vietnamese troops is manageable under the agreement, and I see no reason to repeat all the arguments.

We will proceed next week in Paris along the lines that General Haig explained to you. Accordingly, if the North Vietnamese meet our concerns on the two outstanding substantive issues in the agreement, concerning the DMZ and the method of signing, and if we can arrange acceptable supervisory machinery, we will proceed to conclude the settlement. The gravest consequences would then ensue if your government chose to reject the agreement and split off from the United States. As I said in my December 17 letter, "I am convinced that your refusal to join us would be an invitation to disaster—to the loss of all that we together have fought for over the past decade. It would be inexcusable above all because we will have lost a just and honorable alternative."

267

As we enter this new round of talks, I hope that our countries will now show a united front. It is imperative for our common objectives that your government take no further actions that complicate our task and would make more difficult the acceptance of the settlement by all parties. We will keep you informed of the negotiations in Paris through daily briefings of Ambassador Lam.

I can only repeat what I have so often said: The best guarantee for the survival of South Vietnam is the unity of our two countries which would be gravely jeopardized if you persist in your present course. The actions of our Congress since its return have clearly borne out the many warnings we have made.

Should you decide, as I trust you will, to go with us, you have my assurance of continued assistance in the post-settlement period and that we will respond with full force should the settlement be violated by North Vietnam. So once more I conclude with an appeal to you to close ranks with us.

Sincerely,

Richard Nixon

His Excellency
Nguyen Van Thieu
President of the Republic of Vietnam
Saigon

Publisher's Note: These two letters are reproduced from photocopies of the originals on file at Presidio Press. They are available for examination on request.

Index

WESTMORELAND

THIEU

MCNAMARA

KY

JOHNSON

DIEM

TAYLOR

MINH

HARKINS